D0031516

French Socialists
in Search of a Role
1956-1967

French Socialists in Search of a Role 1956-1967

HARVEY G. SIMMONS

Cornell University Press
ITHACA AND LONDON

First published 1970

Standard Book Number 8014–0540–8

Library of Congress Catalog Card Number 75–87023

PRINTED IN THE UNITED STATES OF AMERICA
BY KINGSPORT PRESS, INC.

To the memory of
my father

Preface

The nature and recent history of the French Socialist party (*Parti Socialiste—Section Française de l'Internationale Ouvrière*, hence SFIO) have frequently been distorted both by the exaggerations of its partisans and by the denigrations of its critics. American observers have found it particularly difficult to sympathize with a group whose position in a multiparty system has frequently led to participation in heteroclite coalition governments, highly flexible electoral tactics, and a defensive organizational strategy. European critics, on the other hand, have often found it quite easy to explain or justify every move of parties like the SFIO in terms of party tradition and doctrine or simply the need for self-preservation.

The complex nature of the French political system under the Fourth and Fifth Republics also creates obstacles for the political analyst. Under the Fourth Republic the political system was characterized by a multiplicity of parties clustering about numerous highly divisive issues, a political culture split along party, religious, and historical lines, and a legislature jealous of its prerogatives, hostile toward the executive, and frequently stripped of its initiative by a powerful and sometimes hostile administrative apparatus.

There are two ways for a political party to survive in this kind of system. The first, chosen by the French Communist party (PCF), is the lonely and friendless road of isolation and opposition. Except for a brief period after the Liberation, the party refused to participate in government and, until 1962, its tactic during legislative elections was simply to run Communist candidates in all districts but to make no electoral alliances. For the PCF this led to a modicum of success during elections, but it also resulted in powerlessness and sterility, for except in local politics the PCF could claim no real share in the achievements of the Fourth Republic after 1947. At the same time, of course, it could not be criticized for the Republic's shortcomings.

There is another and much more difficult way for a party to survive, and this was the way chosen by the SFIO. It is the way of governmental participation, of the acceptance of responsibility for both the achievements and failures that necessarily follow from holding office.

Each choice, each party, was inevitably subject to both approval and criticism. Thus the Communists were praised by some for their consistency and honesty in refusing to "dirty their hands" by sharing the burdens of office in an essentially "unjust" system. Those who supported the SFIO, on the other hand, applauded its willingness to compromise for the sake of immediate—and pressing—reforms. The critics of the PCF attacked it for paralyzing the process of effective government in France, thereby indirectly contributing to the terrible difficulties encountered by the Fourth Republic and to its eventual collapse. The critics of the SFIO castigated its leaders for their "opportunistic" policies and frequently drew attention to the apparent gap between its programs and its behavior and achievements.

Too often, however, those who defended parties for having compromised their ideals assumed that there was no other choice, while those who attacked reformist parties like the SFIO often seemed to assume that all choices were open. Yet the most striking fact of party life under the Fourth Republic was the relatively small freedom of maneuver available to the parties. It was as if each political party was immobilized in a large but sloppily assembled jigsaw puzzle. The pieces could be shifted, but only very slowly and gently, for any sudden or radical move would so disrupt the arrangement that the whole puzzle would have to be reassembled from the very beginning.

If, as Stanley Hoffmann says, France under the Third Republic was a "stalemate society," so too were the parties under the Fourth Republic stalemated. Each had carved out its own slice of the electoral pie; each had a characteristic doctrine or appeal, historical roots, and organization. Radical doctrinal, policy, or organizational changes were simply out of the question, for the risks were much too high. There were too many parties and groups, and there was no large group of flexible independent voters, toward whom even the most ideological of parties will frequently make overtures in stable two- or three-party systems.

In France, the Communists could not move to the right without running up against the SFIO. The Socialists were blocked on their left by the PCF, while the Popular Republican Movement (MRP) and the Radicals barred the road to the right. The MRP was, in turn, ground between the Socialists to the left and various centrist movements on the right, while the dying Radical party underwent schism after schism without any faction emerging powerful enough to revive it. On the center and right, shifting and amorphous parties fought for position and power, but on this end of the French political spectrum the permanent condition seemed to be the impermanence of the groups it comprised.

The party system was finally shocked out of its immobility

not by any internal initiative or impulse, but rather by the overthrow of the Fourth Republic sparked by the army revolt of May 13, 1958. At first the military tried to shift the pieces in the French political puzzle too rapidly and violently, with the result that all the pieces were knocked helter-skelter. When de Gaulle came to power soon after, he and some other new players set about reassembling the puzzle, but in an altered pattern. The political parties then were confronted with the problem of fitting themselves into this new and unfamiliar arrangement. In the case of the SFIO, the changes in the political system, the new constitution, the growing power of the presidency, the declining prestige of political parties, and the decreased interest and participation of the French in political parties all impelled re-examination of party doctrine, strategy, and organization.

Under the Fourth Republic the SFIO had been under constant fire from both internal and external critics. The criticism intensified near the end of the period when a large minority of dissenters quit, accusing the leaders of using dictatorial tactics, of suffocating dissent and free discussion, and of betraying Socialist principles by backing the Fifth Republic referendum. But even this severe break did not shake the larger unity and consensus of the SFIO. Rather it was the continuing evolution of the Fifth Republic that finally led the party majority to look for new solutions to the problems confronting it in the new system. Thus, under the Fifth Republic, after years of study and discussion, the SFIO adopted a fundamental program setting forth for the first time in party history a detailed statement of party goals and methods. Later, Gaston Defferre's meteor flared briefly in the French political sky as he won the SFIO nomination for the 1965 presidential election but then failed in his attempt to lead the SFIO into a federation with certain clubs, elements from the Radical party, and the MRP. Soon after, Guy Mollet reassumed control of the party and led the SFIO into the Federation of the Democratic and Socialist Left (*Fédération de la Gauche Démocrate et Socialiste*). Later, the FGDS began to move hesitantly toward fusion and the constitution of a new force on the French political scene.

This book is concerned with the attempts of the SFIO to work within the French political puzzle. It deals with the SFIO as it tried to maneuver during the later years of the Fourth Republic, defines the broad limits of its actions, and offers some explanations for the choices party leaders made during that period. Then the question of the party's new role in the Fifth Republic is taken up and the many proposals for reform that have agitated the party during recent years are analyzed and discussed. Finally, some of the more important socioeconomic and political characteristics of party leaders and party organization are noted so as to illuminate some of the principal factors impinging on party activities during the period under discussion.

HARVEY G. SIMMONS

Toronto
May 1969

Contents

French Socialists
in Search of a Role
1956-1967

1. Introduction

When the Socialist-led government assumed power in 1956, the Algerian rebellion was on the verge of becoming the most difficult problem any French government had confronted since the war. Flushed with their success in the country and in the National Assembly, however, the Socialist leaders were unprepared for its complexities. In their reactions to the crisis they immediately demonstrated a lack of direction and purpose. Moreover, the Socialist leadership tended to debase whatever intellectual prestige the party possessed by defending any and all government actions, even those seemingly most in contradiction to Socialist doctrine (the Suez operation for example), in terms of Socialist principles.

During the sixteen months it was in power, the government of Guy Mollet seemed both unwilling and unable to take drastic action to initiate promised reforms in Algeria. The resistance of the European Algerians, the recalcitrance of the army and administration in Algeria, and the desire of the Socialist leaders to retain the necessary support of the Independent group in the National Assembly combined to make a mockery of Socialist electoral promises for reform in Algeria. At the same time, however, in keeping with party tradition, the Socialist government worked toward domestic social and economic reforms. When by May, 1957, it became clear that the Mollet government would have to sacrifice further domestic reforms in order to retain support from the right in the National Assembly, the SFIO refused to compromise. Thus, having relied upon the forbearance of the Independents for sixteen months, the Mollet government fell in May, 1957, when the Independents withdrew their support in a dispute over a proposed tax on business and industry.

After the fall of the government, the SFIO's parliamentary tactics remained more or less unaltered. Safely ensconced in its key position on the center left, the SFIO could make or break governments almost at will. Thus its participation or support was a necessary precondition for the success of any government in the remaining years of the Fourth Republic. Although many party deputies and militants were becoming increasingly discontented with the SFIO's continued participation in government after May, 1957, Mollet and his allies were always able to win the support of the party executive committee (*comité directeur*, or CD) or of the party congress or national council. Only when the party was called upon to vote de Gaulle's investiture as President of the Council in June, 1958, did Mollet fail, 49 to 42, to carry the majority of the SFIO deputies. The period of Socialist participation in power had not ended, however, since Mollet, Eugène Thomas and Max Lejeune entered de Gaulle's cabinet. Later, when an Extraordinary National Congress voted to support the constitutional referendum of September, 1958, the schism which had long been threatening the Socialist ranks finally cracked open and a number of leaders and militants left to form the short-lived PSA (*Parti Socialiste Autonome*).

Guy Mollet's domination of the SFIO during the Fourth Republic was ensured because a dissenting minority could not obtain a foothold in the party organization, either by re-establishing proportional representation on the CD or by gaining access to the party press. Thus it was forced to express its dissent in a sporadic and unorganized fashion, either occasionally during party meetings, in the infrequently read party bulletins, or in nonparty publications. In the latter case, however, dissenters were subject to disciplinary sanctions for having violated party statutes forbidding members to express opinions contrary to party decisions in the press. Party meetings were dominated by the large disciplined federations such as Pas-de-Calais, Nord, and Bouches-du-Rhône. When the leaders of these three federations (Guy Mollet, Augustin Laurent, and Gaston Defferre) agreed to support a motion there was almost no chance for the opposition to carry the meeting. Even when Gaston Defferre's federation of Bouches-du-Rhône joined the opposition, the weight of the votes of Pas-de-Calais and Nord was enough to carry the meeting. The domination of the latter two federations was made possible by the fact that the other federations (there were almost ninety in all) were either fractious (as in the case of the large Seine federation) and tended to split their votes on most motions, or because the remaining federations tended to divide more or less equally on each motion, thus assuring the dominance of the large federations which voted in concert.

Although internal party critics focused on the government's Algerian policy from 1956 to 1958, perhaps an even more important controversy concerned the issue of party democracy. More by its action in defeating all requests for a change in party statutes to allow a minority greater means for expression and representation than by explicit argument, the majority's view seemed to be that the primary role of the extraparliamentary party was to defend and support the parliamentary party. Party unity, or at least the appearance of unity, had to be preserved at all costs in order not to damage party prestige and thereby aid its enemies. Given this assumption, the majority fought off all attempts at changing party organization so as to give the minority a larger voice in party affairs.

The minority's view seemed to be that the role of the nonparliamentary party was to maintain a critical independence vis-à-vis the parliamentary party. According to minority leaders such as Edouard Depreux, for example, the extraparliamentary party should control and discipline its "delegates" in the National Assembly and in the government. At the same time, complete freedom of discussion should be allowed within the party, although strict discipline in voting would be required. All party members should have the right to criticize the actions of party representatives in parliament. Depreux claimed that, unless the autonomy of the extraparliamentary party was maintained, the electorate was liable to form the opinion that the activities of Socialist parliamentarians represented the basic program and doctrine of the SFIO. This was an erroneous impression, he felt, for, as Léon Blum had pointed out in distinguishing between the exercise and conquest of power, the exercise of power by Socialists in coalition governments required certain modifications in the Socialist program and the granting of certain concessions to coalition partners. Only if the extraparliamentary party constantly called attention to the differences between the maximum and minimum Socialist program would the electorate be able to distinguish between the two.

The majority-minority confrontation in the SFIO during the last years of the Fourth Republic was in the tradition of French socialism. From Millerand to Mollet there had always been individuals who wished to see the party participate in power and those who wished to keep it uncontaminated by participation in government; those who accepted reformism and those who, while accepting the modalities of parliamentary democracy, wished to keep alive the revolutionary ideals of the Socialist party. This explains why those who left the party in 1958 went neither to the PCF nor to the MRP or Radical Socialists, but either to the PSA or out of party politics altogether. The dissidents felt that the SFIO had betrayed socialism both by debasing Socialist doctrine during the Algerian years, and by suffocating democracy within the party. According to these critics a new Socialist party should be established, one which would embody all the ideals of Socialist doctrine and organization neglected by the SFIO. The dissenters hoped, thereby, to recruit dissatisfied SFIO members and to re-enlist the support of disillusioned former SFIO members and sympathizers who had left the party through the years. These hopes were to be deceived as time passed. The people, it appeared, were not interested in flocking to join or vote for yet another competing brand of socialism. Although the PSA and then its successor, the PSU (*Parti Socialiste Unifié*) did attract many of the young people so conspicuously lacking in the SFIO, the new party soon fell to quarreling over doctrine and organization.

During the Fourth Republic, a few people had begun to question not only the SFIO doctrine but the whole concept of the structure and role of a mass political party in France. Under the Fifth Republic, however, an increasing number of people began to discuss this question, to talk about a regrouping of the parties on the left, to propose new and radical forms of organization, and, most important, to prepare for new forms of political activity within the presidential system.

With the departure of the dissenters for the PSA, the SFIO seemed to recover its unity during the period after late 1958. But dissatisfaction with party tactics and strategy became more apparent as de Gaulle and the *Union pour la Nouvelle République* (UNR), appeared to grow rather than diminish in strength. After the disastrous 1962 election, many SFIO leaders began to engage in soul searching, and one of them,

Gaston Defferre, was eventually led to propose drastic changes in every sphere of party activity. Differences between Defferre and Mollet grew, with Defferre leading the fight for the creation of a new political force that would include the MRP and other non-Communist groups on the left. Guy Mollet, on the other hand, continued to support the notion of an independent, cohesive, and disciplined Socialist party.

With the nomination of Gaston Defferre as the Socialist candidate for the presidency, the Defferre wing seemed on the edge of victory—but subsequent negotiations with the MRP showed that neither the leaders of the MRP nor the Mollet wing of the Socialists were yet willing to risk sacrificing traditional party forms in the hope of winning a wider audience in French politics. The exclusion of the MRP from the newly formed *Fédération de la Gauche Démocrate et Socialiste* in 1965, and the incorporation of elements from the Radical party and of certain political clubs, seemed to suggest that the Socialists were willing to take at least tentative steps in the direction of reform; but the overwhelming weight of the SFIO in the FGDS also demonstrated the unwillingness of the Socialists to give up their essential independence.

The profound effect of the change from the parliamentary system of the Fourth Republic to the presidential system of the Fifth Republic on the Socialist party cannot be overestimated. With a minority of deputies in the National Assembly in 1956, the SFIO was able to head a coalition government for sixteen months. Under the Fifth Republic, with the UNR increasing in number and importance in the National Assembly and with the growing concentration of decision-making power in the hands of the President, the SFIO had little influence on the policy-making process. Under the Fourth Republic the number of deputies a party sent to the National Assembly bore little relation to its ability to participate in power. Under the Fifth Republic, however, numbers became of the utmost importance. This helps explain the agitation in the SFIO after 1958, the suggestions for changes in party tactics and strategy, the brief success of the Defferre campaign, and the ultimate formation of the *Fédération de la Gauche Démocrate et Socialiste.*

At the same time, however, the SFIO remained powerfully rooted in French local politics. More than 45,000 Socialist mayors and municipal and general councilors assured its continued existence on the French political scene. In the Fourth Republic, and then under the Fifth Republic, the SFIO was a party that could afford to wait. It was not likely to be blown away by an electoral ill-wind that occasionally blew through France, and, as the oldest organized political party after the Radical Socialists, with deep roots in French political culture and French history, it did not wither during dry periods. Moreover, the elite and many of the ordinary members of the French Socialist party were political veterans.

The vast majority of Socialist deputies, executive committee members and ordinary party members had years of political experience at either the local or national level in France. They were neither stupid nor stubborn. The contradiction many intellectuals and analysts saw between the revolutionary vocabulary of the SFIO and its profoundly reformist actions was not a real contradiction for most party members. Party doctrine constituted an ideal, the action a means for achieving these ideals. If the means used occasionally seemed in contradiction to the ideal, then of course the party suffered, but this was no reason for abandoning these ideals. If the SFIO seemed to engage in complicated and devious electoral or parliamentary maneuvers, this too was part of the political game in France—a game at which the Socialists were quite experienced. Above all, the Socialists were realists. If party leaders differed, still their differences were based on the fact that

French politics is an exciting and frequently unpredictable game. Parties come and go, republics rise and fall, constitutions are promulgated, interpreted, revised, abandoned; personalities burst on the scene, shine for a moment, and then disappear into oblivion.

The issues confronted by the SFIO in the Fourth and Fifth Republics were complex and confusing. As former Prime Minister Pierre Mendès-France once said, however, "To govern is to choose," and the Socialists were frequently forced to choose between two equally unappealing and difficult courses of action. In the French political system, as in all political systems, the inevitability of choice and action is the essence, the tragedy and glory, of politics.

2. *The Party at the Polls—The 1956 Election*

Prior to the 1956 election the Socialists had become increasingly hostile to the MRP and more friendly to Mendès-France and his Radical Socialist supporters. The SFIO had supported Mendès-France in his various bids for office, and when he was finally elected President of the Council of Ministers in June, 1954, the SFIO provided voting support. In the 1951–1955 legislature, however, a breach was opened between the MRP and Socialists over the sensitive issue of *laïcité* during the voting of the 1951 Barangé Law. This breach was increasingly widened by differences that arose on colonial matters.

The immediate reaction of the SFIO to the dissolution of the Assembly by Edgar Faure was extreme anger. On December 6, 1955, when the National Council met to decide on electoral tactics a motion was voted which spoke of the "party's constructive opposition to the reactionary and clerical majority in the National Assembly" and of its "unfailing support for the Mendès-France government." The SFIO also fulminated against the electoral system, demanding a return to the *scrutin d'arrondissement* with two turns. The party also declared itself "as far removed from the majority of Dien Bien Phu, of the *coup de force* against the Sultan of Morocco, of the Barangé law as from the PCF." Finally, the party declared its opposition to the system of *apparentements* but said it was willing to join with those parties opposed to reactionary parties. The allies of the SFIO would have to agree to a nine-point program which included an affirmation of "democratic liberties, the struggle for peace by negotiation and disarmament, Atlantic defense and the construction of Europe, social progress, economic expansion, organization of agricultural markets, peace in North Africa, the construction of a true French Union, and the restoration of *laïcité*.[1]

If the Socialist program and the various propaganda devices distributed to party candidates soon after the National Council covered numerous subjects from social security reform to *laïcité*, the public seemed to be particularly interested in the problem of Algeria.[2] In the various *professions de foi* or electoral programs which the Ministry of the Interior publishes, the theme of Algeria appeared time and again. In the electoral statement of the Socialist candidate from the second district of Seine-et-Oise, for example, one finds the following statement under the heading, "To construct a fraternal French Union":

The Socialist Party considers the events which are unfolding in the overseas territories of an exceptional gravity and calls for a

[1] Parti Socialiste, *Bulletin Intérieur*, no. 84, May, 1956, pp. 156–57.

[2] For Socialist propaganda in the 1956 election see Association Française de Science Politique, *Les Elections du 2 Janvier 1956* (Paris, 1957), pp. 51–57. (Work hereafter referred to as *Elections, 1956*.) An analysis of the Parisian and provincial press showed that the North African and Algerian problems occupied more space in the newspapers during this period than any other problem. A poll conducted by IFOP also found that the major preoccupation of the electorate in 1955 was Algeria. See *L'Express*, December 16, 1955, for the poll.

profound change in the policy elaborated in the course of these last years by the Pinay-Laniel-Edgar Faure majority. . . .

In Algeria: abandonment of the policy of repression. Free elections as soon as possible. Conversations with the qualified representatives of the Algerians in order to study a new form of relations with the Metropole.

These "new forms" that relations between Algeria and France might assume were, "association, federation or any other organization which might be desired by the populations."[3]

The electoral statement of a Socialist candidate in the department of Nièvre said:

Reaction wants to mobilize new recruits for the Algerian War. You will say "no" to the war in voting Socialist. . . . We wish to remind you that our major demand is peace in Algeria.

In *Le Populaire*, toward the end of the campaign, an article by Christian Pineau entitled "Election Stakes" appeared:

Above all the problems posed in the course of the election campaign, there is one dominant question which is at stake in the election—that is the question of North Africa and, in a general manner, that of the French Union.[4]

In an article published in *L'Express* (at that time *L'Express* was a fervent supporter of the Republican Front and of Mendès-France) on December 19, 1955, the secretary-general of the SFIO stated in answer to the question, "What shall we do in Algeria?":

At first, stop lying, let us not repeat the errors committed in Indochina, Tunisia and Morocco. Let us protect the population to be sure, but let us cease imbecilic and blind repression. Let us search for qualified spokesmen, but let us not leave the task to the administration which might choose from men who will be the so-called "representatives."

[3] Georges Dupeux in *Elections, 1956*, p. 55.

[4] *Le Populaire*, December 30, 1955.

A second major characteristic of the Socialist campaign was its emphasis on personalities and especially on Mendès-France. During this period Mendès-France occupied the center of the political stage, and for many, to vote for the *Front Républicain* was to vote for Mendès-France.[5] An IFOP (*Institut Français d'Opinion Publique*) poll conducted on December 12 for example, found that, in response to the question, "Whom do you wish to see as President of the Council?", 27 per cent wanted Mendès-France, 10 per cent Edgar Faure, 8 per cent Antoine Pinay, while de Gaulle, Thorez, Mollet, and Bidault all received between 1 per cent and 3 per cent.[6] The Socialists made use of the *mendèsiste* wave of support by referring to the fact that the SFIO had supported the Mendès-France government, which, according to one electoral statement, "had restored confidence in the Republic and given hope to the young."[7] This was not an isolated statement by any means; in Meurthe-et-Moselle, for example, the Socialist candidate spoke of his personal acquaintance with Mendès-France and stated, "He has not only made peace in Indochina, but has given a new meaning to French politics."[8] It was obvious that the Socialists were attempting to capitalize on the highly personal appeal of Mendès-France.

In addition to Algeria, Mendès-France, and the record of the outgoing government, the SFIO also emphasized social and economic issues. Scattered among the party's statements on these issues were the usual phrases designed to reassure militants who might fear that the SFIO had forsaken its revo-

[5] *Elections, 1956,* pp. 103 and 295.

[6] *L'Express,* December 12, 1955.

[7] Duverger, *Constitutions et Documents Politiques* (Paris: Presses Universitaires de France, 1957), p. 219.

[8] *Recueil des Textes Authentiques des Programmes et Engagements Electoraux de 2 Janvier 1956* (Paris: 1956, Ministry of the Interior), vol. II, p. 562.

lutionary goal. At the 47th National Congress held at the end of June and in early July, 1955, the SFIO voted on a detailed program. In it the following statement appeared:

> The very existence of a regime founded on profit, the capitalist regime, does not allow society to attain the high living standards otherwise permitted by technical progress.

The statement also noted that the reforms advocated by the SFIO would

> prepare the disappearance of the capitalist regime founded on profit and promote a true economic and social democracy. . . . develop all the institutions where worker's management is beginning to be exercised. It also intends to organize economic education preparing the producers for the tasks of direction and for the responsibilities that will fall on them in a Socialist society.[9]

These statements were also accompanied by concrete proposals for economic and social reform. The proposals were of two kinds: ameliorative proposals designed to humanize or make more efficient existing institutions such as social security or the minimum guaranteed occupational salary (*salaire minimum interprofessionnel garanti*, or SMIG); and proposals concerning structural reforms such as nationalization of steel and atomic energy.

It might be thought that the latter type of proposal would be of more importance to a party whose stated aim was to "prepare the disappearance of the capitalist regime," but such was not the case. By far the preponderant amount of space in the program was devoted to the ameliorative rather than the structural proposals. A final contrast is provided by a selection from the electoral statement of another Socialist candidate, P.-O. Lapie former minister from Meurthe-et-Moselle:

[9] *Bulletin Intérieur*, no. 84 May, 1956, p. 129.

Socialism in France, in the image of British and Swedish Labor parties, wishes in the immediate future, to enact profound and generous reforms in favor of all workers.[10]

When the National Assembly was dissolved in late 1955, the SFIO chose to ally itself with the Radical party, the *Union Démocratique et Sociale de la Résistance* (UDSR), and some elements of the Social Republicans. The alliance took the name *Front Républicain.* The other groups contesting the election were the Communists and assorted parties of the center and right, including the newly formed group led by Pierre Poujade. Jacques Fauvet noted that the Republican Front was mainly an electoral alliance concocted to take full advantage of the electoral system, and that the partners did not have much else in common.[11]

The campaign was organized and conducted mainly by the candidates acting on the local (i.e., departmental or party federation) level. This was due both to the type of electoral system in which the department was the constituency and to the abbreviated nature of the campaign. In effect, the list system of proportional representation allowed the departmental SFIO federation to choose not only the party candidate, but the party deputy. This was true simply because the person who headed the list in a department where the party was fairly strong was almost assured of reelection. Of the ninety-three successful Socialist candidates, sixty-nine headed the list in their department. During the 1956 campaign one observer noted that the national headquarters of the SFIO exercised little or no central control over the campaign in most depart-

[10] *Recueil,* Vol. II, p. 563.

[11] Jacques Fauvet, *La IVe République* (Paris, 1959), p. 304; also *Elections, 1956* pp. 25 and 127 on the tenuous nature of the Republican Front alliance.

ments.[12] Although the candidates were plentifully supplied with material, the use they made of this material and the issues they emphasized were left entirely up to the candidate and his federation. Except for a scanty fifteen-minute broadcast on the radio, and five minutes on television, however, even party leaders limited their campaigns to their own districts.

Results

In 1951 the SFIO had received 2,783,000 votes on the first ballot; in 1956 it received 3,247,000, an increase of 16 per cent. In terms of the number of registered voters, the party received 14.6 per cent of the votes in 1951 and 12.1 per cent of the votes in 1956. The Republican Front received 22 per cent of the total vote while the center-right, including the former government parties, received 26 per cent. The extreme right (including Poujadists) received 10.2 per cent, and the PCF received 20 per cent of the votes. The party sent 93 deputies to the National Assembly.[13]

The geography of the 1956 election seemed to indicate that the SFIO had preserved its traditional basis of support in the industrial north, where, for the first time in ten years, the SFIO received more votes than the PCF (in Pas-de-Calais and Nord). The party also maintained its position in the laic departments of the Center and in the traditionally left regions of the Midi.

The strong local implantation of the SFIO would seem to be one of the reasons for its ability to maintain its positions

[12] Saul Rose, "The French Election of 1956," *Political Studies* IV, (October, 1956), 25–63.

[13] Frequently the number of deputies elected will differ from the number in the parliamentary group during the term of the legislature because of deaths, by-elections, or the addition of non-SFIO deputies who joined the parliamentary group after the election.

during national elections in certain areas of France. Safe in their bastions of local power, parties like the PCF and SFIO could suffer a sharp decline in votes during national elections and still come back again in following elections because of their ability to keep local party personalities and issues before the voters in the districts where the party is strong. Since the parties of the left in France depend on their members for both energy and money, the possession of the mayor's seat in a large city is an important factor in rewarding active members and keeping local party organizations alive and dynamic. Frequently a mayor will subsidize sympathetic party organizations from municipal funds, distribute municipal bulletins free to the population, and make parks and other public facilities available to party-affiliated organizations. All these activities helped the parties in their publicity and propaganda campaigns.[14]

The SFIO, like other parties in the 1956 elections, tended to put forward candidates with local reputations—but the SFIO, along with the PCF, led in this practice, as three-fourths of its candidates were also in local government. The MRP followed with two-thirds, the Radicals with half, and the Moderates with one-third. Almost all the Socialist candidates who headed the lists in their departments were either former deputies, members of the party executive organs, federal secretaries, or members of the federal executive. Of the ninety-three Socialist deputies elected in 1956, fourteen had been elected to the National Assembly for the first time before the war, thirty-six had been elected for the first time either to the Consultative Assembly based in Algiers (later in Paris), eleven had been elected the first time either to the second Constituent Assembly in June, 1946, or to the first legislature of November, 1946, fourteen to the legislature of 1951 and eighteen for the first

[14] Serge Mallet, "A l'Assaut des Municipalités Ouvrières," *France-Observateur*, December 11, 1958.

time to the 1956 legislature. In 1956, of nineteen parliamentary members of the CD, one had first entered the legislature before the war, fifteen immediately after the war in the Consultative Assemblies of 1945 or 1946, or in the first legislature of 1946, while only three first appeared in the Assembly after 1951. On the whole, then, the Socialist parliamentary group was composed of individuals who had made their living in politics for quite some time.

Election polls also seemed to show that predictions of mass desertion of the working class from Socialist ranks had been rather hasty. Mattei Dogan, found that 42 per cent of the total Socialist vote came from working-class voters although the party received only 17 per cent of the total French working-class vote. The PCF received the lion's share of the French working-class vote with 49 per cent, with the other 34 per cent going to the various parties of the center and right.[15] An IFOP poll in 1960 seemed to confirm these figures showing that 39 per cent of the Socialist vote came from working-class voters with white-collar workers (23 per cent) and retired people or people with independent means also comprising an important proportion of the Socialist vote (20 per cent). But those who claimed the SFIO had been slipping into the electoral skin of the Radicals since the Liberation, if not before, had to reckon with the 1956 voting statistics showing some marked differences between the composition of the Radical and the Socialist vote. The Socialists, for example, drew 37 per cent of their vote from persons forty-four years old and under as compared with 31 per cent for the Radical Socialists. In addition, if the Socialists and Radicals both drew 34 per cent of their support from urban areas of 20,000 and above, still the Socialist vote in cities of 5,000–20,000 comprised 26 per cent of the party total for 1956, as compared with 13 per

[15] Mattei Dogan, "Le Vote Ouvrier en Europe Occidentale," *Revue Française de Sociologie*, I (1960), 25–44.

cent for the Radical Socialists; while more than half the Radical Socialist vote (53 per cent) came from areas of 5,000 and below, small towns of this size provided only 40 per cent of the Socialist vote. The working class weighed much more heavily in the total Socialist vote (39 per cent of the vote) than in the Radical Socialist vote (28 per cent). Finally, the lopsided figures showing 65 per cent men and 35 per cent women supporting the SFIO as opposed to the more evenly split 58 per cent men and 42 per cent women voting for the Radical Socialists seemed to evidence continuing differences in the composition of the Socialist and Radical Socialist electorates (see Appendix A.1).

3. *The Socialists and Algeria*

Most observers date November 1, 1954, as marking the beginning of the Algerian rebellion. On that day a number of police posts in Algeria were attacked by the Algerian ALN (*Armée de Libération Nationale*). The reaction of the Mendès-France government was to immediately send three battalions of paratroops to reinforce the approximately 60,000 French troops then stationed in Algeria. Speaking to the National Assembly on November 12, 1954, Mendès-France expressed the sentiments of a majority of the deputies when he said:

> Let no one expect any circumspection in the face of sedition, no compromise with it. There can be no compromise when it is a question of defending the internal peace of the nation and the integrity of the Republic. The Algerian departments are part of the Republic, they have been French for a long time. . . . Between it [the Algerian population] and the Metropole there can be no conceivable secession. Never will France, never will any parliament, never will any government cede on this fundamental principle.[1]

[1] *Journal Officiel,* November 12, 1954, pp. 4960–61.

In addition to the increased military effort both Mendès-France and his Minister of the Interior, François Mitterand, favored a vastly increased program of economic and social reform in Algeria.

On February 5, 1955, however, the Mendès-France government fell and was replaced by a government headed by Edgar Faure. At this point the initiative in Algeria fell to Governor-General Jacques Soustelle, a Mendès-France appointee. Soustelle elaborated a program for the political and economic integration of Algeria into France. He also requested and received more troops, bringing the total to 100,000. In August, 1955, Soustelle initiated a bloody campaign of repression in retaliation for a vicious rebel attack.[2] In the autumn of 1955, 200,000 French troops were in Algeria.

By 1956 the Algerian problem had moved to the center of the French political stage. The newly elected President of the Council of Ministers, Guy Mollet, stated that the government would discuss the future statute of Algeria with representatives freely elected to a single electoral college, and that the French government would initiate economic, social, political, and administrative reforms. "In this Algerian drama where the destiny of France is at stake, the government has a duty to tell the truth to the country and to act accordingly."[3]

Thus began what Guy Mollet appropriately called "the Algerian drama." When, sixteen months later, the Mollet government fell, the rebellion was raging throughout Algeria, and the problem seemed farther from solution than ever before.

The Incident of February 6, 1956

On February 6, 1956, occurred an event which many observers felt marked both the real and symbolic turning point

[2] Thomas Oppermann, *La Question Algérienne: Données Historiques, Politiques, Juridiques* (Paris, 1961), pp. 139–40.

[3] Guy Mollet quoted in *L'Année Politique*, 1956, p. 461.

in the government's Algerian policy and in the course of the rebellion.[4] After his investiture as President of the Council of Ministers, hoping to emulate Mendès-France's dramatic trip to Tunis in 1954, Mollet decided to install General Georges Catroux as minister residing in Algeria. General Catroux was considered to be liberal in regard to colonial affairs. In an interview with Jean Eparvier of *France-Soir* on February 3, 1956, Catroux mentioned that a federal solution for Algeria might be negotiated.

Algeria cannot be considered as a French province. It is necessary to think of a statute which will give satisfaction to the Algerian personality. For example, a large degree of administrative autonomy not involving political autonomy. . . . In these conditions, if in the future, the French Republic, currently one and indivisible, should become a federal republic, Algeria will have its place in it.[5]

The use of the phrase "Algerian personality" and Catroux's statement about the possibility of there being a federal relationship between France and Algeria aroused elements in Algeria adamantly opposed to any change whatsoever in the Algerian statute.

During a cabinet meeting prior to his scheduled Algerian visit, Mendès-France, a vice-premier in the 1956 government, warned Mollet to keep the exact date of his arrival secret so as to keep the opposition off balance, preventing them from organizing their forces.[6] Mollet, however, discounted news reports of scheduled antigovernment demonstrations in Algeria and accused Mendès-France of undue pessimism when the latter warned Mollet about the serious nature of the demonstrations. To a committee of Algerian politicians which he

[4] Fauvet, *La IVe République* (Paris, 1959), p. 316; André Philip, *Le Socialisme Trahi* (Paris, 1957), p. 174; and J. Barsalou, *La Mal-Aimé* (Paris, 1964), p. 264. Barsalou says, "We believe that the day of February 6, 1956 was the key date, the capital day of the Fourth Republic."

[5] *France-Soir*, February 3, 1956.

[6] Fauvet, p. 310.

received in Paris on February 4, 1956, Mollet said of the Algerian demonstrations, "C'est moi le patron" (I'm the boss).[7]

The Socialist newspaper *Le Populaire* noted that the trip was not only intended to inform the government of the situation in Algeria, but that it also had a "symbolic" character.

On arriving at Algiers airport on February 6, Mollet said that he had not brought any "miracle remedies" or "prefabricated solutions." Above all, he said, he had come in order "to listen and be informed by you." Reporters then questioned him.

Question: What is your position on the single electoral college?
Answer: On this point I insist on repeating that I have come to inform myself and that it is only at the conclusion of my trip that I will be able to definitively state a position.

Later, accompanied by Max Lejeune, Secretary of National Defense for Algeria, who had preceded Mollet in order to prepare for the latter's visit, Mollet attempted to lay a wreath at the Algiers war memorial. A crowd of howling demonstrators pelted them with tomatoes and rotten fruit and then with small stones. Cries of "Catroux à la mer" and "Guy Mollet au poteau" were heard. Mollet and Lejeune thereupon beat a hasty retreat to the Summer Palace, seat of the Governor-General in Algeria. The police seemed disinclined to restrain the crowd, but the army impassively protected the Prime Minister as best it could.[8] When Mollet and his entourage reached the Governor-General's palace it was almost 5:00 P.M. Fifty minutes earlier, at 4:10 P.M., General Catroux, having learned of the demonstrations, had submitted his resig-

[7] *Le Monde*, February 4, 1956.

[8] *Le Monde*, February 7, 1956; *Le Populaire*, February 7, 1956; Jean-Raymond Tournoux, *Secrets d'Etat* (Paris, 1960), p. 110, Barsalou, *Mal-Aimé*, p. 262.

nation to President of the Republic Coty. Mollet telephoned Paris at about five and spoke with the people gathered in the offices of the Ministry of the Interior. "I cannot keep Catroux any longer. What do you advise? It is necessary to have a successor immediately."[9] Although Catroux had already submitted his resignation, thus allowing Mollet merely to accept it, no immediate agreement could be reached on Catroux's successor. It was not until two days later that Robert Lacoste was chosen.

In subsequent speeches both in Algeria and France, Mollet spoke about the February 6 demonstrations. Speaking from Algiers, he said: "I regret the lack of understanding of my actions that I read in the eyes of my former fighting colleagues this afternoon."[10] On Algiers radio, February 10, Mollet said of the demonstrations and of his later meetings with various groups in Algeria:

> Above all I have better understood what you feel in your hearts and in your flesh, you Europeans, you Moslems. . . . These men believed that France was going to abandon them. I have understood their despair . . . that is why I say to you that if I have suffered, the painful demonstrations of Monday contained a healthy element. They have been for a great many people, the means for affirming their attachment to France. If this is what the immense majority of men and women at the War Memorial wanted to convey, then let them know that they have been heard.

[9] Conversations reported in Barsalou, *Mal Aimé*, p. 263.

[10] *Le Monde*, February 8, 1956. Gaston-Charles Pignault noted in *Le Monde*, February 8, 1956, that most of the demonstrators were youngsters of high school age and would have been ten or twelve years old at the end of the war. *Le Monde* also noted that the *Comité d'Entente des Anciens Combattants* had ordered its members to abstain from any hostile demonstrations toward the government on February 6. A letter to *Le Monde* on February 15, 1956 from a teacher in Algiers stated that the demonstrators were mostly youths between the ages of thirteen and twenty.

France will remain present in Algeria, the bonds between the Metropole and Algeria are indissoluble.[11]

Mollet went on to say that the political solution to the rebellion could only result from free discussions with representatives of Algeria, and that this presupposed free elections in a single electoral college—"but according to a system guaranteeing the maintenance of an equitable European representation."[12]

Some observers feel that Mollet's actions on February 6, in letting Catroux resign and in endorsing the demonstrations, marked a significant turning point in the attitude of the Moslem and European communities toward the metropolitan government. According to Gaston-Charles Pignault, the demonstrations "aggravated the divorce between the European and Moslem communities." He also noted an increase in tension in Algeria, not among the people, but among the Moslem elite. He observed that the word "independence" was on the lips of many Moslems who, three months before, had never before used it and he reported that many Moslems felt the February 6 incidents had marked a break between the European and Moslem communities—with the initiative for this break being the responsibility of the former.[13]

Reporting from Algeria soon afterward, Philip Minay noted that the actions of Guy Mollet and *Le Populaire*'s

[11] *Journal Officiel*, February 16, 1959, p. 323.

[12] *Le Populaire*, February 16, 1956. In 1956 the Algerian Assembly was composed of two separate houses with 60 members in each. The first house was elected by an electoral college composed mainly of Europeans, the second by an electoral college composed mainly of Moslems. To suggest election by a single electoral college was to imply that the Moslem representatives would outnumber the European representatives. In 1956, in spite of the equal sizes of the two electoral colleges, it was known that the Moslems elected to the second house were elected under European "supervision" in falsified elections. See Oppermann, *Question Algérienne*, pp. 92, 96–98, and 100.

[13] *Le Monde*, February 9, 1956.

acceptance and even endorsement of the antigovernment demonstrations had deceived the French Algerians on two counts. First, the French Algerian demonstrators seem to have been convinced that France was about to negotiate Algerian independence with the rebels. Second, they thought that Mollet's acceptance of Catroux's resignation had proved their first presumption correct. Moreover, news emanating from France was being scrutinized more carefully than ever by the Algerians in order to determine whether there were to be any further changes in government policy and whether the French Algerians should attempt to influence the government by organizing new demonstrations. According to another observer acquainted with Algerian affairs:

The electoral campaign of 1955 and the electoral success of Guy Mollet and Pierre Mendès-France inspired a timid interest among Algerian Moslems and burning despair among Europeans. The total and immediate capitulation of the President on his arrival in Algiers, the spectacular and violent character of the demonstrations which preceded it, unleashed . . . a profound sense of uneasiness among the Moslems, while the Europeans, having become conscious of their strength henceforth desired to use it.[14]

The reason for Mollet's actions on that day remain a source of dispute. For André Philip, they demonstrated how a lack of doctrinal orientation and of information conspired to weaken a man's will in the face of events he did not understand and could not control. Philip maintains that February 6 saw

the internal breakdown of a man who, having arrived with good intentions, persuaded that the origin of the Algerian difficulties proceeded from the bad will of a few great capitalists and landed proprietors, discovered with astonishment that the demonstrations against him were inspired by whites representing the same

[14] Germaine Tillion, *Les Ennemis Complémentaires* (Paris, 1960), p. 169.

social groups which in the metropolitan areas constituted the most solid bastion of his party. . . .

The capitulation of the Prime Minister seems to have had its origin in his ignorance of the general Algerian problem and in the ideological weakness of a conception of Socialism reduced to the notion of the defense of the little fellow against the big one.[15]

In retrospect, there can be little doubt that February 6 was, if not the turning point of the Fourth Republic, then at least one of the most important dates of that era. For years, through timidity, lack of imagination, or weakness, French governments had allowed colonial policy to be shaped by administrators and army personnel who either obstructed government policy or initiated their own. Since both the nation and its governments were divided over colonial policy, the method of *fait accompli* had become the usual tactic of those who wished France to retain the colonies at any price, or of those who wanted to prevent reforms that might injure their position.[16] The demonstrations of February 6 were in that tradition. If the first demonstrations were led by right-wing agitators and student groups, they merely expressed the sentiments of large sectors of Algerian opinion, and, as later events were to prove, the suspicions of administrators and army cadres. By giving way to the demonstrators on February 6, Mollet was to set the pattern of the government's colonial policy during the last years of the Fourth Republic. Finally, whereas prior to the demonstrations it had appeared that the Mollet government would attempt to act as a neutral intermediary between the Moslem and European communities, after the demonstrations the weight of government support came down heavily on the side of the Europeans.

Although some members of the government were unhappy

[15] Philip, *Le Socialisme Trahi*, p. 174.

[16] Raymond Aron, *Immuable et Changeante: De la IVe à la Ve République* (Paris, 1959), pp. 135, 137–39, and 166.

with the results of the demonstrations (Mendès-France was one, but he felt obliged to support Mollet so as not to divide the cabinet in the early stages of office), opposition to Mollet's Algerian policy did not arise until some time after the events of early February. On February 18, for example, *L'Express*, ever faithful to Mendès-France and thus a lukewarm supporter of the Mollet government, declared that Mollet's February 17 speech before the National Assembly proved the government intended to struggle against the "feudal powers" in both France and Algeria. *L'Express* went on to declare it the "duty of all republicans" to support the government.[17]

In that February 17 speech before the National Assembly, Mollet emphasized his belief that a purely military solution to the Algerian rebellion was impossible. He claimed the rebels were exploiting the themes of nationalism in order to organize on the "political and psychological levels." Moreover, he claimed that Algerian nationalism in turn drew much of its strength from "Moslem solidarity" and a feeling of "Islamic fraternity."[18]

For Mollet it was less the misery of their situation that impelled the Moslems toward active or tacit support of the rebels than a sense of injustice before the economic and political inequities of the Algerian situation. A minority of both the European and Moslem populations was deliberately attempting to prevent any reconciliation of the two peoples, Mollet maintained. Thus, among the rebels there were a number of "madmen and criminals who take orders from outside Algeria and serve interests which are not Algerian." Among the Europeans a small minority of "colonialists" supported extremist organizations.[19] According to Mollet, then, the government

[17] *L'Express*, February 18, 1956.
[18] *Journal Officiel*, February 16, 1956, p. 324.
[19] *Le Populaire*, February 10, 1956.

should crush the extremists on both sides and initiate social, economic, and administrative reforms in preparation for free elections which would disengage *interlocuteurs valables*—valid interlocutors—to discuss the future status of Algeria.

On February 28, 1956, on French radio and television, Mollet enunciated the terms of the famous "triptych." It comprised a cease-fire by the rebels, to be followed by free elections held three months after the cessation of "acts of violence and combat," and then negotiations on the future statute of Algeria. Algerian independence, however, would not be subject to negotiation.

In order to secure the country against rebel terrorism and to enact immediate reforms in the face of expected Algerian European opposition, a law granting the government special powers was submitted to and passed by the National Assembly on March 12, 1956. The vote was 455 to 76. The PCF voted unanimously for the law. Article 5, later to occasion much criticism stated:

> The government will dispose, in Algeria, of the most widespread powers allowing it to take all exceptional measures demanded by circumstances so as to re-establish order, to protect people and goods, and to safeguard the territory.
>
> When measures taken by virtue of the preceding lines modify legislation, they will be ordered by decree by the Council of Ministers.

Unwilling to involve itself in debating and passing unpopular measures for Algeria, the National Assembly delegated much of its legislative authority to the government with the passage of the March 12 decree law. As February 6 had presaged, however, the result was not to increase the executive's authority in Algeria but rather to increase the independent power of the minister in Algeria and through him the power of the army and administration.

The Ben Bella Incident

Although the inability of the government in Paris to impose its will on the administration and army in Algeria became common knowledge with the passage of time, the willingness of the government and of Mollet himself to accept and even take responsibility for a policy of *fait accompli* was illustrated in a remarkable fashion when Ben Bella and four other FLN (*Front de Libération Nationale*) leaders were captured by the French in October, 1956.

The immediate circumstances surrounding the capture were these. For a long time the FLN had infiltrated men and arms across the Tunisian border into Algeria, and violent incidents had occurred between French and rebel units near the border. Since Tunisia and France were linked by treaties of cooperation, and since France wished to retain both Tunisian and Moroccan good will, the French initially attempted to persuade Tunisia against aiding the FLN rebels.[20] In October, 1956, however, the Sultan of Morocco officially and warmly received a delegation of FLN leaders in Rabat. On October 22, 1956, the day of their reception, the Socialist Minister for Tunisian and Moroccan Affairs, Alain Savary, sent an official communiqué to the Sultan expressing the French government's decision to suspend its negotiations with Morocco for a treaty of financial and technical assistance. That same day the Sultan and the FLN leaders were scheduled to fly to Tunis where Habib Bourgiba had prepared another warm reception. The French intelligence services had learned, however, that the Sultan and the FLN leaders would travel in separate airplanes, the latter in an American DC-3 owned by Air Atlas, the Moroccan airline. The airplane was piloted by French pilots under charter to the Moroccan government. According to J.-R. Tournoux, the idea of kidnap-

[20] *L'Année Politique*, 1956, p. 222.

ping the FLN leaders originated with the French army and intelligence services. As the airplane carrying the FLN leaders passed within range of French radio facilities, the pilots were contacted by the French authorities in Algeria and asked to land their plane in Algiers. While conversations were taking place between the pilots and the authorities in Algiers, telephone calls were made by Robert Lacoste's cabinet secretary in an attempt to reach Lacoste, who was visiting in Dordogne, but he could not be reached. Abel Thomas, the cabinet director of Defense Minister Maurice Bourgès-Maunoury, was reached, however, and he spoke with the head of the general staff, General Henri Lorillot, who said, "It's a provocation; the army cannot stand by with its arms folded. What should we do?" Thomas answered, "This is the responsibility of the Minister for Algeria. Take the measures you think are opportune, in conformance with international law and the security of the frontiers as defined in the general directives of the government." General Lorillot then spoke with Max Lejeune, Secretary of State in the Ministry of National Defense, and Lejeune approved the kidnapping.

Soon afterward Lacoste was contacted. He flew immediately to Algiers airport, where he was notified of the attempts then being made to persuade the French pilot to land the plane carrying the rebel chiefs in Algiers. Informed that there was still time to countermand the order, Lacoste exclaimed, "Formidable! What a story, by God!" An aide replied, "M. le Ministre, the counterorder can still be given." "Too late, Ben Bella is above Algiers, most of the army knows what is happening and those who are fighting in the field will know tomorrow. This affair is going to cover me with ----, but the rebel chiefs are now above French territory, within reach of my hand. We are at war. At this point my duty is to arrest them."

Later that evening, having been informed of the incident,

Guy Mollet purportedly exclaimed to Max Lejeune, "You are one of the few people to know about Suez, didn't you weigh the consequences of the arrest? The Arabs are going to become very touchy at Port Said and you have created additional difficulties." (The reference of course, was to the impending but still secret invasion of Suez.)[21]

The resignation of the French Ambassador to Morocco, Pierre de Leusse and of Alain Savary followed the arrest of Ben Bella and the other rebel leaders (Mohammed Khider, Ahmed Hocine, Mohammed Boudiaf and Mostafa Lacheraf). As Jacques Fauvet pointed out, their resignation was not occasioned by the fact of the kidnapping, but because, having been informed by the Sultan of Morocco of the messages passing between the French authorities and the pilot of the Moroccan plane, Savary and de Leusse were unable to receive any confirmation from Lacoste until some time after the Moroccan craft had landed and the rebels taken into custody.[22]

The decision to kidnap the rebel chiefs had been made in the beginning of the afternoon of October 22 by the civil and military authorities of Algiers.[23] Yet, in the National Assembly on October 26, 1956, Guy Mollet said that

> the initiative for the arrest of the FLN chiefs, which might have grave consequences in many areas, falls upon the civil and military authorities who finally informed the government.
>
> I do not say this to diminish my responsibilities, but in order to attribute the merit of them to myself. [Lively applause.]

Although the capture of Ben Bella and his compatriots was very popular in France the consequences were less happy.

[21] Jean-Raymond Tournoux, *Carnets Secrets de la Politique* (Paris, 1958), pp. 126–39, gives a complete account of the Ben Bella kidnapping.

[22] Fauvet, *La IVe République*, p. 320.

[23] *Le Monde*, October 28–29, 1956.

Riots soon broke out in Tunisia and Morocco when people learned of the arrests, many French were killed or injured and, as a result, relations between France and both Tunisia and Morocco were damaged. Finally, and perhaps most serious of all, the arrests ended the secret discussions which had periodically taken place between representatives of Guy Mollet and the FLN concerning the possibility of beginning negotiations on a cease-fire and on the future status of Algeria.[24]

The capture of the rebel chiefs was one of the most striking examples of the impotence of the Socialist-led government in the face of the army and administration in Algeria. The acceptance and endorsement by Guy Mollet of the kidnapping certainly illustrated the diminished authority of the government in Algeria. Perhaps Mollet had no other choice; he could not very well have released the rebel chiefs after their capture, since the damage had already been done. To have let the rebels go would have been to risk defeat in the National Assembly. Lacoste had reasoned in approximately the same fashion. The initiative having passed out of the government's hands, there was little else to do but accept the inevitable. The point is, however, that at many crucial points in the history of the Fourth Republic, the government pleaded that decisions taken without its consent or knowledge had to be accepted because to reverse them would be more injurious than accepting them. The difficulty with this reasoning was that it established a precedent for the future, and one whose significance was lost on neither the Algerian rebels nor on those who felt that the Algerian problem could only be solved outside the framework of democratic institutions.

The Suez Attack

If one of the reasons for the longevity of the Mollet government was its refusal to risk parliamentary defeat by cen-

[24] Barsalou, *Mal-Aimé*, pp. 272–74.

suring or disciplining those who made policy without the government's knowledge or consent, another important reason was Mollet's willingness to profit from a revival of French nationalism occasioned by the Algerian rebellion and the nationalization of the Suez Canal.

The Suez affair followed close upon the heels of the rebel leaders' capture. For the first time since it had taken office, the government had an opportunity to demonstrate the strength of its resolution. The capture of the FLN chiefs had met with widespread support in France and it was thought that the Suez invasion would bring glory not only to the army which received most of the credit for the Ben Bella capture, but to the government and to Guy Mollet.

Public opinion was prepared since French hostility toward Egypt had been heightened by the Suez nationalization in July, 1956, and then further irritated by news of the capture of the yacht *Athos* loaded with arms sent by the Egyptian government to the Algerian rebels.[25] *Sondages*, the quarterly public opinion journal, published the results of a poll it had conducted from August 28 to September 4, 1956:

On July 26, Colonel Nasser, Chief of the Egyptian government, nationalized the Suez Canal company. Do you think he had or did not have the right to act thusly?

Had the right	18%
Did not have right	58%
No answer	24%

Do you think that, until now, Egypt has played a very important, a rather important or an unimportant role in the Algerian rebellion?

Very important	48%
Rather important	25%
Unimportant	7%
No answer	20%

[25] *L'Année Politique*, 1956, p. 220.

If events helped prepare public opinion for the Suez invasion, certain comments by Socialists in government also aided this process. Before the National Assembly on March 9, 1956, for example, Robert Lacoste emphasized the fact that the FLN was receiving aid from "certain" Arab states. "Algerian nationalism is already under tutelage." A variation on this theme was enunciated by Marcel Champeix who linked "panarabism" or "panislamism" to historical "pangermanism," a juxtaposition which was to become quite common after the Suez nationalization. Another variation on this theme was stated by Max Lejeune during the 48th National Congress held in June, 1956. Spicing his discourse with some basic Socialist sloganeering calculated to arouse the delegates, he claimed that the French were really at war with "panarabism maintained by the petroleum war led by international capitalism." Lejeune leveled an attack against capitalism and against American oil interests which he felt had always been opposed to the Socialist party.

By early July, 1956, still prior to Nasser's seizure of the canal, Robert Lacoste was saying that the Algerian independence movement had "lost its autonomy," that it was dominated either by Cairo, "that is, by the panarab movement that the USSR is striving to capture, or by a kind of Western Islamism in which the U.S. and other countries are interested."[26] Moreover, according to Lacoste, "one French division in Cairo is worth four in Algeria."[27] This kind of rhetoric was well-seasoned with references to Hitler and to Munich. Nasser was compared with both Hitler and Stalin by Guy Mollet before the National Assembly,[28] and the Suez nationalization

[26] *Le Populaire*, March 9, April 30, and June 29, 1956.

[27] Barsalou, *Mal-Aimé*, p. 267.

[28] *Journal Officiel*, October 23, 1956, p. 4286. In an interview conducted ten years later, Guy Mollet said of his government's conduct during Algeria and Suez, "If I had to do it again, I would do it." And

was considered to present a similar challenge and threat to France as Munich had in 1938. Guy Mollet stated his unwillingness to agree to "peace at any price, the peace of Munich maintained with contempt for justice."[29]

The Socialists found little difficulty in replying to those who wondered about their violent reaction toward an act of nationalization, an act which, in other contexts, it would seem Socialists would applaud. Writing in *Le Populaire*, Henri Lévy-Bruhl stated that the act of nationalization was not an end in itself, but the means to an end. This end was prescribed by socialism and was the freedom of the individual. Nationalization could not be justified, therefore, if its goal was merely to enhance the power of the state to the detriment of the individual. Moreover, when a problem was international in scope, then an international solution was always preferable to a national solution. This was in accordance with the internationalism of the Socialists. Although Socialists were instinctively sympathetic toward nationalization, when nationalization affected the international community in a deleterious fashion, then Socialist doctrine held that "the sovereignty of each country has limits and is respectable only to the degree that it does not intrude upon the legitimate interests of other nations in the human community."[30]

Another article in *Le Populaire* also defended the Socialist action from a Marxist point of view. According to Suzanne Labin, Marx considered capitalists only semiparasites since they contributed something of value to the community. The worst parasite, however, was the landowner who did not

---

he said, "I have never hidden the fact that there is among us in the Socialist party an anti-Munich complex. If in 1938 one had done for the Czech army what one did in 1956 for the Israelis, things would have changed." *Le Monde*, January 26, 1966.

[29] *Le Populaire*, October 1, 1956.

[30] *Ibid.*, September 3, 1956; summary of an article by Henri Lévy-Bruhl.

work at all, but drew a profit from the work of other people. Thus, Nasser was worse than a capitalist semiparasite since, Labin pointed out, nationalization gave to Nasser the fruit of other people's labor. Further, it could not be defended on any other grounds because it would not benefit the Egyptian people who could not vote and who were unfree. As in much of the Algerian analysis of the Socialist commentators, unless a country or a government was a carbon copy of, or attempted seriously to imitate, French democratic institutions, then whatever actions it undertook were subject to the most extreme criticism for being undemocratic and outside Socialist tradition.

When the Anglo-French invasion of Egypt occurred, it was defended by the Socialists as a logical extension of their previous arguments against the nationalization of the Suez Canal. According to Paul Parpaix, one of the editorialists of *Le Populaire* and a member of Guy Mollet's cabinet, the Suez invasion could be justified on a number of grounds: it was intolerable that nations such as Egypt scrap treaties at will, that international agreements hold for some (in contravention of the Suez convention, Egypt had refused to allow Israeli ships to pass through the Canal, and Egypt had refused to heed a United Nations request that it allow the Israeli ships to proceed) and not for others, that the decisions of the United Nations be flaunted and ignored.[31]

According to Guy Mollet, the invasion was based on France's desire to prevent the Israeli-Egyptian conflict from spreading, to assure the security of the Suez Canal and prevent Egypt from hindering the free circulation of traffic through the Canal, to stop Nasser from realizing his dream of establishing Egyptian hegemony over the Arab world and to limit Egyptian expansionism.[32]

[31] *Le Populaire*, November 1 and 27, 1956.

[32] *Journal Officiel*, November 7, 1956, p. 4527.

Within the SFIO both Daniel Mayer and André Philip were prominent among the critics. Mayer pointed out that the Socialist-led government had engaged in preventive war, and that this was contrary to Socialist principles.[33] He also accused the government of having been motivated by the desire to interdict further aid to Algeria from Egypt and to punish Egypt for helping the FLN. Mayer maintained that the government had flaunted the U.N. Charter, ignored international law, and alienated all its allies. Philip accused the government of having united nations in the developing areas as well as the countries of the Arab world against France.[34] Criticism also came from the Socialist International, which condemned Britain and France for the Suez invasion.[35]

Although Mollet tried to salvage some positive results from the abortive invasion, there can be little doubt that it failed to achieve most of the major objectives previously set forth by the government. The Suez Canal was not placed under an international authority, the Algerian rebellion was not in the least affected by the invasion, Nasser's prestige increased because of his seeming ability to withstand and then bring about the withdrawal of the Anglo-French-Israeli forces, and the canal was blocked for weeks by ships sunk by the Egyptians during the attack, thus forcing France to ration fuel. The Suez failure starkly illustrated the difficulties France seemed to confront when trying to act in concert with an ally so apparently beholden to the United States, while de Gaulle purportedly concluded that "if France had had an atomic bomb, it would not have been treated so badly."[36]

As for the SFIO, the absurd lengths to which party propa-

[33] *Le Populaire*, December 17, 1956.

[34] *L'Année Politique*, 1956, p. 110.

[35] *Socialist International Information*, VI, no. 49 (November, 1956), 848–49.

[36] Barsalau, *Mal-Aimé*, p. 272.

gandists went to justify the Suez action in terms of Socialist doctrine could not but hurt the party. If the party had attempted to defend the government's action on the basis of national interest or *Realpolitik*, then perhaps its intellectual honesty would not have been called into question; but it appeared that Socialist doctrine was being pressed into service to justify any and all controversial actions undertaken by the government.

By acceding to and then championing French nationalist impulses, the SFIO not only helped to create a climate hostile toward the Fourth Republic—for many people attributed the Suez failure to the Republic as well as to the Socialist-led government—but, waving the banner of nationalism for the sake of temporary popularity, it was later to discover there were other parties and other personalities better qualified by background and prestige to elicit support because of their assumed devotion to French national interests.

Pacification in Algeria

The anticolonialism of the Socialist party can be documented in a general sense. Jaurès, Blum, and other party luminaries all stated their opposition to imperialism and colonialism at various times, and the SFIO has traditionally supported the establishment of democratic institutions in French colonies.[37] In the case of Algeria, however, Guy Mollet and

[37] Parti Socialiste, *Bulletin Intérieur*, no. 91, June, 1957, pp. 13–17. Jaurès is quoted as saying, when he heard of the destruction by French forces of a village where combatants and noncombatants were killed, "I ask that all possible light be thrown on this affair and I declare that if, unfortunately, certain excesses have been committed, the honor of France lies in not hiding them, not veiling them, not in excusing them, but of being the first in the world to denounce them, criticize them and chastise those who committed them." See also A. Grosser, *La IVe République et sa Politique Extérieure* (Paris, 1961), p. 112: "Until its arrival in power in 1936, the SFIO had made its most definitive state-

his supporters never tired of pointing out that Algeria was a unique case:

Tunisia and Morocco were independent states when France took them under her wing as protectorates. There were sovereigns there going back centuries. There were institutions and local government and local officials receiving their orders from the Bey or the Sultan. But what was there in Algeria when the French took over in 1830? Nothing. No sovereign. No laws. No institutions of any kind that united the anarchic and chaotic conglomeration of villages and poverty-stricken peasants that France united and built up into a territorial unit under the guidance of France.

It was France that gave borders to this territory, gave it existence and spirit. Algeria is a monument to French ingenuity. It was France and only France which raised it from the dust and gave it life. France fathered and mothered it. Without France there would have been nothing. And more than one million Frenchmen have gone there to make their homes and to raise its economic level to that of France.[38]

Thus it was France which had created the Algerian nation, and this certainly made Algeria something more than a colony. The fact that there were eight million Moslems in Algeria, however, and that the Moslems were worse off than the French in practically every sphere of activity also made of Algeria something less than a province of France.

---

ments in the area of anticolonialism. On July 11, 1927 Léon Blum had declared to the Chamber during a discussion relating to Algerian electoral reform, 'As far as we are concerned, we are less interested in granting a larger representation to the indigenous peoples in the parliament, then in seeing colonial legislation lead increasingly toward independence, toward "self-government" [in English] as in the Dominions. I say this, speaking, if not for the party, then for the majority of my colleagues.' " And it should be recalled that as Prime Minister in December, 1946, Léon Blum took the first steps to end the revolt in Indo-China.

[38] H. Luethy and D. Rodnick, *French Motivations in the Suez Crisis* (Princeton, 1956), p. 79.

Algeria, then, was a peculiar case and could not be subsumed under a simple rubric. It was a complex country with complex problems calling for subtle and intelligent solutions. It should not be forgotten that in early 1956 not even the PCF had supported Algerian independence. There was certainly a great deal of debate during that period about granting Algeria increased autonomy within the French Union, but the word independence was taboo.

Prior to the election, the Socialists had freely dispensed prescriptions for the Algerian problem. Guy Mollet had said it was necessary to "stop the lies" and not to "repeat the errors of Indochina, Tunisia, and Morocco." He claimed the people of Algeria had only asked to be French, to be equals in a Republic really based on liberty, equality, and fraternity. "They believed in us and we have lied to them."[39]

After the election Mollet appeared on television and was asked why, since he was a Socialist, he had not tried to grant Algeria its independence. Mollet replied that Socialists were mainly interested in the "liberty of each individual, the independence of each person." He noted that granting independence to a "feudal system" would lead to feudal domination of the individual and thus would be against the tenets of socialism. This notion that the essence of socialism was political democracy was widely trumpeted by Socialist spokesmen after 1956. Claude Fuzier, editor of *Le Populaire* attacked "chauvinistic nationalism and racism" and claimed that the Socialists wished to guide colonial peoples toward "true liberation" rather than let them fall into the hands of an authority "more barbarous than the one they have known."

Mollet went so far as to claim that nationalism was against the current of history and that "interdependence among nations is becoming the rule."[40]

[39] *L'Express*, December 19, 1955.
[40] *Le Populaire*, June 20, 1956, and January 26–27, 1957.

The danger implicit in these kinds of explanations was that it could lead to a total rejection of one kind of chauvinism in favor of another. Thus, J. Riès, writing in the April, 1957, *La Revue Socialiste*, claimed that for Algeria, Morocco, and Tunisia the basic choice was between westernization, which alone would allow the development of democracy leading in turn to socialism, and refusal to westernize, which would lead to economic, political and social regression. For Riès, therefore, as for many SFIO members, nationalism implied regression because it excluded the possibility that some form of acceptable democratic structures might develop after native nationalist leaders assumed power. Moreover, the threatened success of native nationalist movements in the Middle East carried with it the certainty that religious intolerance would spread and impede progress toward socialism. For Riès, only laic democracy in the French colonies should be an acceptable form of government. Any other system should be condemned, and, if possible, France should fight to suppress alternative systems.

the chances of socialism are narrowly tied to an economic transformation which implies, among other things, the end of the European dominators, but also of the feudal masters, the unseating of the ulemas and the students and professors of the Koranic universities.

Thus, not only was France's role to eliminate the big capitalists in Algeria, but to aid in suppressing the conservative and intolerant forces of the Moslem religion. Not only in the underdeveloped areas was religion a threat to French democratic institutions; in France, too, though for different reasons, Riès felt religious groups were dangerous. As he pointed out, left-wing Catholics were undermining the *Union Française* through their misguided criticisms of government policies in

Algeria.[41] For many other Socialists, too, the cruel tactics of the Algerian rebels could be attributed, in part, to their religious fanaticism. Early in 1956, for example, Max Lejeune noted:

There are only a few thousand rebels, inspired by extremely diverse motives: there are the miserable peasants, the unemployed, young people without hope who have joined the rebels and bandits in the mountains; there are the religious fanatics who are the most primitive, full of scorn and hatred for the infidel, and whose cruel character is marked in the execution rites, victims with their throats cut . . . finally, there are, and it seems to me that this is the least important element, the nationalists who aspire to an impossible independence. To the nationalists, to the unemployed it would be easy to respond. To them we promise, we will give dignity, justice and work. To the fanatics we have nothing to say, nothing to give to assassins other than the rigor of the law.[42]

Within the SFIO, however, there were a number of critics who felt that the party leadership tended to analyze the rebellion in an abstract and unrealistic fashion. According to one of the foremost French experts on North Africa, a Socialist member of the Assembly of the French Union, the development of nationalism in North Africa could not be understood if it were separated from the question of Islam. The two were so intermingled that it was impossible to claim the rebels were fighting because of religious fanaticism alone. Their motives were a mixture of nationalism, religion, and other influences.[43]

The difficulty with the Riès interpretation, critics pointed

[41] J. Riès in *La Revue Socialiste*, no. 108 (June, 1957), pp. 46–47. J. Moreau ("En Lisant J. Riès, ou Esquisse d'une Critique Idéologique de Socialisme Occidental," *La Revue Socialiste*, no. 114 (February, 1958), pp. 138–55) notes that Riès's articles represented the view of the majority of party members.

[42] *Le Populaire*, March 15, 1956.

[43] *Le Monde*, May 2, 1956.

out, was that it was ahistorical, conceiving nationalism to be both an artificial and a reactionary phenomenon. By refusing to acknowledge the necessity for a nation to pass through stages of development before attaining both the psychological and sociological levels permitting the establishment of a working democratic system, the government, by attempting to impose French political institutions on an unwilling populace, was creating the conditions for the very dictatorship it claimed it wished to prevent.[44] By denying the possibility of the growth of a genuine sentiment of nationalism among the Moslems, and by characterizing nationalist claims as basically reactionary and deriving from selfish or intolerant motives, the French government had been led to base its policy on a narrow view of Moslem desires. Thus the government exerted extraordinary efforts to improve the social and economic conditions of the impoverished Moslem masses, while, at the same time, it acted rather timidly in the political domain. This led one Moslem to comment bitterly on Jacques Soustelle's policy of distributing free grain to the Algerian Moslems, "We are not merely stomachs."[45]

If the government seemed to emphasize the necessity for giving priority to reform in Algeria as the best means for reducing rebel support, there were some within the government who seemed to place the emphasis elsewhere. For Robert Lacoste, the Algerian rebels won support through a clever mixture of "terrorism and messianism." He felt there was no evidence to support the view that the rebels won spontaneous support from the people.[46]

Many Algerians also seemed to take the position that Lacoste's view of the rebellion differed from that of the majority

[44] Moreau, "En Lisant," p. 143.

[45] Charles-Robert Ageron, "Le Nationalisme Algérien, de l'Islam à la Révolution," *La Revue Socialiste*, no. 99 (July, 1956), p. 131.

[46] *Le Populaire*, March 9, 1956.

of the government. Amédée Froger, president of the Interfederation of Algerian mayors and spokesman for the most diehard sectors of Algerian opinion, said:

Reformism and terrorism, these are two irreconcilable words. Free elections. What foolishness! The terrorists don't want them and never will want them. I am also hurt because the current Moslem representatives, who are our creation, are profiting from our difficulties to ask for advantages that they never had during the period of calm. We are very enthusiastic about the declarations of Robert Lacoste. We must support him all the way and support him we shall.[47]

When pressed to enact reforms that might provoke the opposition of European Algerians (increasing the number of Moslem civil servants, for example—in 1956 there were 145 Moslems in the top ranks of the civil service and in 1957, 239, out of a total of 7,394 in these ranks)[48] Lacoste uttered his famous remark, "I am being fired upon from in front, I don't want to be fired upon from the rear."[49] Jacques Chevallier, *mendèsiste* mayor of Algiers, also noted Lacoste's close relations with Alain de Sérigny, publisher of *L'Echo d'Alger* and one of the most important leaders of the antigovernment, later the *Algérie Française* forces in Algeria.[50]

The controversy surrounding the actual extent of govern-

[47] *Le Monde*, March 1, 1956.

[48] Tillion, *Ennemis Complémentaires*, p. 156.

[49] Fauvet, *La IVe République*, p. 327; *Le Monde*, July 2, 1956; *Journal Officiel*, June 2, 1956, p. 2261. See also *L'Année Politique*, 1956, p. 211, for Lacoste's detailed explanation of his desire not to alienate the Europeans and throw moderate Europeans into the arms of ultras by a "violent and vindictive policy" that "some people had counseled" him to follow in Algeria.

[50] Jacques Chevallier, *Nous Algériens . . .* (Paris, 1958), p. 152. See also Merry and Serge Bromberger, *Les 13 Complots du 13 Mai* (Paris, 1959), p. 73, where they note that Lacoste was unwilling to provoke the European Algerian community by effectuating scheduled reforms.

ment reform in Algeria was soon complicated by complaints about the methods of pacification practiced by the army in Algeria. The government contended that terrorism had to be controlled and calm restored before elections to the dissolved Algerian Assembly could be held. The excesses to which the pacification campaign gave rise were of two general kinds. First, excesses committed during military operations when Moslems were killed indiscriminately because it was very difficult to distinguish between those who were rebels and those who were not. Second, excesses committed by torturing real or suspected rebels or real or suspected FLN supporters.[51]

Another practice, and one condemned by critics, was the attempt to suppress those critics who protested against the use of torture. Thus, Henri Marrou, a professor at the Sorbonne, had his apartment searched by police soon after he protested against torture, repression, and concentration camps in Algeria. By April, 1957, however, the use of torture was confirmed in *Le Monde:* "If maltreatment is not systematic . . . it is too frequently practiced to be called exceptional."[52] Confirmation of the use of torture also came from General Jacques Massu, Commander of the Algiers region.[53]

The usual reaction of the Socialists, in the beginning, was either to deny or to ignore reports of torture. Speaking before the National Assembly on June 3, 1956, Mollet stated:

If the role of the press is to inform us, it also has the duty not to simplify. The entire nation is involved in the Algerian drama, it vibrates to each bit of news and each declaration concerning it.

[51] The literature on torture and excesses practiced by the French in Algeria is extensive, but some of the most noteworthy books are: Henri Alleg, *La Question* (Paris, 1958); Jean-Jacques Servan-Schreiber, *Lieutenant in Algeria* (New York, 1957); and P. Vidal-Naquet, *L'Affaire Audin* (Paris, 1958).

[52] *Le Monde*, April 11 and 12, 1956.

[53] Charles-Henri Favrod, *Le FLN et l'Algérie* (Paris, 1962), p. 217.

. . . France does not answer crime with crime, terrorism with counterterrorism.[54]

Neither *Le Populaire* nor *Populaire-Dimanche* ever mentioned the famous account of torture in Algeria by Henri Alleg, *La Question*.[55]

Even when the SFIO leadership finally acknowledged the existence of excesses it was done in a grudging and accusatory fashion. Thus Claude Fuzier wrote in *Le Populaire* that everything wasn't "idyllic" in Algeria because some tough fighting was going on. But he placed the blame for the continued conflict on the rebels who refused to agree to a cease-fire and who resorted to terrorism and mutilation as methods of war.[56]

In the National Assembly, Lacoste, in his usual bluff and blunt fashion, spoke about the mutilated victims of FLN terrorist attacks in Algeria and then criticized those who had, in the metropolitan French papers, indulged themselves in a "false humanism." Only results mattered for Lacoste, and "one could think what one wanted about it, but our action against terrorism has sensibly decreased the number of victims." To a question concerning Ali Boumendjel, a Moslem lawyer who had purportedly committed suicide while being held incommunicado in Algiers by paratroops, Lacoste replied:

From a juridical and procedural point of view . . . it is certain that, in Algeria, . . . the apparatus of justice is extremely insufficient in means and personnel. That is why we are obliged to have recourse to the procedure against which you have protested, but which is perfectly permissible.[57]

[54] *Le Populaire*, June 4, 1956.

[55] *Tribune du Socialisme*, no. 5, May 15, 1958.

[56] *Le Populaire*, March 27, 1957.

[57] *Journal Officiel*, March 20, 1957, pp. 1783 and 1784–85; March 26, 1957, p. 1866.

By April, 1957, however, the protests against excesses had mounted to the point where the government was forced to create an investigatory commission, the Commission for the Safeguard of Rights and Individual Liberties.[58]

Claude Fuzier commented on its creation by noting that it had been initiated by Robert Lacoste, Max Lejeune, and Maurice Bourgès-Maunoury. He noted that its purpose was to end excesses no matter "how small they might be," but also to end the "systematic campaign of denigration which tends to make of hundreds of thousands of men who are suffering for a new Algeria, just so many torturers."[59]

It is interesting to compare the above statement with one published in *Le Populaire* in December, 1955, prior to the election:

> France has tolerated the exploitation of workers, it has left thousands of unemployed without work, it has rigged elections, it has imprisoned and tortured the opposition . . . ; under the pretext of suppressing the rebellion a ferocious and imbecilic campaign of repression has only multiplied it.
>
> The conscience of the young soldiers rebels against the atrocities they are ordered to commit in the framework of operations called "repression," "mopping up," and "rounding up."

While the government was heavily criticized for its half-hearted attempts to investigate and punish those who committed excesses, it exerted itself in strenuous fashion in seizing or suppressing numbers of newspapers, periodicals, and books which mentioned torture or concentration camps in Algeria. It is interesting to note, for example, that in 1955 the CD of the SFIO protested against "the attacks on the liberty of the press" of the Faure government, while, in 1956, the government seized more newspapers (usually newspapers on the

[58] *L'Année Politique*, 1957, pp. 35–36.
[59] *Le Populaire*, April 6–7, 1957.

left) in both France and Algeria than had the Faure government in 1955.

One of the most flagrant examples of the government's attempt to suppress criticism occurred in November, 1956, when the Mollet government refused to allow *Le Monde* to raise its prices in order to meet mounting costs.[60] The French radio and television facility, RTF, also suffered from the attempt to mute criticism. In December, 1956, the RTF canceled the Free Tribune, a program which brought together journalists of all political persuasions for weekly discussions of government politics. As *Le Monde* pointed out, RTF also was inclined to ignore news which might damage government prestige—as in March 1957, when the controversy between General Paris de Bollardière and the Minister of National Defense was not mentioned. General de Bollardière had resigned from the army in protest against the harsh tactics of repression he had been ordered to practice by his superiors. He was then placed under arrest by the Minister of National Defense for allowing a letter publicizing his views to be printed without first clearing the letter with his superiors. He also offended the government because of his support for Jean-Jacques Servan-Schreiber, editor of *L'Express* and author of the popular and critical *Lieutenant en Algérie*.[61]

On balance the Algerian policies of the Socialist-led government of 1956–1957 were a failure. Guy Mollet assumed the post of President of the Council of Ministers at a time when the rebellion was led by about 12,000 rebels and combated by approximately 200,000 French soldiers. When he left office in May, 1957, the number of rebels had swollen to

[60] Martin Harrison, "Government and Press in France during the Algerian War," *American Political Science Review*, LVIII (June 1964), 278–79. Editorial of H. Beuve-Méry in *Le Monde*, November 8, 1956; also Harrison, p. 280 and n.

[61] *Le Monde*, March 30, 1967.

nearly 60,000 while French forces numbered more than 400,000.

The primary objective of the Socialists in government had been to stop the bloodletting and to demonstrate France's resolve to maintain its ties with Algeria. When Mollet left office the first objective was quite far from being achieved and the second, in spite of Mollet's assertions to the contrary, was weakened by rebel successes and by the growing sentiment on the left and within the SFIO that, eventually, Algeria would have to be granted a large degree of autonomy.

During both the February 6 and the Ben Bella incidents the government had demonstrated its inability to impose its will in Algeria. Germaine Tillion wrote that during the last few months of 1956 people who carefully followed Algerian affairs were aware that the French government "had ceased to be obeyed there."[62] Neither after February 6, nor after the Ben Bella kidnapping were those guilty for the incidents punished or reprimanded. In Algeria the local powers accrued to themselves the authority vested by the National Assembly in the government and, finally, in the office of the Minister in Algeria.[63]

In effect, the Socialist-led government, in spite of campaign promises and rhetoric, was led to practice approximately the same kind of policy as its predecessors. There were a number of reasons for this, not the least of which was the deeply rooted and traditional independence of colonial authorities in

[62] Tillion, *Ennemis Complémentaires*, p. 182.

[63] Claude Panier in *Journal Officiel*, June 2, 1956, p. 2270: "When the question arose of appointing a committee charged with preparing the promotion of Moslems to civil service posts, the cabinet director of Robert Lacoste could only think of nominating as a representative of the veterans' organizations one of the men who was pointed out during the troubled period from February 6 to 10, 1956, as being one of the most violent opponents of the government." The army had been given police powers in February, 1957, by Lacoste.

Algeria. In spite of their strictures to the contrary, the Socialist party itself had been guilty of supporting individuals who flouted the law and condoned rigged elections in Algeria.[64] But, as Robert Schuman once noted, colonial adminstrators found it very difficult not to become captive in a repressive colonial system. "The *fait accompli* is the great and constant temptation. If they don't succumb to it, it is to the credit of the residents-general."[65]

As for the rebels, they knew that they could not hope to defeat the French militarily. They pinned their hopes on demoralizing the French people and the government by forcing the government to pour immense, and finally insupportable amounts of men and material into Algeria in the attempt to crush the rebellion. To counter this tactic the government had to demonstrate to the rebels that its will and resources were inexhaustible and that no French government could or would accede to rebel demands for recognition of Algerian independence. The danger latent in this kind of dialectic was that any sign of willingness to discuss or negotiate with the rebels could be interpreted as a weakening of French resolve. Thus, to allow open criticism of the government policy in Algeria might be interpreted as pointing the way toward a change in government policy—at least this was how some people argued. In any case, this interpretation might help explain the anti-intellectual tone assumed by certain Socialists in the government. Robert Lacoste, for example, criticized those "pretended intellectuals" who claimed that France might be defeated in Algeria. And Guy Mollet attacked those who had "unleashed the odious campaign based on a few isolated cases of brutality." He promised that those who committed brutali-

[64] André Philip, *Pour un Socialisme Humaniste* (Paris, 1960), p. 113.

[65] Schuman is quoted in Philip Williams, *Crisis and Compromise* (Hamden, Conn., 1964), p. 349 and n.

ties would be punished but he announced the "defamers" would also not be spared.[66]

Speaking before the 49th National Congress on June 30, 1957, Max Lejeune criticized the very "intellectual discourse" of Gaston Defferre in which the latter had advocated granting Algeria a certain degree of autonomy. Lejeune remarked: "The discourse of M. Defferre may be compared to Rousseau's essay on the Constitution of Poland."[67]

It should be recalled that in 1956 no French political party, not even the PCF, felt that the Algerian rebels should be allowed to negotiate for Algerian independence. Algeria had been considered part of France for a long time. The statement of Ferhat Abbas that he had "interrogated the living and the dead, visited the cemeteries—no one spoke to me of it [Algerian nationhood]"[68] was repeated on all sides in early 1956. Many people felt the Algerian rebels were artificially attempting to create nationalist sentiment where none had previously existed and where the historical and psychological bases were lacking. Moreover, the presence on Algerian soil of almost a million Europeans of French nationality, a community whose roots in Algeria extended back to the middle of the nineteenth century was a powerful argument against analogizing the case of Algeria with that of Tunisia and Morocco.

Party leaders diagnosed the Algerian rebellion as arising partly from the legitimate demands of the Algerian Moslem population for increased social and economic services and partly from fear of reprisals from the FLN. For Mollet,

[66] *Le Populaire*, January 1 and April 15, 1957.

[67] *Le Monde*, June 30, 1957.

[68] Quoted in Charles-André Julien, *L'Afrique du Nord en Marche: Nationalismes Musulmans et Souveraintè Française* (Paris, 1952), pp. 110–11.

Lejeune, and Lacoste, it was difficult to believe in the appeal of a nationalism inspired by hatred for the colonizer and complicated by the intolerant and regressive influence of the Moslem religion. They refused to believe that a reform program inspired by traditional Socialist egalitarian ideals could fail to win the support of disaffected Algerian Moslems. In their experience, the oppressed of the world usually tended to support Socialist ideals and Socialist parties—when, that is, they were not deceived by Communists who preyed on the discontented for their own selfish ends. For these Socialists, therefore, those who supported the rebels must have been either misled or terrorized. That the appeal of nationalism might have been stronger than the appeal of democratic socialism seemed to have occurred to few people in the SFIO during this period.

4. *Party Democracy and Algeria*

The SFIO was not a stranger to internal dissension and occasional splitting. Before the Second World War there were four important splits, the first giving rise to the *Parti Socialiste Français* in 1919, the second and most important leading to the formation of the French Communist party in 1921, the third occurring in 1933 when a Neo-Socialist wing left the SFIO, and the last occurring in 1939 with the formation of an appeasement faction. After the Liberation, however, there was little serious disagreement in the party, although the left-wing *Bataille Socialiste* group which favored unity with the PCF was excluded from the SFIO in 1944. Moreover, except for the schism in 1921 that gave rise to the PCF, all the groups that left the SFIO to form independent parties soon withered on the vine.

A party commission appointed in 1956 to examine the question of revising party rules commented on the apparent consensus within the SFIO by noting that battles over doctrine or method were unlikely to occur because everyone "agreed with Jaurès on the value of reform, and with Guesde on the limits of its efficacy within the capitalist system." The commission also claimed that the question of government participation was accepted by all as a matter of principle, but only gave rise to controversy when party members differed over the appropriate moment to choose to participate. Finally the commission observed that no one argued now about the party's duty to defend the Republic.[1] In 1956, then, the party gave the impression of being unified on the major issues which had caused dissension in the past. When the SFIO appeared as one of the major victors in the 1956 elections, the Extraordinary National Congress that met soon afterward was unanimous in its support for a motion asking that the Republican Front seek to form a minority government in the new legislature.

By early March, 1956, however, there were signs of growing disagreement within the government. Gaston Defferre, Alain Savary, and Mendès-France had begun to oppose the Algerian policy advocated by Robert Lacoste, Max Lejeune, and Maurice Bourgès-Maunoury. Although the controversy was merely over tactics, not about the long-run objectives of government policy, this first disagreement was to harden into a division between those who took a tough and those who took a conciliatory position on Algerian policy. One of the very first issues that gave rise to disagreement within the government, according to a report published in the March 2, 1956, issue of *Le Monde*, concerned the question of delaying the execution of Moslem rebels accused of having committed capital crimes. Some people like Mendès-France wanted to delay the executions as a conciliatory gesture toward the FLN; others like Robert Lacoste wanted the rebels to be executed as soon as possible in order to set an example.

By March, 1956, Daniel Mayer, former secretary-general of the SFIO and perpetual thorn in the side of Guy Mollet,

[1] Parti Socialiste, *Bulletin Intérieur*, no. 84, May, 1958, p. 9.

stated that only the passage of the so-called Defferre *loi-cadre* (a liberal policy granting increased political freedom to France's territories in Black Africa) was a sufficient reason for the government remaining in office.[2] By June, 1956, the division between toughs and moderates in the party was manifested during a meeting of the Socialist parliamentary group when sixteen members abstained in the vote taken on the question of voting confidence in the government. By late June, 1956, it had become clear that an anti-Lacoste, anti-Mollet wing was taking shape in the Socialist parliamentary group, and that it would attempt to influence government policy primarily by trying to obtain support from the SFIO Congress or National Council. The 48th National Congress held in Lille from June 28 to July 1 finally provided a forum where the party critics could express their grievances.

Daniel Mayer asked that resort to force be ended and that the government take the initiative in seeking negotiations with the representatives of the diverse tendencies of Algerian opinion, including the one represented by the chiefs of the insurrection.

Pierre Rimbert, a former member of the CD and a frequent contributor to *La Revue Socialiste* based his criticism on the financial drain of the Algerian War, stating that the public had not been fully informed of the immense expenses required for successful completion of the pacification campaign.

André Philip questioned the continued willingness of the French people to make the necessary financial sacrifices in order to carry out an intensive military effort coupled with a large-scale program of economic and social reform in Algeria. He asked that the "Algerian national fact" be recognized and immediate negotiations be started between the government and the rebels. He warned that the party was forsaking Socialist ethics in favor of a petty bourgeois realism.

[2] *France-Observateur*, March 29, 1956.

The Socialists listened with great attention to the speeches of Lamine-Gueye, a delegate from Senegal, and to Mostefa Benbhamed from Constantine. Lamine-Gueye said the shooting should stop. He also claimed that it was necessary to silence those who "would like this abnormal situation to continue," and he emphasized that only the Socialists could resolve the Algerian situation.

Benbhamed implied that the war had welded the different ethnic groups of Algeria together into a whole. No longer were there Arabs and Berbers, there were only "Algerians," and any solution to the problem had to take this "birth of a national consciousness" into account. Otherwise the French would be in for further difficulties.[3] Disagreement in the resolutions committee led to the presentation of a majority and a minority motion. The minority motion called on the government to seek to arrange a cease-fire with "all those, without monopoly or exclusion, with whom contacts can be established." The cease-fire would then be followed by "prenegotiations" to arrange for a single electoral college and to outline the principal options to be submitted to the electorate. After the election of representatives, negotiations on a new statute for Algeria would be undertaken.

The majority motion called on the government to struggle on two fronts, against the rebels and against the "ultras of colonialism." The motion went on to outline in detail a number of economic and social reforms the government should initiate and called upon the government to discuss a cease-fire with "those who fight." In contradistinction to the minority motion, however, the majority called for the maintenance of "solid institutional bonds" between France and Algeria, while the minority called for strong "organic bonds." The latter phrase implied looser ties between France and Algeria. More-

[3] *Le Monde* and *Le Populaire*, June 30, 1956.

over, the majority motion asked that arrangements for elections be worked out by a commission controlled by the Algerian and metropolitan political parties. This was a crucial point since the Moslems distrusted the willingness of the French to conduct honest elections in Algeria.[4]

The final vote in the National Congress was 3,308 to 363 with 44 abstentions—a crushing defeat for the minority, although the majority request that the government fight on "two fronts" was an implicit criticism of Lacoste, who had been accused of overemphasizing the military effort in Algeria. Perhaps one reason the majority motion obtained such overwhelming support was that Mollet purportedly told the delegates that a massive vote for the majority Commin motion would reinforce his position in the government.

The Minority and the Concept of the Autonomous Party

The months that followed the National Congress and National Council of June, 1956, saw a number of parliamentarians and party members become increasingly discontented with the policy of the Socialist-led government in Algeria and with the state of party democracy. After the Suez crisis broke, Pierre Rimbert, Marceau Pivert, Jean Weitz, and Jean Rous, all considered to represent the left tendency in the party (and all from the Seine federation), criticized the government's policy during Suez and suggested that the Suez question be put before the United Nations. André Philip also warned the government against undertaking military measures against Egypt, although he applauded the government's firm stand in opposing Nasser.

[4] A. Philip, *Pour un Socialisme Humaniste* (Paris, 1960), p. 113. "The tradition of elections in Algeria is not encouraging, the Moslems have, for a long time, been kept out of the electoral body, then they were shoved into separate electoral colleges; the election results have been falsified. The Socialist Governor-General Naegelen has gone down in history as the great expert in electoral manipulations."

In October, 1956, the SFIO suffered a severe blow to its morale and prestige when Benbhamed, the former Socialist deputy and delegate from Constantine resigned from the SFIO in order to join the rebel forces in Cairo. Explaining that he took this decision because of the "cowardly aggression" the government had committed in capturing Ben Bella and the other rebel chiefs that same month (see above, pages 29–32). Benbhamed went on to note that he had addressed a letter to the CD early in 1956 protesting against certain excesses in Algeria.

In November, 1956, Mme. Andrée Vienot, former deputy from Ardennes, resigned. According to Mme. Vienot it was no longer possible for her to remain in a party whose leaders had not only "denied their electoral promises but all morality and the entire Socialist tradition."[5] On December 6, 1956, seventeen Socialist deputies out of twenty-five Socialist notables signed a letter addressed to interim secretary-general Pierre Commin. The letter stated that the pacification campaign in Algeria had failed and that the Suez expedition had proved to be catastrophic because it isolated France from the western world and allowed the Soviet Union to extend its influence in the Middle East. Among the signatories were Jules Moch, Robert Verdier (president of the Socialist group in the National Assembly), and Alain Savary (former Minister for Tunisian and Moroccan Affairs in the Guy Mollet cabinet). Fourteen of the seventeen deputies who signed the letter had previously broken discipline in 1954 to vote against the European Defense Community.

Minority opposition within the party was not directed solely toward the government's Algerian policy. In January, 1957, speaking before the CD, André Philip bemoaned the fact that the party, instead of being independent of its repre-

[5] *Le Monde,* September 21, October 27 and November 10, 1956.

sentatives in parliament and in the government, had become an organ of propaganda for Socialist ministers. He also criticized the party for not disciplining those who disobeyed party decisions. Believing that the party should be totally disciplined in action, but completely free in discussion, Philip asked that Robert Lacoste be disciplined for not "fighting on two fronts" against the rebels and the ultras, but only against the former. He also asked for the opening of a free tribune in party newspapers and journals so that dissenters might express their views.[6]

These views were quite similar to those put forward six years previously in an article by Edouard Depreux (who stated that André Philip and Gérard Jaquet had expressed their agreement with his thesis). In posing the question, "Do Socialist ministers in government represent the party in government or the government in the party?" Depreux went to the heart of the difficulties the SFIO faced in the Fourth Republic. According to Depreux, the SFIO was "not a party like the others" because its ultimate purpose was to change the regime from a capitalist to a Socialist system, from one where there was private ownership of the means of production to a system of public ownership. For Depreux, the danger for the SFIO was that in exercising power within a capitalist regime, by participating in government, the party would encourage the electorate and especially the working class to believe that it was no different in action or intention from the other parties. This would be particularly harmful to the SFIO since, in fact, its ultimate objectives were revolutionary. Moreover, if the SFIO showed a tendency to shift from its position on the left, the move could only redound to the benefit of the PCF. The SFIO might well become mired on the center-right. The solution to this problem was for the extraparlia-

[6] A. Philip, *Le Socialisme Trahi* (Paris, 1957), p. 219ff.

mentary party to maintain a certain autonomy vis-à-vis the parliamentary party. "Autonomy, originality, incessant propaganda, education and Socialist recruitment are the conditions necessary for the safeguarding of democracy."[7]

Writing nine years later, in 1960, Depreux expressed the same sentiments with reference to the SFIO during 1956–1957. Objecting to the cumulation of the function of secretary-general of the SFIO and President of the Council of Ministers by Guy Mollet, Depreux noted that such a situation

> generated the most deadly confusion between socialism, that is, the *raison d'être* of the party, and the acts of a coalition government acting within a capitalist regime supported by a parliamentary majority of which the least that one could say of it was that it was heterogeneous.[8]

The assumption behind this argument was that the extra-parliamentary party could formulate, and enforce, the voting of policies more in keeping with Socialist doctrine than those foisted upon the party by its parliamentary leaders. The question was how to prevent the latter from exercising undue influence over the party. Neither Philip nor Depreux went so far as to suggest that the participation of parliamentarians in the party hierarchy be curtailed (by, for example, reducing the number of parliamentarians on the CD), but they both felt that the party had become nothing more than a tool of the leadership, since opportunities for dissent and for free discussion of policies were few and restricted.

The problem was, however, that the entire history of the SFIO and, indeed, of most other European democratic parties tended to demonstrate that the parliamentary representatives

[7] Edouard Depreux, "Le Vrai Problème: l'Autonomie Socialiste," *La Revue Socialiste*, no. 42 (December, 1950), pp. 446–73.

[8] Edouard Depreux, *Le Renouvellement du Socialisme* (Paris, 1960), p. 194.

almost always emerged as the dominant force in the party. In the prewar SFIO, for example, as long as Paul Faure, party secretary-general from 1921 to 1940, and Léon Blum cooperated they were able to exercise a determining influence over party policy. In 1938, however, when Faure opposed Blum it was the latter who carried the party despite Faure's position as head of the party bureaucracy.

In the one party where the parliamentary representatives exercised only minimum influence and where party leaders owed their influence and prestige primarily to nonparliamentary position and achievements, it was not the use of technical devices that assured their dominance but the "atmosphere" within the party. In the PCF, according to Maurice Duverger, there were no limits on the number of parliamentarians on the party's controlling organs. Parliamentarians might even hold a majority of the seats on the bureaus and committees but this was of little importance because their status as members of the party's inner circle took precedence over their status as members of parliament.[9] Within the SFIO, since Guy Mollet's accession to power in 1946, the atmosphere had increasingly tended to favor the parliamentarians, to lend them increasing prestige and influence within the party. This was especially true of those parliamentarians, like Guy Mollet, who combined the functions of parliamentarian and extraparliamentary leader.

The minority in 1956–1957 hoped to counter the advantages held by party members in government by forcing the majority to open a free tribune in the party press wherein minority spokesmen could express dissenting opinions. The question of the free tribune was voted upon at the December, 1957, National Council. Minority and majority chose different grounds on which to argue their respective positions.

[9] Maurice Duverger, *Political Parties* (New York, 1962), pp. 196–97 and 202.

Those opposing the free tribune tried to argue less on doctrinal and more on circumstantial grounds. To have argued on a theoretical or doctrinal basis would have equalized the contestants since no one group within the party could claim a monopoly of knowledge about party theory or doctrine. To argue on the basis of financial or material possibilities, as the majority did in fact tend to argue, was to lead from a position of strength. From this point of view the majority, which included party leaders in government and party administration, could marshal facts and figures not readily available to the minority.

The party secretariat argued that there was no need for a free tribune since the members could already express themselves freely, except for limitations imposed by the "demands of party fraternity and respect for the declaration of principles" (i.e., the member was required to publicly defend party decisions no matter what his own opinion might be). The secretariat also argued that sufficient material was available to keep members informed of issues, but that it would be prohibitively expensive to send internal bulletins directly to the members as the minority requested. Moreover, the secretariat claimed that the existence of a free tribune in party publications would undermine cohesion by stimulating debate over past decisions. Finally, the secretariat argued that it would be impossible to allow all viewpoints to be expressed, since this would necessitate the creation of an editorial committee that would provoke the formation of artificial factions.

The proponents of the free tribune argued that both *Le Populaire* and *Populaire-Dimanche* merely noted party decisions and gave no space to dissenters. Moreover, the minority claimed that section secretaries did not always distribute internal bulletins containing minority motions; thus the members usually were uninformed about dissenting views. As for undermining party cohesion through the creation of a free tribune, the minority pointed out that the existence of a free tribune before the war had not damaged the party. Besides, they argued, it was contrary to elementary democratic procedures to suffocate open discussion. Since party meetings were open to the press, it was also demeaning to require members to defend in public policies that they were known to have attacked at meetings. Finally, the minority argued that the creation of a free tribune would stimulate interest in the party.[10]

In the end, the motion advocating a free tribune was defeated by 2,539 to 1,196, with 119 abstentions. Gaston Defferre's federation of Bouches-du-Rhône voted with the minority.

The Minority Increased

Prior to January, 1957, minority leaders such as Edouard Depreux, Daniel Mayer, and Robert Verdier had protested against government policies by supporting motions in party meetings and by occasional public statements of dissent. Unable to win any support within the party, prevented by party statutes from publicizing their dissent in the nonparty press, and unable to express themselves in the party press, a number of Socialist personalities met to form the Socialist Study and Action Committee for Peace in Algeria (*Comité Socialiste de l'Etude et de l'Action pour la Paix en Algérie*) on January 29, 1957. Animated by Daniel Mayer, Robert Verdier, Edouard Depreux, Oreste Rosenfeld, André Philip, Marceau Pivert, Charles-André Julien, and Jean Rous, the committee grouped together people who had been associated with the right (André Philip, Daniel Mayer) and the left (Jean Rous, Marceau Pivert) wings of the party.[11] Ignoring party statutes

[10] *Bulletin Intérieur*, no. 97, December, 1957, pp. 23–31.

[11] *Le Monde*, February 27, 1957, and *France-Observateur*, June 20, 1957.

(articles 17 and 19), the Committee sent out a bulletin of information to SFIO militants attempting to show that the Socialist ministers in government were acting contrary to the principles of socialism in supporting the government's Algerian policy. The party executive reacted immediately by calling for the dissolution of the committee by April 10, 1957. The committee was not dissolved and continued to function in defiance of the party's executive committee.

In spite of increased support for the minority position manifested in the National Assembly by Socialist deputies, party members continued to support the leadership at Congress and Council meetings. In the country, too, they saw the government's Algerian policy reaffirmed in the results of a widely publicized partial election in Seine where the Socialist candidate maintained his position while the Poujadist, Communist, and *mendèsiste* candidates lost votes in comparison to the 1956 figures.

On May 12, 1957, a one-day National Council meeting was held—the first since December, 1956. Most of the speakers devoted themselves to a discussion of the Algerian problem. Many of those supporting the government bitterly attacked Mendès-France, who had criticized the government's Algerian policy at the May 3 Congress of the Radical party. The majority motion was circumspect, noting that the party had become aware of the complex problems facing the government and complimenting the Socialist parliamentary group and the Socialist ministers in government for having acted so well in such "exceptional circumstances."

The minority motion presented by Edouard Depreux moved that the resolution voted at Lille had not been applied. It asked that new measures be taken in Algeria to inspire the masses with confidence in the party, that a tax-reform bill be submitted by the government, and that a free tribune be opened in all the press organs of the SFIO.

The vote was 2,997 for the Commin majority motion, 401 for the Depreux motion; there were 435 abstentions. Most significant was the abstention of the Bouches-du-Rhône federation and its 347 votes. It had been apparent from the very first that Gaston Defferre was at odds with Lacoste, Lejeune, and Mollet over the government's Algerian policy, and his dissatisfaction was apparently increasing.

Between the May 12 and June 3, 1957, National Council meetings, the Mollet government fell. Subsequent events demonstrated a number of things. First, they showed that the SFIO minority would probably remain a minority as long as its criticism of the Mollet leadership was bound up with its opposition to the government's Algerian policy, and as long as the Socialists participated in government. Once the Socialists ceased participation, however, party delegates were more inclined to vote with the minority since this no longer affected Socialist ministers. Second, the ability of Guy Mollet to influence the party was demonstrated in striking fashion when he was able to convince the party it should support Bourgès-Maunoury in his successful attempt to form a government, even though the new Prime Minister's views on preconditions laid down for Socialist support of any new candidate at the National Council of June 3, 1957, had not been determined.[12] Third, most controversies within the party were seen as arising over differences of strategy, not of doctrine. Since Socialist ministers could usually argue more persuasively on questions of strategy or circumstance, the minority was in a difficult position. Unless the minority wished to revive doctrinal issues, its position was weakened. This may explain why the minority obtained more support on questions that were either basically doctrinal (participation versus nonparticipation) or could be discussed in terms that brought in threads of

[12] *France-Observateur*, June 8 and 9, 1957.

party doctrine. The minority always managed to win more support in its struggle for more party democracy than in its attacks on the government's Algerian policy.[13]

Participation versus Nonparticipation

The Bourgès-Maunoury government that succeeded Mollet's lasted from June 12 to September 30, 1957. For the following thirty-five days, no majority could be found to elect another government. Guy Mollet then attempted to win the support of the National Assembly on October 28, 1957. In his investiture speech Mollet emphasized, among other things, his desire to see increased power granted to workers' committees in nationalized industries and to see the workers share in profits. He also affirmed his support of the Gazier bill proposing reimbursement of 80 per cent of physicians' fees by social security. These demands aroused the ire of the Independents, who, instead of abstaining on the vote as had been expected, voted against Mollet, thus scuttling his chances for forming a government. The high priority put on domestic reform policies by the SFIO was, this time, an unacceptable basis for the Independents to grant support.

A new government headed by Félix Gaillard was finally approved on November 6, 1957. Neither Gaston Defferre nor François Mitterand, both known opponents of Lacoste's Algerian policy, entered the government. Robert Lacoste remained as Minister for Algeria, while Gérard Jaquet, Christian Pineau and Max Lejeune also remained in the new government. The National Council called to decide on Socialist participation on November 3, 1957, had voted 2,087 to 1,732, with 20 abstentions, for participation. The SFIO was obviously unhappy at the prospect of Socialists engaging in government by the side of the Independents in the Gaillard cabinet. Again Bouches-du-Rhône voted with the minority.

[13] *Bulletin Intérieur* no. 102, May, 1958, p. 151.

The presence of Socialists in what appeared to be a government of national union (a government including all shades of political opinion represented in the National Assembly except the extreme right and extreme left) needed a good deal of explanation. In an elegiac defense of participation Paul Parpaix, former member of the Mollet ministerial cabinet, noted that Mollet was able to convince the delegates at the November National Council of the desirability of Socialist participation in the Gaillard government

> because, more than anyone in the party, he knows about the real situation in France.
>
> Because, more than anyone else, he has knowledge of the French reactionaries who would undermine our system.
>
> Because, finally, he knows perfectly well what the conditions are for maintaining a system where the working classes can express themselves, a system to which the Socialist party has committed itself.[14]

Speaking in Pas-de-Calais in December, 1957, prior to the December 14 National Council, Mollet said the Socialists had participated in the government because they feared the Republic was on the verge of collapse. But he felt the public had still lost faith in the Republic, and he noted the appearance of "Rightist Fascism as well as Stalinist Fascism."[15] When this question of participation came up in two successive National Council meetings held in early December, 1957, and early March, 1958, the party majority defended participation because it felt that preserving the normal procedures of parliamentary government was the best way to defend the Republic.

Thus those who supported participation in the Gaillard government based their argument on two assumptions: first,

[14] Barsalou, *La Mal-Aimée* (Paris, 1964), p. 289 and *Le Populaire*, October 30, 1957.

[15] *Le Populaire*, November 4 and December 9, 1957.

that the system was so threatened that a continuing crisis provoked by the refusal of the SFIO to join the government might bring about its collapse; second, that Socialist participation assured the working classes that their demands for social justice would be heard, thus lessening the danger of a disaffected working class joining a popular front that might arise outside and against the party system.

Confronted by this argument the antiparticipation minority could only argue that the government had not met Socialist demands for social justice and that continued participation in power represented more of a danger to the Republic than nonparticipation. Thus Gaston Defferre:

> I think that the Republican regime is threatened more by bad government and bad policies with Socialist participation than by a ministerial crisis no matter how long it might be!

In spite of the tactical advantage enjoyed by the participationists (the fact that, being present in ministerial posts, they could argue—combining prestige of position with greater access to information—more authoritatively about the relative advantages of participation), the final vote was 2,650 for participation, 1,121 against, and 83 abstentions. Bouches-du-Rhône, Seine, and the federation of Var together contributed 43 per cent of the minority vote. Seven federations contributed 40 per cent of the majority vote.

Again, in March, 1958, the party debated the question of continued participation in the Gaillard government. Albert Gazier pointed out that the SFIO was confronted with two equally unappealing choices. Because the Communists and the Poujadists together held 200 votes out of the 596-vote National Assembly, the Socialists could join these two in opposition. But to join the Communists and Poujadists in sterile opposition—given the extreme differences separating the Socialists from both these groups—was almost as unappealing as supporting a government that inevitably drew a great deal of participation and support from the center and moderate right in the National Assembly.

At this same March National Council, the existence of some disagreement between Lacoste and Mollet was revealed when Mollet corrected Lacoste for implying that an appeal for a rebel cease-fire necessarily meant unconditional surrender by the rebels.[16]

It soon became apparent that the party leadership was gradually moving away from a position of complete support for the military effort in Algeria. Between the March Council and the fall of Félix Gaillard on April 15, 1958, a series of strikes broke out in the public services. An editorial in *La Revue Socialiste* signed "xxx" expressed the sympathy of the SFIO and stated that the Socialists were tired of seeing the workers forced to sacrifice for the Algerian campaign while those who advocated an all-out effort in Algeria were the very ones who refused to support the financial burden. The reference was obviously to the Independents.

On April 29, 1958, in London, Mollet accepted a resolution of the Socialist International calling for negotiations in Algeria without preconditions, that is, without excluding the prospect of Algerian independence from the scope of discussion.[17] By the time of the May 2, 1958, National Council, therefore, moderation of Mollet's position on Algeria and a toughening of the Socialist position on domestic economic policy weighed heavily against further Socialist participation in government. Although Guy Mollet was favorable to continued participation, most of the SFIO was opposed. Thus

[16] *Bulletin Intérieur*, no. 100, March, 1958, p. 24; no. 101, April, 1958, pp. 19 and 27; no. 102, May, 1958, p. 175.

[17] Serge Hurtig, "La SFIO face à la Ve République: Majorité et Minorités," *Revue Française de Science Politique*, XIV (June, 1964), 526–55.

when René Pleven was proposed as the next Prime Minister to succeed Gaillard, Mollet, sensing the rising antiparticipationist sentiment, decided not to advocate participation. Moreover, many militants and leaders alike had become dissatisfied with Lacoste's continued presence as Minister for Algeria, especially since people were beginning to talk about the "Lacoste policy" for Algeria.[18] This was May, 1958, however, and very shortly the pieces in the French political puzzle were to be violently shaken from their positions by military rebellion and the threat of civil war.

[18] *L'Année Politique*, 1958, p. 50. "Among the reasons the party voted against participation was the desire to remove M. Lacoste from Algiers—although this was not explicitly affirmed." See also the statement of Max Lejeune before the National Information Conference of July, 1958: "We met during the National Council at Puteaux. The majority of the party wished to be discharged of governmental responsibilities, a feeble minority of us wished to remain. It is certain that many of us were anxious to see Lacoste leave Algiers, the Socialists, leave their governmental posts, that certain others, more impressed by the European Socialist meeting in London wanted to change Guy Mollet's triptych" (*Bulletin Intérieur*, no. 105, July, 1958, p. 63).

It is interesting to note here that Lejeune felt the moral weight of the Socialist International was an important factor in the gradual shift of the party majority away from its original position on Algeria. Most likely, however, the SFIO was more open to criticism from the Socialist International when the party was either out of power, or participating in government in a minor capacity. The condemnation of the Suez invasion by the Socialist International had little effect on the Mollet government or on the party majority in the last months of 1956.

5. "*To Govern Is to Choose*"

In the face of the Algerian and Suez problems and threatened by crumbling support in the National Assembly, how was the Socialist-led government able to remain in power for a record time of sixteen months?

One of the reasons was that the 1956 elections gave the SFIO a key position in the National Assembly. On the left sat the PCF with 150 votes and on the extreme right the Poujadists with 52 votes. Thus the two extremes together held approximately one-third of the total vote of 596. No government could possibly be formed under the leadership of either the PCF or Pierre Poujade's *Union et Fraternité Française* (UFF), and so a government of the center left or center right was necessary. Among them, the remaining parties held about 400 votes. The Republican Front (SFIO, *mendèsiste* Radicals, UDSR, and Social Republicans) together held 182 votes. It was logical then that the President of the Council be chosen from among these parties.

Although Mendès-France would probably have been the choice of the electorate, his strong personality and the hostility of the MRP eliminated him from the running. The obvious choice then was Guy Mollet, secretary-general of the SFIO, an able politician and leader of the largest party in the Republican Front. Once Mollet was chosen as President of the Council of Ministers the problem was to determine the kind of support the government should seek. Two broad choices were open: an alliance of the Popular Front kind grouping the PCF, *mendèsiste* Radicals, and the SFIO with a total of 302 seats—a bare majority—or a government of the center right based on the support of the SFIO, UDSR-RDA, MRP, Social Republicans, *Rassemblement des Gauches Républicaines* (RGR), and Independents, with an overwhelming majority of 384 votes. Neither the *mendèsistes* nor the Socialists were willing to ally themselves with the PCF because of the precarious nature of such a coalition, because such an alliance would have been forced to endorse an Algerian policy to the left of the one then advanced by the Republican Front, and, above all, because of the traditional Socialist reluctance to bring the PCF into government.

An alliance of the second type was hardly more conceivable since there was no possibility of cooperation between the RGR and the Radical Socialist groups, the split between Edgar Faure and Mendès-France being too deep. Further, the hostility of the SFIO toward the right was even greater than its dislike of the PCF, thus precluding a lasting alliance of this type.[1]

[1] The possible future of a Popular Front alliance was illustrated in early 1956 when the issue of changing the Barangé Law split the Assembly. When the question was put before the National Assembly of setting a date for debating the Barangé Law, the SFIO, PCF, and some Radicals and members of the UDSR voting together were defeated 288 to 279. A second time the vote was 273 to 260. In each case a number of Radicals and members of the UDSR deserted the laic bloc in order to prevent the question from reaching the floor. The issue was raised again in October, 1956, and again dissenters in the ranks of

The only alternative then, barring these two alliances, was the formation of a minority government supported by alternating majorities which would change according to the issue posed before the National Assembly. No negotiations, no agreements, would be undertaken between the members of the Republican Front and the other parties. The resolution voted at the Extraordinary National Congress meeting January 14 and 15, 1956, stated clearly that

> the Republican Front ought to form a government alone, and refuse all compromise, all negotiation, all alliance with the adversaries of democracy as with the parties of reaction which are, consciously or not, its accomplices.

This formula proved successful. For the first six months of the legislature the PCF supported the government. During this time the Independents also supported the government on its Algerian policy and on the issue of extending paid vacations for workers in public enterprises to three weeks. The Independents did oppose the government on increasing old-age pensions but this opposition was more than compensated for by the support of the PCF. By July 31, 1956, however, as the PCF went into opposition, the Independents provided crucial voting support, fearful that opposition might provoke a serious governmental crisis and lead to a change in Algerian policy.

Thus, Guy Mollet was able to trade off a reformist domestic policy against an increasingly harsh Algerian policy. During its tenure, the Mollet government was supported by the PCF on practically all its reform measures (except some sections of the agricultural reform bill of December, 1956). In some cases the PCF provided the crucial margin of support on a vote of confidence as, for example, on two votes on the

---

the Radical party and the UDSR prevented the issue from being debated. See *L'Année Politique*, 1956, pp. 27 and 105.

National Fund for the Aged on May 5, 1956, and on June 21, 1956. The votes were 260–138 and 263–124, with the Independents voting against the government in both cases.[2] When the PCF went into opposition, therefore, the fate of the government lay in the hands of the Independent group. The Independents finally did bring about the fall of the Mollet government on May 21, 1957, because they refused to agree to the government's proposed tax measures. Once the government fell, the crisis that was to lead to the collapse of the regime began.

Relations between the SFIO and PCF

In spite of the period of tripartism when the MRP, SFIO, and PCF governed together uneasily during 1946–1947, relations between the PCF and SFIO had been marked by extreme caution and often hostility. The dismissal of the Communist ministers from the Ramadier government on May 5, 1947, and the entry of the PCF into opposition that year ended the brief period of cooperation. In 1956, however, with the success of the Republican Front, the PCF left opposition and voted Mollet's investiture. The PCF continued to support Mollet for six months. During this time the PCF repeatedly appealed to the SFIO for the establishment of a common program of action. The PCF tactic was explained by Laurent Casanova before the National Assembly:

> During the investiture debate, the PCF program was defined in a clear fashion. We established that there was a difference between this government and the preceding ones because it was directed by a Socialist and bound by the formal engagement of the massive majority which resulted from the January, 1956, elections.
>
> We warned the government about its refusal to agree to unity of action with the forces of the workers and the forces of the left

[2] *L'Année Politique*, 1956, pp. 110, 482 and 486.

in the country and in parliament, but we refused to practice the tactic of all or nothing.

We considered it most urgent to support all steps toward the re-establishment of peace in Algeria and the satisfaction of the demands of the workers. . . .

We went to the extreme limit in time and acts—until the June 6, 1956, debate, to be exact—and we refused to allow the government a pretext permitting it to diminish its own responsibilities in the eyes of Socialist workers and democrats who had voted for the Republican Front. This being done, we wish to maintain open against your maneuvers, the perspective of unity of action between Socialist and Communist workers, because this unity constitutes the necessary condition for a policy of the left in France.[3]

During the early part of the legislature the PCF seems to have supported the Socialist Algerian policy for a number of reasons. First, since their Ivry Congress in 1954, the PCF had been calling for unity of action with the SFIO, and the PCF might have felt that the appeal for a new Popular Front would be more tempting if the SFIO was forced to rely on PCF voting support to get the SFIO's ostensibly liberal Algerian policy through the National Assembly. Second, the leaders of the PCF had not forgotten the break in SFIO voting discipline occasioned by the European Defence Community issue, and by holding out the promise of assured support in the National Assembly for a liberal Algerian policy, the PCF might have hoped to attract the sympathies of Socialist deputies disenchanted with the government's Algerian policy. Third, the PCF approved the liberal Socialist policy toward Tunisia and Morocco since this policy was directed toward maintaining a French presence in these countries and thus preventing Arab nationalism from being exploited by the U.S. Fourth, the PCF risked losing support in the country by opposing the government's Algerian policy (although given the history and nature

[3] *Journal Officiel*, March 20, 1957, p. 1735.

of the PCF's activities through the years, this consideration was probably a minor one). Fifth, the Soviet Union evidently did not wish to alienate France completely, since it hoped to injure the Atlantic alliance by dangling Russian neutrality and PCF support for the government's Algerian policy in front of the SFIO as bait for closer relations between the two countries.[4]

The SFIO was quite cool toward suggestions that it cooperate more closely with the PCF. Prior to the 1956 elections the CD set forth its reasons for refusing to agree to join Communist-Socialist election lists and for its refusal to consider the possibility of unity of action between the SFIO and PCF. Since, according to the SFIO explanation, the PCF was a "simple instrument of Soviet diplomacy" and the tactics of the PCF were based on the demands of Soviet, not French national interests, the PCF would have to do a number of things before the SFIO would consider discussing the possibility of close cooperation between the two parties. First, the PCF would have to democratize its internal structure; second, it would have to denounce all crimes against liberty, concentration camps, and imprisonment of democrats which took place in the countries where the Communists had come to power; third, it would have to renounce the one-party regime; fourth, it would have to agree to fight for a revolution in

[4] Speaking at the PCF National Congress in July, 1956, Mikail Suslov endorsed closer relations between the PCF and SFIO: "The positions of Communists and Socialists in numerous countries are veering toward one another at present. The Soviet party wishes to tighten its links with its brother parties at the same time as it develops closer contacts with Socialist parties and notably with the French Socialist party" (*Le Monde*, July 21, 1956). Jean Boireau in "Les Conditions d'une Solution à la Crise Algérienne," *La Revue Socialiste*, no. 100 (October, 1956), suggested that it was in the Soviet interest to maintain a French presence in Africa so as to prevent the United States from gaining power in North Africa through France's losses.

France for the benefit of French workers and cease to be a simple tool of Soviet diplomacy in France.[5]

The watershed of Communist support for the Mollet government was Suez. From left to right in France the nationalization of the Suez Canal was condemned in the severest terms, but *L'Humanité* noted that "the nationalization of the Suez Canal is an historic event of the first importance. . . . It is a new blow against the colonial system."[6] And during a debate on government policy Guy Mollet was provoked into making his famous remark to the Communist group in the National Assembly: "There is something frightening about you, gentlemen; it suffices that a cause be anti-French for you to make it your own."[7]

This remark was not completely true, however, for the PCF had encountered some difficulty in attempting to maintain cordial relations with the Algerian Communist party since the latter backed Algerian independence while the PCF was trying to walk a narrow path between supporting Socialist policies in Algeria and soothing angry militants anxious to see the PCF come out for Algerian independence.[8]

If the PCF had ever entertained hopes that its support of Socialist policies in Algeria might lead to a call for closer SFIO-PCF relations from Socialist deputies dissatisfied with the increasing harshness of the government's pacification campaign in Algeria, this hope was finally shattered by the PCF's support of the Soviet repression of the Hungarian rebellion. At a time when many influential Socialist deputies were at odds with party leadership over the Suez invasion, weakened bonds of party loyalty were strengthened as all Socialists united to deplore the repression of the Hungarian rebellion.

[5] *Bulletin Intérieur*, no. 84, May, 1956, p. 166.
[6] *L'Humanité*, July 28, 1956.
[7] *Journal Officiel*, August 3, 1956, p. 3870.
[8] *Le Monde*, May 3, 1956.

At a Socialist-sponsored meeting on Hungary held in November, 1956, both those who were considered dissenters and those who supported the party majority in the National Assembly unanimously condemned the Soviet intervention and castigated the PCF for its endorsement of Soviet actions. Edouard Depreux, at that time highly critical of the government's policy, appealed to Communist militants to leave the "pseudo-Communist" party in order to join the SFIO.[9]

Relations between the SFIO and the Independents

In a sense, the role played by the Independent group (including the Independents and Peasants of Social Action, and the Peasant group—a total of 95 votes) during the life of the Mollet government complemented that of the PCF. While the PCF supported the government during the first six months of its existence, the Independents tended to vote sometimes for, sometimes against, the government, depending on the issue. The Independents supported government policy on Algeria and backed a government measure increasing paid vacations from two weeks to eighteen days. But on all other issues the Independents either voted against the government on votes of confidence, or abstained. Thus, on eight votes of confidence that occurred prior to July, 1956, when the Communists entered opposition, the Independents voted for government policy eight times, four times on the paid-vacation issue and four times on the government proposal to grant Algerian administrative authorities special powers. But on nine votes of confidence on increasing old-age pensions, the Independents either voted unanimously against the government, or voted against it by a large majority. On the final vote on old-age pensions on June 27, 1956, a large majority of the Independents abstained.

[9] *Le Populaire*, November 10–11, 1956.

After the PCF went into opposition as a result of the government's reaction to Nasser's nationalization of the Suez Canal, it appears the Independent group was careful to support the government. On October 25, 1956, for example, on a vote of confidence on the foreign policy of the Socialist-led government, the Independents voted for the government by a large majority (see Appendix B.1). Thus the support of the center now compensated for the loss of PCF support. Later, on votes of confidence on government-sponsored agricultural reform legislation, the Independent and Peasant group either supported or was careful to abstain. In December, 1956, for example, the Independent and Peasant group deliberately abstained so as to prevent the government from resigning (see Appendix B.2). A concerted effort by the Independent and Peasant group to bring the government down would have succeeded at almost any time after the PCF began systematically to vote against the government. It was not until May 21, 1957, however, that the Independent and Peasant group joined the PCF and other parties in opposing the government, thus forcing its resignation.

The support of the Independent and Peasant group was given mainly because Lacoste's Algerian policy was very popular on the center and center-right in the National Assembly. In addition, there were some on the center and right who early in 1956 feared that the defeat of the Mollet-led government would lead to the formation of some kind of Popular Front majority. After Suez and then Hungary, this was no longer even a remote possibility. By May, 1957, the SFIO had become committed to an Algerian policy approved and supported by groups that normally were quite opposed to the Socialists on other matters. Robert Lacoste had become the living symbol of this policy and, in May, 1957, the Independent and Peasant group's leaders may have felt they could risk a governmental crisis since any future government would find it extremely difficult to change an Algerian policy that had been followed for almost a year and a half by the Socialists.

The Party and De Gaulle

The demonstrations of May 13, 1958, signaled the beginning of the end for the Fourth Republic. The first response of the SFIO was to advocate "Republican defense." In Paris, the Pflimlin government was invested by a vote of 274 to 129, with the PCF abstaining. When the gravity of the crisis became clear, Mollet decided to participate in government by assuming the post of Vice-President of the Council of Ministers. Jules Moch became Minister of the Interior, a move that symbolized the determination of the government to defend the Republic against potential enemies of both the extreme right and extreme left. Albert Gazier became Minister of Information.

The period between the investiture of the Pflimlin government and the eventual investiture of de Gaulle was confused and tense. The Socialist parliamentary group was wracked by indecision, first voting against and then for de Gaulle; at one point voting to join with the PCF in manifesting Socialist support for the Republic, then refusing to cooperate with the PCF.

On May 16, Guy Mollet posed three questions in a letter to de Gaulle: Do you recognize the current government as the only legitimate one? Do you disavow the promoters of the Committes of Public Safety in Algeria? If, one day, you were asked to form a government, would you appear before the National Assembly as would any other candidate, present your program to it and consider yourself responsible before it if invested, and retire from it if not?[10] No answer was forthcoming from de Gaulle, who had, the previous day, stated his

[10] *Le Populaire*, May 17, 1958.

willingness to "assume the powers of the Republic."[11] By May 24, Georges Bidault and Antoine Pinay had both rallied to the support of de Gaulle and Corsica had fallen to a detachment of paratroopers, meeting only token resistance from a few Socialists. Jules Moch found himself unable to exercise any control over the police and security troops (*Compagnies Républicains de Sécurité*) during this period—a fact that must have weighed heavily in the minds of many Socialist deputies when time came to vote on de Gaulle's investiture.

On May 25, Mollet secretly sent a letter to de Gaulle. Noting that on two occasions, he had been contacted by Olivier Guichard, an associate of de Gaulle, Mollet expressed his fear that de Gaulle's assumption of power would serve the interests of "bolshevism" in a "quasi-irrevocable" manner.

> Why do I think that your coming to power would be a mistake? Because you have not said, you cannot say neither how nor why you request power. Because the instinctive fears of the masses toward a personal regime would, one day, cause the people to rise up against you or your memory.

Mollet noted, however, that

> the essential difference between you and the . . . [Bolsheviks] is that you know yourself to be temporary, mortal, while they believe themselves eternal; that you want to act directly on the present while they think only of what they call history, the fatal march of time. . . . If the Communists can pass themselves off as having been the sole defenders of liberty and the Republic—a Republic they really despise and which has been undermined by your supporters although not threatened by you personally—and if, hypothesizing your success, they can wait for a time of disillusion, and of difficulties that will inevitably occur, then they certainly think they will succeed you.[12]

[11] *L'Année Politique*, 1958, p. 58.
[12] Guy Mollet, *13 Mai 1958–13 Mai 1962* (Paris, 1962), pp. 8–10.

Later, in July, 1958, defending himself before the party from the accusation that this letter had begun the process whereby de Gaulle assumed power, Mollet claimed that the letter was merely intended to demonstrate to de Gaulle that his accession to power would constitute a danger to the country. Mollet contended that only after he realized a government of national unity could not be formed, did he find himself faced with the problem of choosing between de Gaulle and a government of colonels.[13] The ambiguous nature of the Mollet letter could, however, have given rise to other interpretations, and if Mollet refused the interpretation that his letter was a veiled invitation to power, de Gaulle himself seems to have read it in just that fashion. His reply of May 26, 1958, read, in part:

> Your letter leads me to believe that we are very close to agreement on the basic things. I regret that you did not follow through on your intention of seeing me. It seems that, in the name of the unity of the country—and soon, of its independence, everything points toward a direct contact, as discrete as one desires—which should urgently take place between the government and myself so as to evade an aggravation of the situation.

On the same day, former President of the Republic Vincent Auriol wrote to de Gaulle, calling on him to disavow the seditious elements in Algeria and France and holding out the prospect of Socialist support as a reward.[14] That same night Pflimlin secretly met with de Gaulle in Saint-Cloud. The following day, May 27, 1958, de Gaulle stated that he had "begun the regular process necessary for the establishment of a Republican government capable of assuring the unity and independence of the country." He concluded his statement by asking the armed forces to remain under the commands of

[13] *Bulletin Intérieur*, no. 105, July, 1958, p. 43.
[14] *L'Année Politique*, 1958, p. 538.

their chiefs. This extraordinary statement, seemingly based on nothing but the General's ambition and imagination, led the Socialist group to vote 112 to 3, with one abstention, a motion stating that "the legal government must remain, the party will in no case support the candidacy of General de Gaulle in the form currently posed."

Rumors soon began to circulate that de Gaulle had made the statement in order to forestall a threatened invasion by paratroops from Algeria.[15] On May 28, confusion reigned. The Socialist parliamentary group declared its support for the PCF and CGT, which had called for a strike and demonstration to show support for the Republic. The CD, however, voted 17 to 9 against associating the SFIO with the strike.[16] On May 28, 1958, a demonstration march was held by the National Committee for Republican Defense. The Committee had been formed May 24 by elements from the SFIO, the Radical party, and the UDSR-RDA. On the day of the demonstration, numerous members of the PCF and the *Confédération Générale du Travail* (CGT), mingled with the marchers, whose number was estimated at 200,000. Although the march was impressive, it did not dispel the memory of May 17 and May 19, when CGT workers had failed to strike in protest against the army coup in Algeria.

By the end of May, the pressure had become unbearable, and on May 28, at 4:00 A.M., Pflimlin resigned as Prime Minister. On May 29, President Coty threatened to resign if the National Assembly did not invest de Gaulle as President of the Council. On May 30, the Socialist parliamentary group voted 62 to 29 to approve the Auriol letter sent to de Gaulle on May 26, signifying that the Socialist group was ready to negotiate with de Gaulle. On the evening of May 30, de Gaulle received first Vincent Auriol and then Guy Mollet

[15] *Bulletin Intérieur*, no. 105, July, 1958, p. 7.
[16] *Le Monde*, May 29, 1958.

and Maurice Deixonne. After the encounter, Mollet commented, "I have lived one of the greatest moments of my life."[17] De Gaulle had agreed to ask for complete powers for a period of six months, instead of two years as he had originally demanded, and he agreed to appear before the National Assembly to answer questions on his proposed course of action. During the Mollet-Deixonne-de Gaulle meeting, de Gaulle confirmed what Mollet already suspected, that an invasion of Paris had been prepared in the event de Gaulle was not asked to form a government.

On the evening of May 31, de Gaulle met with all the parliamentary leaders and asked Mollet to participate in his government, making of Mollet's presence one condition for his acceptance of leadership. Mollet thereupon offered to resign as secretary-general of the SFIO and from the CD, but he was asked to remain until the next party meeting.

The Socialist group in the National Assembly finally voted 42 for and 49 against de Gaulle when he was presented as a candidate for the President of the Council of Ministers. The vote found all those who were later, in September, 1958, or soon after, to join the Autonomous Socialist Party (PSA) voting against de Gaulle. Many of those opposing him did not leave the SFIO, however, since people like Gaston Defferre, Albert Gazier, and Félix Gouin remained loyal in September, 1958. In addition, voting for de Gaulle were men like Jules Moch and Pierre-Olivier Lapie who had opposed Mollet in the past and would oppose him in the future.

At a National Information Conference held on July 6, 1958, a number of explanations were given for the vote on de Gaulle. Once again, as in previous meetings, those who supported the leadership tended to explain their vote on circumstantial grounds, to avoid larger issues of party theory or

[17] *L'Année Politique*, 1958, pp. 65, 66, and 211.

doctrine. Thus Gérard Jaquet stated that the divergence between those who voted for and those who voted against de Gaulle was less serious than many believed. Moreover, Jaquet pointed out that it was "more our intuition than our reason that guided us," since the party could only guess at the possible consequences of either supporting or rejecting de Gaulle.

A member of the minority faction, Charles Lussy (deputy from Vaucluse and former president of the Socialist group in the National Assembly), sadly noted that differences in the party went deeper than the division between those who supported and those who opposed de Gaulle. Rather, claimed Lussy, the differences were "based on the very conception that we hold of socialism." The main point of difficulty was that the party had moved away from both the humanism of Jaurès and the "intransigent Marxism" of Guesde only to "subordinate the *raison d'être* of the party to its purely parliamentary and governmental actions."

Once again, then, the notion of the autonomous party was suggested. Edouard Depreux and Antoine Mazier also criticized the CD and the party for allowing its secretary-general to join a government whose investiture had been opposed by a majority of Socialist deputies. No matter that the secretary-general of the SFIO joined the government solely on a "personal" basis and that the party disclaimed any responsibility for its members in government; the fact was, Mazier contended, that most people would believe that when a party authorized its secretary-general to enter the government the entire party was associated with this move.

For Depreux, the commitment of the SFIO to governmental participation over the past three years had virtually eliminated whatever chance the SFIO might have had to attract disaffected Communists. By refusing to allow the extraparliamentary party to lead an independent and critical existence, it had become identified with a discredited and ineffective regime. The public could no longer distinguish between the ideals of socialism and the actions of Socialists in government. The party was about to betray its original ideals and to sacrifice socialism to the exigencies of government. Depreux said:

> There is something I love better than the SFIO and that is democratic socialism . . . and I hope with all my heart that none of us are ever, under any circumstances, obliged to choose between our fidelity to democratic socialism and its essential principles, and fidelity to the SFIO.

Most of the speakers at the Conference agreed that a new political era was about to begin in France. The coming of de Gaulle had interred the Fourth Republic, the new Constitution was yet to come, and the SFIO faced the problem of determining the role it would play in the Fifth Republic. Some of those speaking at the Conference (Albert Gazier, for example) wished to see the SFIO act in a constructive fashion—but outside the de Gaulle government. Max Lejeune, on the other hand, felt that the SFIO could best act in a constructive fashion inside, rather than outside, government. Others (Arthur Notebart, for example) wished to see the SFIO undertake a recruitment drive among the trade unions and cooperative movements in order to create "the great party of the left that this country needs."

If the prescriptions for a new role were vague, the reason was simple. No one knew what the new political system would be like, although most people seem to have assumed that some simplification in the party system on the right would take place as the right united behind de Gaulle. Even this was not certain, however, for as Pierre-Bloch pointed out, some extreme right-wing journals had already begun to criticize de Gaulle. But Pierre-Bloch was hopeful and asked if the day might not soon come when, as after the Liberation, the SFIO would find its slogans echoed throughout the entire country. And Guy Mollet said of de Gaulle:

I would like to say what I think, not of the man . . . but of his method. As astonishing as it may appear, because I did not believe this at the beginning, this man of the north is much more of a pragmatic Anglo-Saxon than a Latin constitutionalist. . . . He isn't the kind of man who writes or says what he intends to do before he does it. He isn't the kind of man who locks himself inside great theoretical constructions.[18]

Thus to the nebulous nature of the new political system was added the unpredictable nature of the man who was to hold vast powers in it. No wonder that the SFIO was unable to outline a basic course of action. In the Fourth Republic, the party system was stable, in spite of the eruption of movements like Poujadism or the RPF, and the SFIO focused its energies on conserving its position in that system. Suddenly faced with an apparently new situation where the entire regime was called into question, where there was a good possibility that the party system might be drastically altered, the desire of many Socialists to see the SFIO constitute the center of a democratic Socialist opposition sprang to the fore. The problem was, however, that any regrouping of the parties would have to take into account the fact that de Gaulle himself had become a political factor of immense importance, and in the summer of 1958 no one knew what his position was or would be.

Schism in the Party

Controversy within the SFIO increased as the text of the new Constitution was released and the SFIO prepared for the September National Congress. Many Socialist parliamenta-

[18] *Bulletin Intérieur*, no. 105, July, 1958, passim.

rians were dissatisfied with the draft Constitution and, on August 7, 1958, the Socialist parliamentary group voted, unanimously except for one vote and three abstentions (the abstentions were those of the three Socialist ministers in the de Gaulle government), a motion holding that the text of the Constitution seemed to harbor grave dangers for the Republic. Expressing its misgivings to de Gaulle on August 20, 1958, the Socialist parliamentary group stated its hostility to Article 14 (later to become Article 16) and to the restricted composition of the electoral college.

Assuming that hostility toward the Constitution was increasing in the party, and looking toward the September National Congress, Edouard Depreux was encouraged to write to a comrade, "It will depend on a few votes; we can hope for a majority which will vote 'no' if we all work extremely hard."[19] On July 27, 1958, representatives from forty-one SFIO federations had met in Paris in order to elaborate a minority text for the National Congress. Félix Gouin and Francis Leenhardt, both deputies from Defferre's Bouches-du-Rhône federation, spoke against the Constitutional draft.[20] Depreux's hopes were to be cruelly deceived, however, for on September 6 and 7, *Le Provençal*, the Marseille newspaper of Gaston Defferre, carried the news that both Defferre and Leenhardt had decided to vote for a "yes" on the Constitution. Explaining his decision, Defferre made five points. First: Algeria was the most critical problem facing France; second, de Gaulle was liberal in colonial matters, as his recent voyage to Africa and his decision to recognize the right to independence of the overseas territories proved; third, de Gaulle had decided to end the Algerian War because he could not ignore the logic linking it to the future of black

[19] Daniel Ligou, *Histoire du Socialisme en France, 1871–1961* (Paris, 1962), p. 624.

[20] *Tribune du Socialisme*, no. 9 (September 25, 1958) and *France-Observateur*, September 11, 1958.

Africa; fourth, this same logic would push Algeria into the same category as black Africa, the ultras felt this, and this explained their growing hostility toward de Gaulle; and fifth, de Gaulle not only wanted, but would be able, to negotiate on Algeria if he obtained a striking success on the referendum, and since he would no longer need the support of the men of the 13th of May and of the military, he would be able to force the first to come to their senses and the second to obey.[21]

The September National Congress was one of the most bitter ever held. Debate concerned not only the Constitution but party activity since 1956. The real point of argument between those who supported and those who opposed the Constitution was the constant participation of the SFIO in government since 1956. Although everyone seemed to agree that the SFIO was not, and could not be defined as, a party "like the others" because of its revolutionary vocation, the Congress was divided over the best means for making the party into a truly "revolutionary instrument."

One of the speakers claimed that the party was based on a "profound confusion": on the one hand, he noted, SFIO doctrine claimed the party's object was to transform the existing society into a collectivist or Communist society, while, on the other hand, the party affirmed its desire to safeguard the regime and to perfect it. From this it seemed to follow that if the regime was perfectible there were no reasons for any radical changes. Thus "the greatest evil" was that the party appeared to the public like any other party. Moreover, the speaker went on, the party's local sections had devoted themselves solely to electioneering, and, aside from the brief period when local and national elections were being prepared, the sections met infrequently or not at all.[22]

Jules Moch emphasized the lack of doctrinal activity in the

[21] *France-Observateur,* September 11, 1958.

[22] Parti Socialiste, *Compte Rendu,* 50th National Congress, 1958, pp. 145, 149.

party and called for a modification of party doctrine in the light of new developments and theories in areas such as teaching, nationalized industries, worker's councils, and economic planning.[23]

In 1960, with regard to the National Congress and Defferre's last-minute decision to support the Constitutional referendum, Edouard Depreux wrote bitterly:

> When we had to organize our opposition in the SFIO, I proposed an objective that experience has demonstrated to be singularly ambitious: to disengage a Socialist majority. Was it utopian? Would we have attained it if a modern Joan of Arc from Marseille hadn't suddenly heard voices which, at the decisive moment, deprived us of his support?[24]

Once Defferre had made his decision, the outcome was preordained. The party general report was voted by an overwhelming majority of 3,146 to 598, with 136 abstentions. The vote on Algerian policy was 3,370 to 611, with 43 abstentions. The majority motion moved even further toward conceding the possibility that Algerian negotiations might lead to granting Algeria a large degree of autonomy. In this case, Bouches-du-Rhône voted with the majority. The vote on the Constitutional referendum was closer with 2,786 voting to support it, 1,176 voting against. As expected, Bouches-du-Rhône voted with the majority. The size of the minority vote, approximately equal to the best minority vote from 1956 to 1958, concealed the fact that the minority received support from elements in federations such as the Nord with 92 votes, Pas-de-Calais with 32 votes, and Haute-Vienne with 42 votes. All these federations had, in the past, voted unanimously with the party majority.

[23] *Le Populaire*, September 12, 1958.

[24] Edouard Depreux, *Le Renouvellement du Socialisme* (Paris, 1960), p. 17.

At the conclusion of the National Congress, Depreux called a press conference and read the text of a statement in which he announced the creation of the Autonomous Socialist Party (*Parti Socialiste Autonome*) whose goal was to

> bring back into the great and democratic Socialist family all those who have turned away, to give them some reason for hope and to demonstrate to them that they will still have an opportunity to be effective, as long as they are non-Communist but still wish to suppress the capitalist system.[25]

The schism had long been brewing in the heart of the party and was not simply the result of discontent with the leadership of Mollet during the closing days of the Fourth Republic. The events of May 13, 1958, and the subsequent decision to support the Constitutional referendum provided the opportunity for a break that might have come in any case. The minority had really organized itself on January 29, 1958, when the Socialist Study and Action Committee for Peace in Algeria first came into existence. Although the party Bureau had called for its dissolution on many occasions, the Committee had remained active.[26] By January, 1958, the minority had begun to publish *La Tribune du Socialisme*, a monthly newspaper devoted to expressing the minority viewpoint and to elaborating alternate policies. This was certainly in keeping with the concept of the "autonomous Socialist party." The newspaper frequently criticized the "bolshevization" of the SFIO and complained about the elimination of dissenters from the executive committee and the hostility to criticism and dissent evidenced by many party leaders and militants. It criticized the average militant, who, it claimed, argued in the following way during the period of the Socialist-led government:

[25] *Tribune du Socialisme*, no. 9 (September 25, 1958).

[26] *Bulletin Intérieur*, no. 102, May, 1958, p. 191; no. 94, June, 1957, p. 11; no. 99, February, 1958, pp. 23 and 27.

He . . . found himself confronted with a government directed by the secretary-general of the party, by a man who, par excellence, had the confidence of the militant. From this moment on, whenever the secretary-general-President of the Council initiated a policy, even if contrary to all election promises, the militant tended to reason as follows, "He knows what to do better than me; consequently, I'll follow him."[27]

La Tribune du Socialisme held that the leadership had violated Socialist principles by its "nationalistic and racist" policies in Algeria and Suez, suffocated party democracy by denying the minority both the opportunity and the right to express itself, and made of Socialist doctrine nothing more than a rationale for the grossest kind of opportunism.

Initially, the minority had felt that their mission was to renovate the SFIO, not to form another left-wing splinter group. In early January, 1958, for example, *Le Monde* reported that the Socialist minority had sent a letter to party militants saluting the "recent regroupment" on the left in the form of the *Union des Gauches Socialistes* (UGS was the result of a merger between the left-wing Catholic *Jeune République* group founded by Marc Sagnier in 1912 and the *Union Progressiste*, a neutralist group led by Gilles Martinet, director of *France-Observateur*.) The letter went on to state that "it is tomorrow, in the heart of a renovated SFIO . . . that all energies will be found to provoke a salutary change in policies." In March, 1958, *La Tribune du Socialisme* editorialists were still protesting against SFIO accusations that they had formed a *tendance* or a faction, and they pointedly noted that the *Tribune* would open its columns to all party members regardless of their views. In April, the editorialists called on the extraparliamentary party to distinguish between the "march toward socialism" and the compromises forced on the party by its presence in the National Assembly.

[27] *Tribune du Socialisme*, no. 6 (June 20, 1958).

By June, 1958, however, the minority had changed its tactic as a call went out for the formation of "action groups" which would parallel regular party structures at section, federation, and national levels. These action groups were designed to appeal to active as well as former SFIO members to struggle against all forms of "totalitarianism, militarism, or the regime of the single party." They would thus attempt to "disavow the policy followed by SFIO party leaders, to express opposition to the regime of personal plebiscitary of caesarian power." An attempt would be made to organize a National Conference of these organizations in order to make "definitive decisions." Obviously this appeal was a direct challenge and threat to the SFIO and in complete contravention of party rules forbidding the formation of a "permanent group of relationships" within the party (Article 19). It was, however, in keeping with the notion of an autonomous Socialist party actively aware of, and critical of, the policies of the party leadership and free to inform and arouse party militants.

By this time it had become obvious that the minority had lost all hope of winning majority support in party meetings. For the dissidents, therefore, the only alternative seemed to be to leave the SFIO and found a party that would hew more closely to Socialist ideals. They maintained that they had left the SFIO "in order to return to it." [28] The departure of the minority dealt a severe but by no means mortal blow to the SFIO. The leaders of the PSA—Edouard Depreux, Alain Savary, and Daniel Mayer—were all from the Seine federation, and the bulk of PSA membership came from the Seine. The federations of Ardennes, Ardèche, and Côtes-du-Nord also furnished leaders and militants for the new party, but since these federations had always been minority federations

[28] Title of an article by Charles Lussy in *Tribune du Socialisme*, no. 10 (October 15, 1958), "Quitter le Parti, Non. Y Revenir!".

in the SFIO, the immediate effect of the departure was to strengthen the hand of the party leadership.

The effect the schism had on membership is difficult to calculate. Party records show that between September, 1958, and July, 1959, paid-up membership dropped by approximately 1,600. On the other hand, the PSA claimed a membership of 8,000 by July, 1959.[29] It is likely that many of these were former SFIO members or sympathizers. In November, 1959, Mollet said the SFIO had lost one-tenth of its membership, while party figures seemed to show a loss of about 3,000 members in 1959.[30] In 1960, the PSU (*Parti Socialiste Unifié*, the successor to the PSA) counted twenty-one former SFIO parliamentarians in its ranks, but by then the new party had ceased to grow as rapidly as in the first years of its existence.

[29] *France-Observateur*, July 16, 1959.

[30] *Bulletin Intérieur*, no. 110, May, 1959, p. 15.

6. *The Party at the Polls— The 1958 Election*

The SFIO approached the Constitutional referendum campaign in a desultory fashion both because the outcome was certain and because of a lack of enthusiasm on the part of members who found themselves allied with men like Georges Bidault and Jacques Soustelle. The SFIO emphasized the themes stated by Guy Mollet at the Congress in September. To vote "no" was to vote for chaos; to vote "yes" was to vote for a liberal approach to the colonial problems confronting France.[1] Guy Mollet said he decided to support de Gaulle's return to power in June, and to back the Constitutional referendum since the alternative might have been civil war. In addition, Mollet claimed de Gaulle was the only one who could solve the crucial Algerian problem.[2]

There can be little doubt that most Socialists had mixed feelings about supporting de Gaulle. In a poll taken prior to the referendum, asking whether the proposed Fifth Republic Constitution pleased or displeased them, 30 per cent of the

[1] *Le Populaire*, September 19, 1958.

[2] Guy Mollet, *13 Mai 1958–13 Mai 1962* (Paris, 1962), p. 4.

Socialist respondants said they did not know, 61 per cent were pleased, and 9 per cent were displeased.

Obviously, many of those who either did not know how they felt or were displeased decided to vote for the Constitution since a later poll showed that the Socialists had voted "yes" by 71 per cent, "no" by 7 per cent, with 5 per cent abstaining and 10 per cent refusing to answer. Yet there were still misgivings on the part of many Socialists, for in reply to the question, "Does the adoption of the new Constitution appear to you as a victory of the right, the left, or both?" 37 per cent answered a victory of the right, 5 per cent a victory of the left, and 46 per cent a victory for both or neither.

If one assumes that most Socialists did not wish to support something that would be a victory for the right, and one subtracts the 7 per cent of the Socialists who voted "no" from the total of 37 per cent who considered the Constitution a victory for the right, it still appears that 30 per cent who either voted for the Constitution, abstained, or refused to answer questions, considered the Constitution a victory for the right.[3]

Two days after the massive vote for the Constitutional referendum, *Le Populaire* launched a slogan which the party hoped would help preserve its 1956 vote and perhaps win increased support from the center and center-right. The slogan was "The Socialist Party in the Avant-Garde of the Fifth Republic." Temporarily at least, the SFIO had hitched its wagon to the rising Gaullist star. Ironically, during a period when the Socialist party had suffered a serious split, when the leadership was divided over the question of supporting de Gaulle and confused about the future role the party would

[3] Association Française de Science Politique, *Le Référendum de Septembre et les Elections de Novembre, 1958: L'Etablissement de la Cinquième République* (Paris, 1958), pp. 152–55. (Work hereafter referred to as *Elections, 1958*.)

play in the Fifth Republic, there seemed to be a faint hope that the SFIO had a chance to broaden the base of its support in the country and to win away some support from the PCF. The request of Communist party members Pierre Hervé and Auguste Lecoeur to join the SFIO on October 21, 1958, might have led some Socialists to believe that the SFIO could win away disaffected PCF voters who wished to support de Gaulle. (But in an interview published in the Italian newspaper *Corriere Della Sera* and reprinted in *Le Populaire* November 22 and 23 Mollet said he thought Communists who voted "yes" on the referendum would then vote for "Fascists" in the legislative election.) A poll had shown that 26.5 per cent of the Communist voters voted "yes" on the referendum.[4]

Le Populaire noted that the results of the referendum had signaled the "disintoxication of the working class" and on October 11 and 12, 1958, René Naegelen in an article entitled "Le Vent en Poupe," called on party members to send him the names of people who might be interested in joining the party, claiming the party had "the wind in its sails" and that it was the appropriate moment to increase recruitment efforts.[5]

A National Council held October 26, 1958, discussed election tactics. On the second ballot federations were asked to withdraw candidates so as to erect "barriers to the enemies of democracy." A Socialist candidate should step down only if the best-placed candidate had been in favor of a "liberal policy in Algeria and overseas, for a policy of economic expansion, for full employment and the defense of buying power."

At the meeting, Guy Mollet made it clear that no alliance with the Communists was envisaged. "There can be no possi-

[4] *Le Populaire*, September 30 and November 22–23, 1958, The poll was published in *Elections, 1958*, p. 24.

[5] *Le Populaire*, October 2, 1958.

ble compromise with the Bolsheviks," he said. Mollet went on to call for voting support from the center left by appealing for votes from "believers." "We are not one-way laics. There is room among us for agnostics, for Catholics, or Protestant Christians, for the Jew and the Moslem." (Mollet's appeal for support from nonlaics occasioned some controversy since *L'Humanité* reported Mollet suggested that a curé might become the secretary of a Socialist section. This led to quick denial by the Socialists that Mollet had said any such thing.)

After the formation of the UNR, the SFIO launched a new slogan, "Votez Utile, Votez Socialiste" (Vote usefully, vote Socialist). In *Le Populaire* Claude Fuzier wrote that those who voted Socialist knew for whom and for what they were voting, while those who voted for candidates from the right did not know whether their candidates were ex-RPF, ex-ARS (*Action Républicaine et Sociale*—a dissident Gaullist group), or ex-PRL, (*Parti Républicaine de la Liberté*—a small conservative party formed at the Liberation).[6]

In its electoral statements the party tended to be defensive about its participation in power from 1956 to 1958. The party excused such participation by talking about the "necessity to defend the Republic," to "express the collective interest of the nation," and to "preserve national independence."[7] In the five minutes allotted by French radio and television facilities to the political parties contesting the election, Georges Brutelle attempted to calm those he thought might be frightened by the image of French socialism drawn by the extreme right and the extreme left. According to Brutelle, "I know that they [the French people] do not contest our democratic and patriotic qualities."[8]

Themes emphasized by the various Socialist candidates var-

[6] *Le Populaire*, October 27, November 3 and 17, 1958.

[7] *L'Année Politique*, 1959, p. 614.

[8] *Le Populaire*, November 15–16, 1958.

ied from district to district. Most, however, emphasized their support of de Gaulle, some by pointing out they had supported de Gaulle's investiture, (René Dejean in the second district of Ariège), others by linking the preservation of democracy to the presence of both Mollet and de Gaulle at the head of the government (Fernand, in the twentieth district of Nord), still others by pointing out that de Gaulle was best able to arrive at an equitable and peaceful solution to the Algerian problem (Leenhardt, in the sixth district of Bouches-du-Rhône).

Another theme common to many Socialist candidates was the necessity to "renovate the Republic," a process best carried out by both de Gaulle and Mollet cooperating to direct the government. In fact, the same phrase—"for national and republican renovation to which, by the side of de Gaulle, Guy Mollet and the Socialists have devoted themselves"—appears in the statements of Jean Durroux (Ariège, first district), Maurice Pic (Drôme), and René Schmitt (Manche, fifth district). It is interesting to note that the nice distinction drawn by the party in June, 1958, when Mollet joined the de Gaulle government solely on a "personal" basis without in any way committing the party, seems to have disappeared by November, 1958. Guy Mollet obviously represented more than himself, and the SFIO hoped to capitalize on this fact in the election.

The Socialist candidates also tended to dwell on local issues. The new electoral system (*scrutin d'arrondissement*), by limiting electoral districts to 93,000 voters, tended to magnify the importance of local controversies and problems. Thus Henri Darras of the eleventh district of Pas-de-Calais, in his electoral statement, devoted a great deal more space to local problems than had the candidate from Pas-de-Calais in 1956.

As in 1956, then, the SFIO tended to avoid controversial issues and tried to associate the party with a leading personality. Although many candidates said that de Gaulle could be expected to solve the Algerian problem, no candidate specifically stated just how he was to do this. On the whole, most candidates tended to deal either with popular personalities or to speak in generalities. Charles Privat of Bouches-du-Rhône, for example, stated that his program was based on the desire "to liberate the individual from all servitudes and allow him to develop and obtain concrete liberties which assure happiness and dignity." As in the 1956 campaign, no candidate mentioned the fact that the party's declaration of principles defined it as "essentially revolutionary," nor did any candidate mention that the party wished to substitute a collectivist system of property ownership for the capitalist system.

Mollet cautioned against being too optimistic about the election results, although he did not preclude the possibility of the party obtaining 130 to 150 seats.[9] Obviously, the party hoped to become the center of the moderate left group in the new government, or as Guy Mollet put it—using a phrase of Albert Gazier's—the "head of a constructive opposition."[10]

Results

The results of the first turn were surprising. The UNR, which had only been officially formed on October 1, 1958, received 15.2 per cent of the vote, giving it second place behind the Moderates, who received 16.5 per cent of the vote on the first turn. The SFIO received 11.7 per cent of the registered vote.

As compared with 1956, the SFIO lost a total of only 50,000 votes on this ballot, although there were perceptible movements both into and out of the Socialist ranks on the local level. In Ardennes, for example, where it might have been expected that the SFIO would lose a large number of

[9] *L'Année Politique*, 1958, p. 140.
[10] *Le Populaire*, November 22–23, 1958.

votes due to the loss of its deputy, Guy Desson, to the PSA, and where former deputy Mme. Andrée Vienot had publicly resigned from the SFIO in protest over its Algerian policy, it appears that the vote went neither to the PSA nor to the UFD (another left-wing splinter group) but to the UNR. This can be demonstrated by comparing the total votes of the various parties in the 1956 and 1958 legislative elections in the department of Ardennes.

The total for the entire left in 1956 (PCF, SFIO, MRP, and Radical Socialists) was 105,426; in 1958 it was 73,936, a loss of 31,490 votes. The total for the right in 1956 (Independents and Poujadists) was 28,201 votes; in 1958 the total for the right (now the Independents and the UNR) was 55,605. Thus the right picked up 27,404 votes from 1956 to 1958. The general movement of votes from 1956 to 1958 would appear to have been toward the right. In addition, the candidate of the PSA (Desson) appears to have made only a small dent in the SFIO totals in 1958, despite the fact that he was the incumbent deputy. (See Appendix C.)

Thus the SFIO did not succeed in filling the role of "avant-garde" party in the Fifth Republic, nor did the PSA win much support from disaffected Socialists. Even well-known former Socialist national leaders running for the PSA were unable to draw very much support away from the SFIO candidate. In the 54th district of Seine, for example, Edouard Depreux, former minister, deputy, and member of the party's executive committee, ran on the PSA ticket and encountered as an opponent Maurice Dolivet of the SFIO. The results were: Depreux, 7,111; Dolivet, 6,298. In 1956 the SFIO had received a total of 10,480 votes in this area. Thus the SFIO candidate in 1958 received 60 per cent of the Socialist vote of 1956. On the whole, then, the PSA did little damage to SFIO positions even where it might have been expected that a strong PSA candidate would attract disaffected Socialist votes. As François Goguel pointed out, the Socialist vote in 1956 revealed a "multitude of variations, often contradictory, within the same department."

With reference to the relation between their position on de Gaulle and the vote obtained in 1958 by Socialist candidates, no clear pattern was evidenced. On the one hand, only four of the deputies who voted for de Gaulle as President of the Council lost votes (Victor Provo in the seventh district of Nord lost 2,000 votes), while some who voted against de Gaulle gained votes (Mme. R. Lempereur gained 1,000 votes in the second district of Nord). Goguel cites Stuart Schram, who reported from the department of Gard that "if one compares the number of cantons in which the diverse Socialist candidates have equalled their percentages of 1956, partisans of 'yes' and partisans of 'no' follow one another without any advantage going to one or the other." Goguel also found that in some areas, in Nord or Somme, for example, votes coming from the PCF compensated for Socialist votes lost to the PSA and other groups of the UFD. The reason for this was that, in Nord and Somme, at least, the SFIO appeared as the worker's party which had voted "yes" on de Gaulle's investiture and on the referendum. On the whole, however, Goguel notes that the SFIO gained little from PCF voters. Goguel also noted that in the Midi and the Center, party losses to the UNR were compensated for by votes coming from the right.[11]

The electoral strategy of the SFIO was a logical extension of its stand on the referendum and of its action in the National Assembly since 1956. The party took a firm stand against concluding any alliances with the PCF for the second ballot, and it placed itself squarely among the supporters of the new regime. The difficulty was that the UNR, not the SFIO, was best fit to win the support of those who wished to vote for the

[11] *Elections, 1958*, pp. 159, 236 and 339–342.

party which would be in the "avant-garde" of the Fifth Republic. The result of the Socialist tactic was to place it in opposition to the PCF in many districts where Socialist candidates needed votes from the right in order to win on the second ballot. In 210 districts, the PCF and SFIO candidates faced each other during the second turn. The PCF withdrew only thirty-seven candidates in favor of a candidate of the left on the second turn. In the 178 districts where the SFIO withdrew its candidate, it did so in favor of the MRP or Radicals, not in favor of the PCF. Of the forty successful Socialist candidates, thirty-eight won on the second ballot. Of these, eleven fought against one other party on the second ballot, eighteen against two other parties (including the PCF) on the second ballot, and nine fought four-way contests (including the PCF) on the second ballot. The parties in the thirty-eight second-ballot battles won by Socialists were as follows:

PCF, SFIO	10
SFIO, UNR	1
PCF, SFIO, UNR, (or other Gaullists)	6
PCF, SFIO, MRP	4
PCF, SFIO, Independents	3
PCF, SFIO, Radicals	3
PCF, SFIO, diverse right	2
PCF, SFIO, UNR, Radicals	2
PCF, SFIO, UNR, and other right	6
PCF, SFIO, UNR, MRP	1

In ten contests where the PCF and SFIO faced each other alone, the candidates on the center and right withdrew in favor of the Socialist candidate who then beat the Communist candidate. In the three- and four-cornered contests, support for the SFIO candidate on the second ballot came equally from the right and the moderate left (MRP, Radical Socialist, Autonomous Socialist) elements, even in some cases when the right or moderate left party maintained its candidate. Not only did the Socialist candidate often receive votes from the right when there was a close contest between the Socialist and Communist candidates, but Socialist voters sometimes hesitated to vote for the Communist candidate when there was a choice between UNR and Communist candidates. The general refusal of Socialist voters to cast their votes for the Communist candidate on the second turn in cases where the Socialist candidate had withdrawn accorded well with a poll taken by *Sondages* in which the following question was posed: "Certain parties lost a number of seats in the elections. Would you please say for each of these parties if these losses please you?" The results of the poll were as follows:

	PCF		*SFIO*		*Radical*		*Poujadist*	
	Yes	*No*	*Yes*	*No*	*Yes*	*No*	*Yes*	*No*
PCF	0	92	37	31	34	23	66	3
SFIO	62	11	7	71	22	25	75	1

Except for the Poujadists, then, no party seems to have been as unpopular among Socialist voters as the PCF, and this hostility was mutual.

The flexibility of the Socialist electorate and its variegated nature demonstrated once again that, in spite of party rhetoric, the SFIO was indeed a "party like the others." It was considered a safe party to vote for by those on the right who were occasionally forced to choose between PCF and Socialist candidates, while its supporters inclined more toward the parties of the center left and right when faced with a choice between the extreme left and other parties. If any party could be defined as a "party unlike other parties," defined not by empty party rhetoric but by the reactions of the electorate toward it, then the PCF, not the SFIO, was that party.

The 1958 elections showed that the composition of the Socialist vote had remained pretty much the same. The most significant change was the evening out of the percentage of men and women voting for the SFIO. The increase in the number of women may have had something to do with the Socialist support for de Gaulle—although statistics show a decline of only three percentage points—from 45 per cent to 42 per cent—of the women's vote when the party moved to oppose the Gaullists in 1962. The only other marked change was the drop in voters in towns of 2,000–4,999 from 14 per cent of the Socialist vote in 1956 to 7 per cent in 1958. There were some disquieting signs. The newly created UNR drew 48 per cent of its support from the forty-four-and-under age group, while the SFIO drew only 41 per cent of its support from this group. The Socialist figures were not bad when compared with those of the Communists, who drew 40 per cent of their vote from these voters, and certainly they were quite good when compared with the Independents' 31 per cent; but in a country experiencing a rise in the birth rate and having, in 1958, almost one-third of the population under nineteen years of age, the difference between the figure for the Socialists and the UNR was a disheartening one. But the party maintained its position in the working class, for, as Mattei Dogan noted, the SFIO received 19 per cent of the total working-class vote in 1958, while, according to his figures, out of the total Socialist vote, 44 per cent came from working-class voters.[12] Interestingly enough, Dogan calculated that the Communist share of the working-class vote declined by 13 per cent from 1956 to 1958, for while in 1956 the PCF received 49 per cent of this vote, in 1958 it received only 36 per cent of the working-class vote. The working class still cast a large proportion of the total Communist vote, 71 per cent in 1956 and 70 per cent in 1958 (See Appendix A.2).

[12] Mattei Dogan, "Le Vote Ouvrier en Europe Occidentale," *Revue Française de Sociologie*, I (1960), 25–44.

For the SFIO, the elections of 1958 were not particularly encouraging. Although the party had preserved its voting strength in the country, it had not won support, as its slogan had wishfully implied that it would, as the "avant-garde of the Fifth Republic." Its traditional areas of voting strength in the northern industrial area, in the center, and in the southern areas continued as party strongholds on the electoral map in spite of sympathetic noises made by Guy Mollet toward Catholics and Gaullists. It was true that, on the second turn of the ballot, many Socialist deputies received the support of non-Socialist voters, but this was due more to an anti-Communist reflex than to pro-Socialist sentiment. Anti-Communist impulses also accounted for the movement of Socialist voters toward candidates of the center and right on the second ballot.

The loss of more than half of its parliamentary seats also boded ill for the SFIO, since it was obvious that the UNR was certainly better qualified than the SFIO to attract Gaullist votes. By suddenly emerging as a major political force, the UNR threatened to secure a firm position by unifying the right and overwhelming the fractured left.

7. *In Search of a Role*

Under the Fifth Republic the SFIO tended to react to events rather than to take the initiative in dealing with the changed realities of the presidential system. The participation of the Socialist ministers in the de Gaulle government until late 1958, for example, was in keeping with the principle of "Republican defense." Although the party was by no means united on this policy, the departure of the PSA minority in 1958 and Defferre's rally to de Gaulle and the Fifth Republic meant that the leaders of the major SFIO federations all supported de Gaulle. Some party leaders, such as Christian Pineau and Albert Gazier, tended to be more critical of de Gaulle and the Debré government than were the majority, but these men had no real support in the federations and their voices were generally drowned out by the supporters of Mollet, Laurent, and Defferre.

On Algeria there still existed some serious division of opinion, although here again the departure of Mollet from the post of President of the Council of Ministers and then of the Socialist ministers from the de Gaulle government allowed the party to be much more critical of the government's Algerian policy than in 1956–1957, when the Socialists had led the government. On one side Max Lejeune from Somme tended to support an Algérie Française position, while on the other side Tanguy-Prigent from Finistère advocated giving Algeria a large degree of independence. Neither of their federations was very large, however, and these views never received much support in the party.

On the whole, the militants seemed to share the sentiments of Francis Leenhardt who noted, at a National Congress held January 12, 1959, that the SFIO was not interested in forcing de Gaulle to depend solely on the UNR. Rather, he suggested, the SFIO should take a position such that de Gaulle would feel that there was an "alternate" majority in the National Assembly. In any case, Leenhardt maintained, the Constitution had allowed the "parliamentary game" to continue. Gérard Jaquet also suggested that the SFIO be prepared to assume governmental responsibilities, or, at the least, be ready to replace the UNR as de Gaulle's support in the National Assembly. Jaquet suggested that members take into account the possibility that de Gaulle might drop all "equivocation" and decide to follow an Algerian policy more in conformity with the views of the SFIO. In any case, he said, the SFIO would have to come to the support of de Gaulle while at the same time actively criticizing Prime Minister Debré. Thus Jaquet envisaged a situation in which de Gaulle would be forced to turn to the SFIO for support for a liberal Algerian policy if the right wing of the UNR emerged triumphant in that party.

For many in the SFIO, it was apparent that de Gaulle's views on Algeria were more liberal than those of many in the UNR. Thus some Socialist leaders began to think about the possibility of supporting a strong executive against the parliament, a reversal of the suspicion with which the French left had traditionally regarded a strong executive.

The Socialists were in a peculiar position, for it appeared

that opposition to de Gaulle might open the way to a renewed threat of intervention from the army. By withdrawing support for de Gaulle and his Algerian policy, the Socialists might force de Gaulle to follow an Algerian policy to the right of that suggested by the Socialists. And, as many Socialist leaders reiterated, de Gaulle had retained a democratic framework in the French political system. A successor or replacement might look much less kindly on democratic procedures than de Gaulle did. Thus the case for Socialist support for de Gaulle appeared quite sound. But not everyone in the party agreed that the French Fifth Republic was as much of a democracy as its supporters claimed. At the July, 1959, National Congress, Jules Moch, Christian Pineau, and Albert Gazier all criticized the government and de Gaulle. Moch castigated the majority motion which held that essential liberties had been preserved that allowed for a "free party in a free country." For Moch, the country was not free when the rights of free men were not respected, when opponents of the regime were treated as if they were traitors to France itself, and when parliament was increasingly deprived of its rights.

According to Gazier it was no longer possible for the party to support President de Gaulle while opposing Prime Minister Debré. Gazier claimed that on "political, economic, and social" questions the SFIO disagreed with de Gaulle, and he maintained it was "false" to believe that only de Gaulle could solve the Algerian problem. Gazier concluded by reminding the audience that, in spite of his criticism of party policy, this criticism should not be construed as an attack on Secretary-General Mollet, since the latter had always been approved by three-quarters of the party and to criticize him would thus be to criticize the party itself.

During the early years of the Fifth Republic, however, the majority of party members seemed to agree with Mollet and others that the SFIO should constitute a "loyal opposition":

I believe that, without compromise on either side, the government can maintain contact with the loyal and constructive opposition as in Great Britain. The SFIO represents a political force considerable enough to merit being informed in certain areas, in particular, international affairs.[1]

For a while, de Gaulle did maintain contact with the SFIO through Mollet, who sometimes visited with the President—on May 12, 1959, for example, when Mollet expressed Socialist support for de Gaulle's foreign policy but had reservations about admitting Spain to NATO.[2]

The beginning of 1960, however, saw the SFIO unwillingly continue its support of de Gaulle on his Algerian policy and his maintenance of government legitimacy in the face of open rebellion from the army and subversion from OAS forces. Many in the party were becoming irritated at the continued decline of parliament and de Gaulle's refusal to remain within the role of "arbiter" assigned to him by the Constitution of the Fifth Republic.

When a rebellion broke out in Algeria in early January, 1960, the SFIO created a Committee for Liaison and Understanding for the Support of General de Gaulle's Actions (*Comité de Liaison et d'Entente pour le Soutien de l'Action du Général de Gaulle*). But in March, when de Gaulle refused to convoke the National Assembly in spite of the presentation of a petition signed by a majority of deputies in accordance with Article 29 of the Constitution, SFIO opposition stiffened. On April 28, 1960, the Socialist group deposed a motion of censure against the government, and on May 5, 1960, Guy Mollet effectively attacked Prime Minister Debré in a debate over the refusal to convoke the Assembly.

Although the SFIO was not yet ready to ally itself with the

[1] Cited in *Le Monde*, April 1, 1959, from an interview with Guy Mollet in *L'Aurore*.

[2] *Ibid.*, May 12, 1959.

PCF or PSU in opposition, by the middle of 1960 it had begun to reconsider the whole question of cooperation with the Gaullists. This was clearly demonstrated in the June 21 and 23, 1960, elections to the Paris Municipal Council when the Socialist candidate did not step down in favor of the UNR candidate as he had done in 1959. It took three ballots to elect the Independent candidate over the Socialist. At the same time, however, Georges Dardel was warned by the party for having accepted the support of the PCF and PSU in being re-elected President of the General Council of the Seine.

The breakdown in negotiations between French officials and representatives of the FLN at Melun also fed the fires of opposition in the SFIO. A text presented by Albert Gazier and Christian Pineau for the 52nd National Congress scheduled for June 30 to July 3, 1960, asked that the SFIO disengage itself completely from the regime and cease concentrating on tactical preoccupations in order to create a new society where socialism would "flourish." Then, since the motion was aimed at party delegates, the fairly orthodox suggestion that the party enter into complete opposition was phrased in language recalling that the Socialist mission was "the destruction of the capitalist regime, replacing the exploitation of man by man." It was also suggested that a new Constitution be prepared, for "most people" doubted the Constitution would survive the President of the Republic. Attacking the notion that the SFIO should support the regime in accordance with the SFIO's principle of "Republican defense," Gazier said that "too often we have tended to fly to the rescue of the 'sick mother' even if it is only a 'cruel stepmother.' "[3] And again: "General de Gaulle has many merits, but he is trying to save capitalism while our goal is to end it."[4] In spite of these resounding calls to repair to revolu-

[3] *Le Populaire*, July 2–3, 1960. [4] *Le Monde*, July 2, 1960.

tionary banners, the majority motion opposed the idea that the SFIO enter into systematic opposition but suggested that the party keep a watchful eye out for any "injury done to the institutions" of government.

The Party in Opposition

By early 1961, Guy Mollet had explicitly rejected the possibility that the SFIO would participate in government—except, of course, if the nation or the Republic was subjected to a mortal threat or if the SFIO was called to participate by virtue of a victory in legislative elections. At the same time, Mollet too began to emphasize the revolutionary strain in Socialist tradition:

> It is necessary to get rid of the cause of human suffering and capitalist profit-making and substitute another regime for the capitalist regime. To change an economic regime is called a revolution. We are thus "an essentially revolutionary party." Revolution is a change in regime and is not necessarily synonymous with bloody revolt. In 1956 France underwent a revolution without bloodletting when the colonies were granted autonomy and independence.[5]

In September, 1961, an Extraordinary National Council was called to discuss increased OAS violence and the continued fighting in Algeria. The Council unanimously condemned the government for its attitude on the *force de frappe*, on Europe, and on the U.N. The party also claimed that the government had never "seriously" negotiated on the Algerian question. It criticized the government for scorning the nation's representatives and for "recoiling" before violence and street demonstrations. It maintained that the government's "successive and abusive" interpretations of the Constitution forced all "democrats" to prepare to renew de-

[5] *Le Populaire*, February 17 and March 4–5, 1961.

mocracy, and it called on all "democratic formations" to form a cartel for democratic action that would present a precise program as an alternative to the government's policy and prepare the way for its successors.

By 1962, therefore, the SFIO seemed on the verge of entering systematic opposition. One of the major signs of SFIO disaffection from the regime was its decision, taken in January, 1962, to join a National Action Committee against the OAS, (*Comité National d'Action contre l'OAS*). The committee included Radicals, members from the Independent Center, the Jacobin Club, and various antifascist and antiracist organizations. At a National Council meeting held in May, 1962, the party approved the text of a resolution on general policy condemning de Gaulle for his "anti-European and anti-Atlantic policies." It also criticized the Pompidou government for its policy of "social regression."

Finally, when de Gaulle decided to hold a referendum changing the method of presidential election after the near success of the assassination attempt at Petit-Clamart, the SFIO stated its absolute opposition. At the October 7, 1962, National Council meeting, the party unanimously voted a motion noting that it was "inconceivable that the President persisted in violating the Constitution against the opinion of the Senate, the National Assembly, and the jurists on the Council of State and Constitutional Council." According to Guy Mollet, the choice was clear: "Either we will allow a monarchy to be installed and dictatorship will inevitably follow, or we will save democracy in leaving open the chances for a Socialist democracy."[6]

There were many reasons for the return of the SFIO to opposition but there can be little doubt that de Gaulle's attitude toward the parties and the Constitution was a key factor.

[6] *Le Populaire*, October 8, 1962.

As the Constitution gradually took hold in the country and as de Gaulle was able to win dominance over the recalcitrant army in Algeria, to bring about negotiations, and then to arrive at a settlement of the Algerian problem, the direction of his policies became clear. Although the National Assembly had been relieved of many of the powers it had held under the Fourth Republic, it had been assumed by many Socialists—Guy Mollet particularly—that the parties in the National Assembly would continue to exercise an important influence over government policy. It soon became apparent, however, that de Gaulle was not content to play the role of arbiter and that circumstances—the continued rebellion in Algeria, army indiscipline, the OAS—all demanded a high degree of presidential leadership and authority. Thus the parties in the National Assembly found themselves relegated to a minor role in the national political life of the Fifth Republic. In addition, the surprising success of the UNR in the 1958 election upset Socialist calculations that de Gaulle might be forced to rely on the SFIO for a liberal Algerian policy in the National Assembly. The amorphous nature of the UNR had also aroused Socialist hopes, for many guessed the new formation would collapse as de Gaulle's intentions became clear. But the continued loyalty of the UNR—even in the face of the President's remarkable maneuvers to bring about negotiations on Algeria—proved that many Gaullists in the National Assembly put their loyalty to de Gaulle above whatever convictions they might have held on Algeria.

When, therefore, in 1962, it became apparent that the end of the Algerian rebellion would lead not to a reduction in presidential powers but rather to an increase, the Socialists and other opposition parties reacted with intense hostility.

8. The Party at the Polls— The 1962 Election

If the prelude to the 1958 election was agreement within the SFIO on the necessity to support de Gaulle as the only alternative to an armed confrontation between the left and the army, the prelude to the 1962 election was the SFIO's hostility to both de Gaulle and the Fifth Republic. Two events that occurred between 1958 and 1962 played a major role in the SFIO turnabout. The first was the end to the Algerian War and the ratification of self-determination by 90 per cent of the electorate on April 8, 1962. The SFIO had supported a "yes" vote on the referendum at the March 24, 1962, National Council meeting by a vote of 2,974 for "yes," with only 2 votes opposed and 107 abstentions. But the motion also warned that the party did not endorse by this vote, the "erroneous and dangerous" policy the government was following, nor did it constitute approval of "successive violations" of the Constitution.

The second important event influencing the party's reversal of attitude was de Gaulle's decision, after the attempt on his life at Petit-Clamart on August 22, 1962, to submit a referendum to the electorate asking that the method of electing the president be changed from an indirect method by a small electoral college to direct election by the entire electorate. Whether the decision to call a referendum on this point directly stemmed from the assassination attempt, or whether the attempt merely provided an opportunity for de Gaulle to change the Constitution in a manner presaged by his experience as President since 1958, is still an open question.[1] The point is that the proposed change in the election procedure was viewed by most of the parties except the UNR as an unwarranted attempt by de Gaulle to further increase the already crushing power of the presidential office. For the SFIO, the call for a referendum was the culmination of de Gaulle's successive violations of the Constitution. Even before the proposed change was made public, the SFIO had become critical of the "successive and repeated violations" of the Constitution. The party noted that power had become increasingly personalized so that the parliament was losing control not only over the course of French politics but over the government as well.[2]

The negative reaction aroused by the Constitutional referendum extended from the far left to the right and included the Radical party, the Independents, and the MRP. Within parliament, under the aegis of Paul Reynaud, the leaders of these parties met late in September to draft a Constitutional counterproposal. Unfortunately, however, the counterproposal finally elaborated by the opposition parties was so encumbered with amendments that its effect would have been to

[1] François Goguel, "Les Circonstances du Référendum d'Octobre, 1962," in Association Française de Science Politique, *Le Référendum d'Octobre et les Elections de Novembre, 1962* (Paris, 1960), p. 10. (Work hereafter referred to as *Elections, 1962.*)

[2] Parti Socialiste, *Bulletin Intérieur*, no. 127, March, 1963, p. 222.

restore the practices of the Fourth Republic.[3] Eventually the MRP refused to accept the opposition counterproposal, and the parties were then forced to submit a censure motion based on the alleged unconstitutionality of the government's amendment procedure. On October 4, 1962, the censure motion received 280 out of 480 votes and therefore met the requirements of Article 49 of the Constitution. The government being forced to resign, it was a foregone conclusion that de Gaulle would take the opportunity to call for dissolution of the National Assembly and for new elections. Thus the opposition parties ensured a confrontation between themselves and de Gaulle.

Tactics

As the October 28, 1962, referendum approached, the parties of the *Cartel des Non,* as the grouping of opposition parties came to be called, closed ranks. The parliamentary alliance among the parties that had signed the censure motion —Radicals, Independents, MRP, Socialists, and the tiny Liberal party—was extended to the point where the leaders of the parties soon constituted a "permanent delegation" composed of the presidents of the various parliamentary groups and party leaders.

The SFIO remained deaf to the appeals of both the PCF and the PSU to elaborate a common program for the coming legislative elections or to elaborate a common electoral strategy.[4] The SFIO had already chosen to work with the parties in the *Cartel des Non.* At the October 7, 1962, National Council meeting held in Puteaux, the party had passed a unanimous motion authorizing federations not to present a

[3] *Elections, 1962,* p. 33.

[4] See article by Claude Fuzier rejecting these proposals in *Le Populaire,* October 16, 1962.

Socialist candidate where there were candidates who had chosen during debates in the National Assembly and the vote on the censure motion to "assume major responsibilities" in the defense of the Republic. The motion also authorized the federations to assure the election of the "most favored candidates" belonging to one of the formations that had signed the censure motion. The PCF had not been one of the signatories of the censure motion, although the ten PCF deputies had, of course, voted in favor of censure.

The results of the referendum were muddy. The "yes" vote obtained only 46.44 per cent of the registered vote, but 61.75 per cent of those voting. The "no" vote obtained 28.75 per cent of the registered voters and 38.25 per cent of those voting. Both the Gaullists and the opposition were disappointed, and both expected the situation to be clarified during the legislative elections.

Just prior to the elections, however, an event occurred that was to completely change the strategy elaborated by the parties in the *Cartel des Non.* In effect, whether aware of the long-range consequences of his statements or not, on November 7 and November 9, Guy Mollet suggested that under no circumstances should those sympathetic to the opposition vote for a Gaullist candidate on either the first or the second ballots of the legislative election.[5] The Gaullists immediately claimed that Mollet was suggesting that those who supported the *Cartel des Non* should vote PCF rather than UNR-UDT if that were the only choice. By November 12, 1962, in an effort to clarify his position, Mollet reaffirmed his support of the *Cartel des Non* and expressed skepticism that there would be many cases of a duel between Gaullists and Communists on the second ballot. But he did maintain that in those "ten or twelve" districts where such a development was liable to

[5] *Elections, 1962,* p. 79ff.

occur, he would vote to beat the UNR-UDT candidate.[6] This tactic also implied that the PCF could withdraw its candidate on the second ballot, throwing support to the Socialist candidate in those districts where the Socialist obtained more votes than the Communist on the first ballot. In Mollet's case, Communist support was necessary on the second ballot because the Gaullist in his district was sure to win if the two left parties split the vote by competing against each other on the second ballot. Thus, Mollet was accused by his opponents of seeking a change in electoral tactics during this election mainly to save his own skin.

The immediate result of Mollet's statement, however, was to irritate the partners of the *Cartel des Non,* who were not at all willing to vote for a Communist as against a Gaullist if they were forced to choose. Thus, prior to the election, the opposition strategy seemed to have broken down, for if there was agreement on first-ballot tactics, on the second ballot it was apparently every man for himself.

Results

Nationally, the SFIO lost 895,057 votes compared with its first-ballot total in 1958, and the 1962 elections marked a low ebb in SFIO electoral fortunes since the war. Only one Socialist deputy was elected on the first ballot (R. Bayou from the fourth district of Hérault), while the UNR-UDT elected forty-six. Contrary to Guy Mollet's prediction, there were not ten or twelve cases of a second-ballot runoff between a UNR-UDT candidate and a PCF candidate but ninety cases. Mollet took account of this situation between the first and second ballots and noted that while thirty or forty Communist deputies in the National Assembly would not threaten democracy in the Fifth Republic, the election of thirty or

[6] *Le Populaire,* November 14, 1962.

forty additional Gaullist deputies would mean the end of the representative system.

Between the two ballots a number of tacit agreements were concluded between the PCF and SFIO for one or the other's candidate to withdraw for the candidate receiving the most votes on the first ballot. At the same time Socialist spokesmen vehemently denied that any explicit agreement had been reached on common strategy by the two parties. According to Gérard Jaquet, the PCF was "multiplying" its efforts to induce the Socialists to organize joint demonstrations and to work together on other activities. But, Jaquet noted, the party was unhesitatingly rejecting all such propositions.[7]

This did not mean, however, that Socialist spokesmen stopped evoking the terrible dangers of a UNR victory. Claude Fuzier noted that "the UNR-UDT represents the right in its most detestable and dangerous form."[8]

What had happened to the more than 800,000 voters who had voted Socialist on the first ballot in 1958 but had not voted for the SFIO on the first ballot of 1962? According to a study of Georges Dupeux, about 5.5 per cent of the 1958 Socialist voters abstained and approximately 30 per cent voted for other parties.[9] According to Dupeux, 7 per cent of those who voted Socialist in 1958 voted PCF in 1962, 6 per cent for the PSU, 3 per cent for the Radicals, and 14 per cent for the UNR-UDT on the first ballot.

In 1958, in 37 of 40 districts where a Socialist deputy was elected, the SFIO candidate faced Communist opposition on the second ballot, while in 1962 the Socialists and Communists dueled in only three districts where the Socialist candidate

[7] *Elections, 1962*, pp. 82–84.

[8] *Le Populaire*, November 15, 23 and 24–25, 1962.

[9] Georges Dupeux, "Le Comportement des Electeurs Français de 1958 à 1962, d'après une Enquête par Sondage," *Revue Française de Science Politique*, XIV, no. 1 (February, 1964), 61.

was successful on the second turn. In six cases the successful SFIO candidate won out over both a PCF and a UNR-UDT candidate on the second ballot. In 53 of the 63 second-ballot battles where the Socialist candidate won, the fight was between a Socialist and one or more candidates from the center-right or the right. Thus, the second-ballot battles seemed to resemble more the left-right battles of the Third Republic than the electoral battles under the Fourth Republic, when the SFIO frequently allied itself with the Radicals or other moderate parties against the PCF. Moreover, according to the Communist party, 53 of the 64 Socialist deputies were elected only because the Communist candidate withdrew and threw his support to the Socialist.[10]

The actual degree of cooperation between the PCF and SFIO varied from one department to another. In some cases there was a tacit agreement between the two parties to withdraw their candidates in favor of the best-placed candidate. Frequent examples of this tactic occurred in Nord, Pas-de-Calais, and Seine. In Nord cooperation between the two parties on second-ballot battles occurred in all but one of the twenty-three districts. In Pas-de-Calais, hostility between the two parties led to a three-cornered fight in three districts among the PCF, SFIO, and UNR-UDT. The PCF won one of these battles and the SFIO two, the Socialist candidates winning because of votes from the UNR-UDT electorate, a small fraction of which usually transferred to the SFIO on the second ballot to allow the Socialist to beat the Communist. In most cases, however, as François Goguel pointed out, the Socialist electorate followed the course advocated by the party in the electoral district.[11]

[10] *Cahiers du Communisme*, no. 12 (December, 1962), p. 321.

[11] François Goguel, "Le Référendum du 28 Octobre et les Elections des 18–25 Novembre, 1962," *Revue Française de Science Politique*, XIII (June, 1963), 317.

The movement of Socialist votes into the Communist column on the second ballot in 1962 may seem contrary to the tendency of Socialists, as in the 1958 elections, to support the right or center when faced with a choice between the moderate right and the PCF. Two factors may account for the change. First, in many districts the SFIO did not enter candidates on the first ballot because of agreements with other members of the *Cartel.* Thus in many districts the Socialist voter could support a non-Communist candidate from the very beginning. Second, the decline in the Socialist vote may have been due not only to the abstention of those without a Socialist candidate to vote for but also to the refusal of many Socialists to vote in an election where they were being asked to support the PCF on the second ballot. In a study of political behavior during the 1962 campaign, Guy Michelat found that only 64 per cent of those who claimed to feel closer to the SFIO than to any other political party actually voted Socialist on the first turn of the ballot. Nineteen per cent of those who felt closest to the SFIO voted PSU, 13 per cent Radical Socialist, and 5 per cent PCF on the first ballot. This would seem to substantiate the impression that many Socialist voters voted PSU in districts where no Socialist candidate was presented. The 13 per cent who voted Radical Socialist probably represented Socialist voters who chose the laic candidate in areas where there was no Socialist candidate or where the Socialist candidate was regarded as having no chance in the election. The low figure of 5 per cent voting for the PCF on the first ballot serves to demonstrate the continuing hostility most Socialist voters felt toward the PCF. Thus, as in 1958, the historical enmity between the SFIO and PCF on the left, and the laic barrier on the right, formed two insurmountable barriers within which the Socialists were constrained.[12]

The election of 1962 was a clear defeat for the SFIO and

[12] Guy Michelat, "Attitudes et Comportements Politiques à l'Automne 1962," in *Elections, 1962,* pp. 218–220.

for the opposition parties, and a victory for de Gaulle and the UNR-UDT. De Gaulle's personal intervention in the campaign and his support for the UNR-UDT had forced a confrontation between the opposition parties and the President.[13] The massive vote for the UNR-UDT (31.94 per cent of those voting) and the election of 229 UNR-UDT deputies who, combined with the sympathetic Independents, composed a majority of the National Assembly was a crushing defeat for the opposition in the parliament as well.

For the SFIO the election of sixty-four Socialist deputies could not conceal the decline in the Socialist vote nor the fact that Communist support was largely responsible for their success. A number of other things had become apparent. The Socialist party still was unable to capture the votes of young people—and this was particularly important since the average age of the population was quite young and getting younger. The SFIO also had to face the fact it could not expect to present itself as a working-class party when it was outdistanced by both the PCF and the UNR-UDT in terms of total working-class voting support and when a minority of its total vote came from the working class. The support of the working class in Nord and Pas-de-Calais could certainly be used as evidence of some working-class support, but in fact their vote was forthcoming largely for reasons of tradition—the two departments had historically been Socialist since the days of Guesde—and because the SFIO was locally strong in the *mairies*, in *Force Ouvrière*, and in the departments that had long been considered Socialist fiefs. The problem facing the SFIO, however, was not to maintain existing positions—although that was important—but rather to extend its influence. The 1962 election only seemed to show the party was shrinking further within the traditional borders of Socialist support.

[13] See Jean Charlot, "La campagne et la tactique des partis," in *Elections, 1962*, pp. 77–79, on de Gaulle's intervention in the electoral campaign.

Even the large proportion of successful deputies who were at the same time powerful local politicians seemed to show not that local SFIO power was transferrable to the national level, but that, taking account of the fact that Communist support was necessary to elect most of these deputies, *even* strong local roots were not enough to win national office for Socialist candidates.

The Electorate

In 1962, the Socialists still ranked low in terms of the percentage of its vote cast by young people. According to figures cited in the 1962 election study by the *Fondation Nationale des Sciences Politiques*, except for the Radical Socialists, who drew 21 per cent of their vote from those aged thirty-four and under, the Socialists were the lowest with 26 per cent of their vote coming from that group. This does not compare badly with the equivalent figures for the UNR-UDT (28 per cent) but it certainly shows very poorly beside the Communists with 35 per cent, the PSU with 35 per cent, and the MRP with 32 per cent of their votes cast by voters aged thirty-four years and under. For these elections, Mattei Dogan estimated that the SFIO and the PSU together received 22 per cent of the working-class vote, with the Communists receiving 38 per cent. The difficulty with this calculation, however, is that Dogan includes all the wives of working-class voters, whether they were actively employed or not. Judging the proportion of the total working-class vote on the basis of sample survey figures, however, one arrives at the figure of 13 per cent of total working-class votes received by the SFIO.[14] According to an IFOP survey, 27 per cent of

[14] Mattei Dogan, "Le Vote Ouvrier en Europe Occidentale," *Revue Française de Sociologie*, I (1960), 25–44 and my own calculations from election results for the 1962 election, cited in *Elections, 1962*, p. 239.

the SFIO vote was cast by working-class voters. But 32 per cent of the Socialist vote came from retired people or those "without profession" (housewives). In contrast, the Communist party received only 25 per cent of its vote from retired people and housewives, while the MRP received 31 per cent of its votes and the UNR-UDT 38 per cent from this category. In addition, the increase in votes from the farmers as a proportion of the total Socialist vote seemed to indicate that the Socialists were drawing much of their support from those sectors of the economy that were either in decline or inactive (see Appendix A.3).

9. The Socialists, the Communists, and the Regrouping of the Left

Soon after the election of 1962, Gérard Jaquet noted that, in order to survive, the parties "must make an effort to reorganize and regroup. . . . The permanent drama of French politics originates in the multiplicity of parties."[1] If, by this time, most party leaders agreed with Jaquet, there still seemed to be confusion as to the exact form that the regrouping would assume and exactly who would be involved. The most ambiguous proposal came from Guy Mollet who said: "French 'laborism' [*travaillisme*], yes, now that is the principal objective."[2]

Soon after making this statement, however, Mollet seemed to change his line. At the December 16, 1962, National Council meeting, he first defended himself against the attack of Francis Leenhardt, who accused him of having contravened the decision of the National Congress by asking Socialists to vote for Communists on the second ballot of the legislative election. Leenhardt pointed out that the Communists, since they had not been signatories of the censure motion, were not

[1] *Le Populaire,* December 3, 1962. [2] *Ibid.*

eligible for Socialist support under the terms of the resolution voted on October 7, 1962. Mollet denied that he had contravened the sense of the motion and said he acted as he did because he feared some federations would enter into written agreements with the Communists and this would have caused these federations to break party discipline. On the question of regrouping the parties Mollet noted that the right had "disappeared," and that the MRP was "on the way." The Radicals could be dealt with, but the big problem remained the PCF. Then came a remarkable analysis and proposal. Mollet stated that it was acceptable to conclude defensive alliances with the PCF when the Republic was menaced by fascism or in order to resist "personal power." But although unity in the worker's movement would be achieved some day, it could not be expected to happen at that particular moment. Mollet's reason was that in 1962 as in 1921, the PCF was still obligated by the twenty-one conditions it had accepted when it joined the Communist International. As for the future course of the SFIO, Mollet pointed out that de Gaulle—or any mayor, for that matter—could do as much for the people in terms of social and economic reform as Socialists. This was especially true when the economic circumstances were favorable. The only alternative left to the SFIO, then, was to

> say the truth, tell the citizens that they are being deceived . . . that the Revolution does not consist in the amelioration of the conditions of everyday living, but the transformation of the structures of society. . . . This Congress ought to choose between the two extremes, to recreate an aggressive, pure, and tough party, or to create some sort of large democratic party, agreeing on some great principle with a man to present for the presidency of the Republic.

As for himself, Mollet chose the first alternative. Moreover, he made it clear that he was also opposed to the presidential regime as de Gaulle had shaped it:

I hope the party doesn't deceive itself on the urgency of certain problems. The most important problem is not to know if the next president of the Republic will be elected by one side or the other, but it is to make sure that the next president loses the powers that the current one has usurped.

At the December 16, 1962, National Council meeting, other suggestions for regrouping were also presented. Georges Brutelle, assistant secretary-general of the SFIO and former supporter of Guy Mollet who now increasingly was convinced that the SFIO had to seek new doctrinal and organizational frontiers, suggested the formation of a "new force" based on the SFIO but including all who agreed on the fundamental principles of socialism. This would include militants from the CFTC, the Radical party, and the PSU, and all those people sympathetic to socialism but not attached to any organization. Brutelle's suggestion formed the basis of the *Colloques Socialistes*, a series of meetings held to discuss Socialist doctrine with interested representatives from other parties, trade unions, and clubs during 1963 and 1964.

Gaston Defferre suggested that once some kind of *rassemblement* was achieved, the political situation might be radically altered if the new formation nominated a "young, new man for the presidency."

Gazier suggested that any regrouping take place primarily on the left, with the PSU included but not the PCF. He stated that he did not believe in *travaillisme* and said that only when a regrouping on the left or center-left had been achieved could serious negotiations with the PCF be undertaken with a view toward future cooperation.[3]

Relations with the PCF

The tactic of mutual withdrawals during the 1962 election marked a profound change in the electoral relations of the

[3] *Le Populaire*, December 17, and March 14–15, 1962.

PCF and the SFIO. The extreme hostility manifested by Mollet toward the UNR-UDT during the 1962 elections showed a rather obvious evolution in his attitude, for he explicitly stated that the greatest danger to democracy in France came not from the PCF but from the UNR-UDT. In addition, from 1962 on he became less and less hostile to suggestions that the SFIO and the PCF might cooperate on certain occasions. Whereas in December, 1962, he had stated that such cooperation could only take place when fascism or "personal power" menaced the country, in July, 1963, he envisaged the possibility of SFIO–PCF cooperation during specific limited periods for "defensive" reasons; for example, during the miners' strikes of that period. Later he specified that not only were electoral alliances with the PCF possible, but that common action was also possible when "on a precise point, one of our freedoms is threatened." Here Mollet cited common action by the PCF and the SFIO under the aegis of the National Committee for Laic Action (CNAL) in the event *laïcité* was threatened.

As for the PCF, its violent criticism of the SFIO diminished as the latter party grew increasingly hostile toward the Gaullists. In February, 1962, for example, *Cahiers du Communisme* had stated:

> Partisans of the Algerian war defending the colonial privileges of a minority, partisans of the Atlantic Pact and of a European policy which makes of the German *revanchards* the spearhead of anti-Soviet aggression, Guy Mollet and his reactionary allies wish to preserve the Gaullist regime and its Constitution.[4]

But as the violence of the OAS provoked criticism from the SFIO, and as this criticism began to extend to the regime

[4] V. Johannes, "Le Parti et la Cinquième République," *Cahiers du Communisme*, cited in *Revue Française de Science Politique*, XIV, no. 1 (February, 1964), 76–77.

itself, so too the PCF began to moderate its criticism of the SFIO. For both parties, the referendum of April 8, 1962, marked the end of an era. The "yes" vote on the Algerian referendum marked the last time the major parties of the left (including the PCF) would find themselves obliged to support a major Gaullist policy. By the end of 1962 the PCF was appealing to the SFIO to join it either in "common or parallel" actions.[5]

On March 14, 1963, speaking before Socialist mayors, Mollet analyzed the various "categories of men" with whom it would be possible for Socialists to work. The members of the PSU and other Socialists and left-wing Catholics all were invited by Mollet to join the SFIO. As for the PCF, Mollet observed that "the essential differences between us do not reside in issues which oppose us to each other today, over foreign or domestic policies, although they remain grave, but in the reasons that caused the split in the worker's world." Then Mollet asked the PCF the following questions:

> What remains of Zinoviev's conditions?
> Is it still true that we are the essential enemy, the 'chicken' to be plucked?
> Is it still true that the end justifies the means?
> Is it still true that the taking of political power and holding it, if need be, by dictatorship, is the real objective?[6]

In *France Nouvelle* of March 20, 1963, François Billoux replied to these questions by saying, in essence, that there was a profound difference between the situation in 1963 and that which had obtained in 1920, that there were no party "theses" on the single party or on the unconditional submission of the PCF to Moscow. Later, in *Le Populaire*, Claude Fuzier took

[5] M. Thorez before the Central Committee, December 13–14, 1962, cited in *ibid.*, pp. 80–81.

[6] *Le Populaire*, March 14–15, 1963.

note of Thorez's statement that (1) it was possible to escape the necessity of a violent revolution if one took account of the weakness of capitalist forces and the power deriving from the unity of democratic and Socialist forces; (2) the Soviet method was not the only one which could be envisaged for ending capitalism; (3) the dictatorship of the proletariat would last only for a provisional period involving no diminution of democracy for the workers; (4) a plurality of parties would be possible both during the period of proletarian dictatorship as well as during the construction of socialism.[7] But Fuzier was dissatisfied with the concepts of democratic centralism and of proletarian dictatorship, both of which retained their "totaliarian implications."

On July 1, 1963, Guy Mollet granted an interview to *France-Observateur* in which he said:

> The Communists and Socialists both condemn the system based on capitalism, profit, and enrichment. We both want to hasten its replacement by another founded on collective progress. But they [Communists] have attempted to build new systems by violence, by sacrificing millions of men, entire generations. . . . We don't accept that. . . . If the PCF is seriously considering preparing for a Socialist revolution by democratic means, then we are deeply interested.

In September, 1963, the Socialists were invited to visit Moscow by the Soviet government. Mollet noted that he hoped to determine whether there had been any evolution in the Communist party of the Soviet Union, not only in its conception of relations among states but also in the principles on which it based its actions.[8]

While in Moscow the SFIO delegation (including Guy Mollet, Gaston Defferre, Albert Gazier, Gérard Jaquet, Augustin Laurent, Jean Pitée, Marcel Champeix, Robert Pontil-

[7] *Ibid.*, May 18–19, 1963. [8] *Ibid.*, September 17–18, 1963.

lon, and Roger Quilliot) met with Khrushchev and spoke to students at Moscow University. The correspondent of *Le Monde* noted that the Soviets had reserved a warm and cordial reception for the Socialist delegation, thus apparently underlining Soviet desires for a *rapprochement* with the Socialists and implying that they might be worthy partners in electoral alliances with the PCF. The *Le Monde* correspondent also observed that the Socialists were no longer insultingly labeled "social traitors" as they had been in the past by the Soviet press.

Upon the delegation's return from Moscow, Mollet, acting as spokesman for the group, reported that the Soviets claimed there were many roads for the construction of a society with a Socialist character including a peaceful and even a parliamentary road. He also noted that, in a personal conversation, Khrushchev seemed to manifest a desire to see democratic centralism become more democratic.[9] But differences over the question of the dictatorship of the proletariat and the single party remained.

The exact nature of the proposed cooperation between the PCF and the SFIO during this period remained unclear. Mollet rejected the idea that they could reach agreement on a common program,[10] while the PCF also was careful to note that it was not necessary for potential allies to agree to the PCF program in order to work with the PCF.[11] Although the PCF did attempt to emphasize areas of agreement with the SFIO and with the Radicals, and to mute or conceal potential areas in which there was disagreement, events in the fall of 1963 were to delay for a year and a half further serious attempts to elaborate closer relations between the two parties.

[9] *Le Monde*, November 5, 1963.
[10] *Le Populaire*, December 18–19, 1963.
[11] Roger Garaudy quoted in *Le Monde*, December 10, 1963.

Suggestions for Reform—The 54th National Congress

The 54th National Congress was held from May 30 to June 2, 1963. Both in the preparations for the Congress and in the motions voted it is possible to discern the beginnings of a quarrel within the party over the future strategy it should pursue and over questions of organizational reform.

In one area, however, and it was a vital one, the party was united. The party unanimously voted a resolution stating that the SFIO would decide "at the appropriate moment" whether or not it would present a candidate for the presidency of the Republic. The motion was short and said nothing about the possible method the party might use in nominating a candidate. Its unforeseen result was to leave the door wide open to Gaston Defferre in his later campaign to win the SFIO presidential nomination.

The Congress was asked to vote on four separate areas of concern: public institutions, program, tactics, and structures. The motions on the party's program and the final resolution were eventually voted unanimously. The motions on public institutions and on party structures were not submitted to the Congress since they had given rise to such conflict that no compromise motion could be drafted.

The question of public institutions revealed a fundamental difference of opinion within the party and one that was to have profound effects on it in the immediate future. Of the two principal texts relating to public institutions, one was presented by André Chandernagor, deputy from Creuse, and the other by Guy Mollet. The Chandernagor text was entitled, "For a Presidential Regime," and in it Chandernagor argued that public opinion in France was in favor of political efficacy and stability and that the people had demonstrated a marked preference for the possibility of choosing their leaders directly. He noted that the presidential system, with its simplification of political choice and the possibilities it opened for effective action had taken immediate hold in France. Moreover, he approved of the fact that the presidential system had influenced the parties to consider regrouping. His motion asked that certain modifications be suggested in the system—that the National Assembly be elected at the same time and for the same duration as the President, that the duration of the Economic Plan be limited to the Assembly's tenure, that the office of Prime Minister be eliminated as well as parliament's right to censure or overthrow a government—and he further suggested that, in the event of a quarrel between the legislature and the President the latter might go to the people to resolve the situation by means of a referendum. If paralysis occurred because of irreconcilable conflict between President and legislature, either could vote for new elections and both would have to go before the country. Aside from these revisions Chandernagor accepted the new system of the Fifth Republic. Gaston Defferre was one of the signatories of this motion.

A completely different motion was presented by Guy Mollet. Although hedged about with qualifications regarding the ultimate uselessness of constitutional texts in the face of a changing party system, Mollet came down squarely on the side of parliamentary government: "I am very tempted by a regime comparable to that of the mayors, with a program, a contract, a plan and a triennial or bienniel budget." Mollet emphasized that the President of the Council of Ministers should be the chief executive and pointed out that although

> certain comrades are oriented toward the presidential regime, the temptations would be, in our opinion, too great for a man, invested with public confidence, to believe himself charged with the mission of assuring the people's well being. We do not believe that one can allow one man to have the responsibility or the right

to dispose of the fate of a people, its progress, its life, or its death.[12]

With certain modifications (voting a motion of censure against the Prime Minister would invoke automatic dissolution of the National Assembly), Mollet seemed to be advocating a return to parliamentary government. Twenty-nine of the fifty members of the CD signed this motion, among them Albert Gazier and Jules Moch.

This was not the first time the SFIO had been forced to discuss the question of a presidential system in the looming shadow of Charles de Gaulle. The party had functioned under de Gaulle when he was chief of the Consultative Assembly that assumed power after the Liberation. It then fought a running battle with him when, five months after he resigned as President of the Council of Ministers on January 20, 1946, he attacked the Constitutional referendum and offered his famous Bayeux "constitution" as an alternative. Léon Blum stated party objections in *Le Populaire* in October, 1946, when he claimed there were no theoretical contradictions between a presidential system and democratic principles, but rather that "in our country and at the present moment, the strongest objection to the presidential idea consists of General de Gaulle himself."

What is this due to? To the very stature of the person, to the exceptional character of the role he has played in the most terrible crisis in our history, to his military habits, to the nature of his ascendency, to the fashion in which he conceives authority and practices command. He believes himself democratic because, in full sincerity, he would like to be democratic. But everything in his political behavior is repugnant to the needs and necessary practices of republican life.[13]

[12] Parti Socialiste, *Bulletin Intérieur,* no. 128, April, 1963, *passim.*

[13] Léon Blum in *Le Populaire,* October 9, 1946; also in Blum, *L'Oeuvre de Léon Blum* (Paris, 1958), p. 315.

Blum mentioned other objections to installing a presidential system in France: the unitary French system meant the President would have immense power unchecked by the counterweight exercised by a federal system; the tradition of direct election for a chief of state was dangerous because of the plebiscitary overtones associated with it; and the lack of unanimous support for the presidential system in France would dangerously undermine its effectiveness and threaten its democratic nature.

On the question of party tactics and structures, the motion sent to the members prior to the Congress took the form of a list of forty-six points. The first thirty-five dealt with tactics, the remaining eleven with structures. Although there was unanimous agreement on most of the points, disagreement did occur and was represented by two separate but parallel texts in the *Bulletin Intérieur*. On the whole, there seemed to be general agreement that the SFIO had suffered a decline in votes and popularity not only because of its meager resources but also because of its close association in the public mind with the discredited Fourth Republic, because party propaganda was undynamic and anachronistic, and because the party had a conception of parliamentary democracy closer to the practice of the preceding century than to the Fifth Republic. There was also general agreement that the SFIO ought to examine the possibility of changing its methods, vocabulary, and structure, and that an attempt should be made to discuss, with other organizations of the left, the possibility of establishing a "large Socialist force." This new force would act on the basis of a common program, and no action would be undertaken until agreement had been reached on this program. On the future relations with the PCF the organization should expect to have, the motion stated that the Socialists did not exclude resort to revolutionary means in order to "realize a Socialist society," but that the rights of minorities had to be respected. Moreover, the motion noted that the PCF had not yet furnished satisfactory answers to Socialist questions on the single party, the structures of a Socialist state, relations with the USSR, democratic centralism, and the role of unions. It was agreed that the SFIO would join the PCF against a "declared peril" and that this time it would not be caught in the "trap" of refusing to join with the Communists in order to save the "bourgeois Republic." It should be noted, however, that in the final draft of the motion submitted to the Congress, the phrase "bourgeois Republic" was eliminated as well as the phrase referring to Socialist defense of the Republic as a "trap."

On the question of reforms to be worked in party organization, disagreement was serious. Two main groups confronted each other on this question. One group included Mollet, Moch, Brutelle, Jaquet, and Pineau, while the second group included Defferre, Leenhardt, and Loo, all members from Bouches-du-Rhône.

The first group felt that the announcement of reform in all aspects of party activity would "reawaken opinion" and contribute to the "resurrection" of political life in France. The second group contended that the announcement of a profound "renewal" of the party in all areas of its activity might well cause a healthy reaction in public opinion, but that this announcement and the reaction were only a precondition to a revival of political activity in France. Although the differences in wording between the two texts may appear minimal, the second text in effect implied that much more would have to be done both within and without the party before public apathy toward the SFIO could be diminished.

A second bone of contention concerned the question of renaming the party. Defferre supported the name "Party of Socialist Democracy" (*Parti de la Démocratie Socialiste*), while the first group reserved judgment on this question—although, given Mollet's penchant for traditional party symbols, it is unlikely that he sympathized with the suggestion. Finally, Defferre and the other cosignatories of the motion proposed that the party alter its organization so that other independent organizations—trade unions, cooperatives, and so on—might join the SFIO in a confederal arrangement. Defferre also proposed that the militants of these organizations be offered the possibility of becoming fully qualified party members. On this point the first group merely proposed study of the question of organizational reform.

At the Congress debate also centered on the question of regrouping the parties and the possible direction this regrouping should take. Mollet advocated a continuing dialogue with the PCF but warned against establishing any other contacts as long as the PCF did not respond to SFIO questions. Others, Leenhardt and Boutbien, for example, attacked even the idea of discussing the possibility of cooperation with PCF and condemned the notion of a PCF–SFIO alliance.

At the concluding session Mollet spoke for two hours. The general point of his speech was that the party's "revolutionary ardor" had been reaffirmed and that it ought to seek new recruits from both the left and the right, from the PSU and from among Catholics also sympathetic to the SFIO. Mollet added:

> I have questioned myself and I am continuing to question myself about my presence in the post of secretary-general. I do not want to be like those old people who are not aware they aren't what they used to be. I don't feel myself to be an old person. The day when a sufficient number of friends say to me that I am not rendering service to the party, on that day, be sure of it, I will leave. I have sufficient love for the party not to pose an obstacle to an eventual renewal.

The final resolution approved unanimously by the delegates proposed that the SFIO ought to open a dialogue between its national organs and several men of the left, belonging to organizations or parties of a Socialist tendency, and who affirm themselves in agreement with us on our basic preoccupations. . . . Despite great difficulties, Socialist unity in the same party is a task of high priority because its success is the necessary condition for our *redressment* and that of the French left.[14]

The procedure for achieving "Socialist unity" was, however, to be conducted in stages. The first task would be to win support for a number of reforms proposed by the SFIO and based on its fundamental program, although a concession was to be made by elaborating a program that "could be accepted by democrats of the left." The program consisted of ten points, none of which were particularly radical even in the French context. The SFIO asked for political democracy conciliating continuity of government action and the demands for control of the executive by parliament; liberalizing laws on radio and television; democratic reform in education; democratic planning; reform of the Plan, including "certain" nationalizations; political and economic integration of Europe; collective security and suppression of national *forces de frappe;* general and controlled disarmament; and international agreement on a pact of solidarity against world underdevelopment. The resolution ended by noting that a "coalition of democrats of the left" would constitute an important political force but one that could not realize its program without Communist support. The resolution also noted that the Socialists and "democrats of the left" did not have the right to run the risk of preparing the ground for a popular democracy. Thus the PCF was to be confronted with two choices, either to cling to its line, thereby "playing the game of the right," or to support the proposed democratic formation of the left.

[14] *Bulletin Intérieur*, no. 135, April, 1965, *passim.*

10. *In Search of Mr. X*

From its beginnings in 1958, the presidential system of the Fifth Republic evolved rapidly and continually. De Gaulle showed that he did not intend to limit himself to the neutral position of arbiter sketched out in the Constitution. At first the parties had simply chafed at de Gaulle's interpretation of the office, but after the end of the Algerian rebellion in 1962, they had become increasingly hostile.

Although the opposition parties were crushed in the 1962 legislative elections, and despite the fact that presidential elections were three years away, the opposition parties were so unused to the new system and so unwilling to believe either in the permanence of presidential powers or in the continued loyalty of the UNR-UDT that they had made no real progress toward elaborating a method for nominating presidential candidates as late as the fall of 1963. This was not difficult to understand.

Under the parliamentary systems of the Third and Fourth Republics, the choice of executive took place only after the legislative elections when the parties had entered the National Assembly and bargained with each other for necessary votes. The fact that voters might have looked more to the personalities of leading politicians during the elections (as with Mendès-France in 1956, for example), hoping these men would be leading candidates for Prime Minister, made little difference when the Prime Minister was being chosen in the National Assembly. What counted in parliament was party support. For the voters, therefore, the election may sometimes have been viewed as a popularity contest; in fact, it was the parties that chose the leader of the government.

For the opposition in 1963, therefore, the most logical procedure seemed to be to give primary attention to negotiating alliances among the various parties and then proceed to the nomination of a common candidate. But the parties would negotiate first, and afterward the people would be presented with the candidate or candidates.

In the summer of 1963, the Socialist party had decided to delay making a choice until the question of possible future alliances and a common program could be ascertained. Thus the SFIO set about opening a dialogue with the PCF. At the same time, however, a group of people decided that the nomination of a presidential candidate should precede, not follow, the negotiation of a common program.

The great degree of uncertainty that surrounds politics in France, the unstable nature of political institutions and governing coalitions, gives rise to an atmosphere in which gossip abounds. This was illustrated in the fall of 1963 when rumors began to circulate that de Gaulle might consider resigning from the presidency in order to call new elections and run for a second seven-year term before the parties had time to organize themselves for a presidential election.[1]

The appearance of these rumors was important because

[1] *France-Observateur*, September 12, 1963. See also statements of Charles Hernu and Alain Guichard in *Le Monde*, September 17, 1963; Gilles Martinet in *L'Express*, December 19, 1963; and Roger Quilliot in *L'Express*, December 24, 1963.

they helped to precipitate the campaign that finally led to the nomination of Gaston Defferre as the presidential candidate of the Socialist party.[2] According to Roger Quilliot, when Guy Mollet declared himself unwilling to run for the presidency, "several Socialists" settled on Defferre as best qualified to represent the SFIO in a presidential race. On September 19, 1963, the weekly *L'Express*, run by Jean-Jacques Servan-Schreiber, a former supporter of Mendès-France and a man very much impressed by American-style pragmatic politics and campaign methods, began a press campaign that was to lead directly to Defferre's nomination. Its form was quite simple. Each week, Jean Ferniot, a correspondent of *L'Express*, interviewed a mysterious Monsieur "X," who, it was suggested, would eventually be the common candidate of the left. In these interviews "X" gradually outlined a moderate Socialist platform that included reforming the social and economic structure of France and placing primary emphasis on improving and democratizing national education.

At the same time, Defferre began to make frequent speaking appearances, and it soon became an open secret that he, in fact, was Mr. "X." At a speech in Paris he was questioned on this point and said: "There is talk of a certain Mr. "X." . . . It is said I am Mr. "X." To be President of the Republic is to assume very heavy responsibilities."[3] By this time, the "X" campaign had become extremely popular, and not a day passed without some press comment on it. Even *Le Monde* gave it top coverage.

On December 11, 1963, Maurice Duverger wrote a front-page column in *Le Monde* entitled "The Transparent Mask." Duverger stated that it was time for "X" to unmask himself since his main purpose was to familiarize a public unused to presidential campaigns with his person as well as his program.

[2] *L'Express*, December 24, 1964.

[3] *Le Monde*, November 21, 1963 and *Le Monde*, November 29, 1963.

Three days later, on December 14, *Le Monde* reported that Gaston Defferre had asked the SFIO executive committee for authorization to declare his candidacy for the Socialist nomination for the presidency.

How did the Defferre nomination come about? Three main factors were involved. First, Defferre had consistently been interested in revising and reforming the SFIO in all areas of activity, and in this he was joined by leading SFIO personalities such as Georges Brutelle, Gérard Jaquet, Christian Pineau, Roger Quilliot, and Albert Gazier. In addition, Defferre's leadership of the powerful Bouches-du-Rhône federation made him a very appealing figure to all those outside the party who nevertheless felt the SFIO held the key to revitalizing the French left. Second, Georges Suffert, former secretary-general of the *Club Jean Moulin*, has written that several members of the club's executive committee were convinced that Defferre was potentially an excellent candidate to oppose de Gaulle in the event elections were called in advance of their scheduled date. Third, beginning in February, 1963, according to Georges Suffert, Gaston Defferre had met with Jean-Jacques Servan-Schreiber, publisher, and Jean Ferniot, editor of *L'Express*, with the latter two trying to talk Defferre into openly declaring himself a candidate for the Socialist presidential nomination. By the fall of 1963, with pressure coming from a number of political clubs (with the *Club Jean Moulin* in the vanguard), from his allies in the SFIO, and from Servan-Schreiber and *L'Express*, Defferre decided to announce his candidacy.[4]

Whatever the exact circumstances of the campaign, one point is clear. The initiative and basic support for Defferre's campaign for the nomination came not only from the Socialist parliamentary party, but also from influential forces outside

[4] On the Defferre campaign, see Georges Suffert, *De Defferre à Mitterand* (Paris, 1966).

the party. Within the party most of Defferre's support came from party personalities known not because they headed large federations—indeed the leaders of three of the largest, Mollet, Laurent, and Fuzier were opposed to the Defferre nomination—but because of their reputations as ministers in the Fourth Republic. This was the case with Albert Gazier, Gérard Jaquet, and Christian Pineau, all former ministers. Other prominent supporters were André Chandernagor, deputy from Creuse, and Francis Leenhardt from Bouches-du-Rhône. Moreover, for the first time in the SFIO for many years, perhaps since the days of Léon Blum, the party was on the verge of endorsing a proposal advanced by men not particularly powerful either in the party bureaucracy (only Georges Brutelle among those who supported Defferre was a member of the Secretariat) or in the federations. On the whole, it was the pressure brought to bear on the SFIO from outside that led to the eventual nomination of Defferre. Thus from the beginning the Defferre camp was turned more to a constituency outside the party community—and in the end, this was the essential weakness of his ill-fated campaign to found a new Socialist Democratic Federation.

In 1963, however, Defferre's star was rising over the French political scene. He was popular outside the SFIO mainly because he was not closely identified with the traditional leadership and because, during the Fourth Republic, he had taken a liberal stand on Algeria. In addition, since his rally to de Gaulle before the referendum in the fall of 1958 he had been a supporter of the presidential system. Finally, the Defferre campaign came at a crucial point in time; under other circumstances the field might not have been so wide open. When the SFIO postponed making a decision on the method and opportunity for nominating a presidential candidate at the June, 1963, Congress the party leaders found themselves caught short later when the rumors about de Gaulle's resignation began to circulate. Thus when Defferre began to act as if he were, in fact, a candidate for the Socialist nomination, there was little that potential opponents could do. There was no possibility of blocking Defferre by appealing to precedent or to party regulations, because there were none. Nor was there any possibility of proposing alternate candidates, since the natural choice, Guy Mollet, had already taken himself out of the race. The decision on Defferre could not be postponed because the rumors about de Gaulle made action imperative. The only alternative open to skeptical leaders like Mollet and Fuzier, therefore, was to back Defferre in the interest of party unity and then try to direct his campaign in the desired direction.

On December 19, 1963, the SFIO executive committee met and unanimously agreed to call an Extraordinary National Congress to meet February 1 and 2, 1964, to decide whether to nominate Defferre as the party's candidate for the presidential election.

The Extraordinary National Congress of February, 1964

The atmosphere in which the Extraordinary Congress opened differed greatly from previous party congresses. Reporters from European newspapers and magazines were present and the press gallery was almost full. Lights from movie and television cameras were focused on the platform where Mollet, Defferre and other party leaders were seated.

During the Congress a number of people showed themselves less than happy about the "X" campaign and the circumstances surrounding the convening of the congress. They resented the manner in which the "X" campaign had been supported by the political clubs, *L'Express*, and other organizations. In addition it was also apparent that Guy Mollet, Claude Fuzier and Augustin Laurent were skeptical about Defferre's candidacy. According to Mollet, the "number one objective is to put an end to the regime." Given this hypothesis Mollet assumed that a "political personality" like Defferre would lose votes against de Gaulle and that the best candidate would be a "moral personality." Mollet suggested someone like Albert Schweitzer as a candidate. According to Mollet, parties both to the right and the left of the SFIO were evolving and the chances of socialism were getting better. He contended that when de Gaulle disappeared there would be a reaction against the "personal regime" and that everything even slightly resembling it would be condemned. According to Mollet, if he were a "presidentialist," that would be his greatest fear.[5] Thus, he claimed, short- and long-term objectives should not be confused, because in the long run it was necessary to reinforce the SFIO and preserve its "personality."

There also seemed to be some confusion about the extent to which Defferre should be subject to the party's control in his campaign. A distinction was drawn by Defferre between the policy the presidential candidate would elaborate and carry out once elected, and the program of the Prime Minister. The President would merely outline the grand objectives the government should pursue; the details of choice would be left to the Prime Minister and the majority in the National Assembly, who would elaborate the specific legislation and methods of application of the broad policies enunciated by the President. Thus Defferre implied he would not be bound by the SFIO if it attempted to elaborate a detailed program for his campaign.

In a long speech to the Congress (which had been previously mimeographed and was handed out to the press by members from the Bouches-du-Rhône federation) Defferre elaborated on the policy he called "Horizon 80." The speech was characterized by clarity, simplicity, and empiricism. In

[5] *Le Monde*, February 4, 1964.

contrast to much of Socialist literature and speeches, Defferre tried to take account of the changes that had occurred in French society since the end of the war and that had apparently blocked the road to socialism. More remarkable was the almost complete absence of Marxist vocabulary in the speech.

Divided into two parts, Defferre's speech dealt both with the methods to be used by the candidate and with the objectives he hoped to attain. The priorities of the "Horizon 80" campaign were to be national education ("the priority of priorities"), housing, and increased aid to farmers. In the area of foreign policy Defferre advocated strengthening the European Community and criticized the *force de frappe* as an "illusion." He also advocated moderate protection against American business and products and a strengthening of the policy of coexistence. To attain these objectives Defferre claimed that an increase in the rate of growth and a more equitable distribution of revenue would be necessary. Moreover, he advocated democratizing the French Economic Plan (providing for the participation in its elaboration of those previously excluded) and using the threat of nationalization when necessary to force private enterprise to conform to national economic objectives. Defferre did advocate the immediate nationalization of business banks and of land near cities where public housing might be constructed.

Interestingly, much of the "Horizon 80" program seems to have been inspired by a document published some time before after a meeting of several political clubs (among them *Club Jean Moulin*, *Cercle Tocqueville de Lyon* and *Citoyens 60*) and unions (CFTC and CNJA) in December, 1963. The statement claimed:

> The French will support a candidate who will . . . speak clearly and without demagogy, who will not give the impression that he or his party know everything and have an answer for everything and that life will be transformed from one day to the next by

prefabricated reforms. As much as the content of his proposals, it is his tone that they will judge, his sense of dialogue.[6]

The club documents also asked that the candidate invite professional and union organizations to conclude a "national contract for progress" when a government was formed. This same phrase, "national contract for progress," appeared in the "Horizon 80" speech, where Defferre spoke of associating the economic and social forces in the elaboration of the French Economic Plan. The document presented by the clubs and unions also expressed the hope that the presidential campaign would see the two great "currents of French democracy" (the Socialist and Christian currents) agree on a candidate and that the division between "laics" and "clerics" might be surmounted.

On this latter point Defferre was silent during the Congress. He had, however, elaborated on some of these points in January, prior to the Congress, when his Bouches-du-Rhône federation had met to approve his candidacy. Speaking of his "tone," Defferre stated he would attempt to be simple, frank, and clear. He stated that he would avoid a flamboyant style and would not indulge in personal or negative criticism. He added:

> Through a curious turn of circumstances, it was my taste for concrete realizations, the desire to do something useful and the tasks I have accomplished here [as Mayor of Marseille], that led several political men, movements, and clubs to think of me as a candidate for the presidency.

On the question of the PCF, Defferre stated his unwillingness to discuss or even negotiate with them because of his total disagreement with their methods and objectives.

The Congress unanimously nominated Defferre as the SFIO candidate for the presidency. On the question of pro-

[6] *Ibid.*, December 17, 1963.

gram the resolution included a number of points Defferre had mentioned in his speech—democratizing the Economic Plan, giving priority to national education, and pushing forward toward the political and economic integration of Europe. The motion also stated that the SFIO and the candidate would *conjugate*, conjoin, their efforts (rather than "assure," as in a motion offered by Mollet) toward the mobilization of support for Defferre. For the moment, at least, the revolutionary mission of the SFIO seemed to be forgotten, for the motion stated that the party would retain freedom for the day, "without doubt quite distant," when the question of reforming all institutions would be posed.[7] The majority also agreed not to interfere in the candidate's campaign, although the party would continue to devote itself to the task of "preparing the march to socialism," affirming its own objectives and "personality." As Raymond Barrillon, correspondent for *Le Monde* observed, the best moments of Defferre's speech at the Congress recalled the time when Pierre Mendès-France had addressed his party in exalted tones. Defferre seemed to be appealing to the country rather than exclusively to the SFIO, speaking in terms quite different from those the members were used to hearing at party meetings.[8]

Toward the Presidency

From February, 1964, to June 25, 1965, Defferre campaigned throughout France for support in his drive to win the presidential election scheduled for December, 1965. But his campaign soon became dedicated to a second purpose—to influence the SFIO and the MRP to join together in a new party federation. In general, however, both the organization and program of the Defferre presidential campaign were de-

[7] *Ibid.*, January 13, 1964.

[8] See statement of a Socialist militant in *Le Monde*, January 14, 1964, "Defferre is our Kennedy; a new style, a new democracy."

signed to appeal primarily to the people rather than to the parties, and to the so-called *forces vives*, the trade unions, clubs, and other organizations that had proliferated and grown more powerful as the parties on the center and left had declined in influence and prestige under the Fifth Republic. During his campaign Defferre and his supporters attempted to project an image of modernity, dynamism, and clarity that they felt was lacking in the SFIO. They created a series of "Horizon 80" committees, beginning with a national committee that included sixty political, professional, and union personalities. In June, 1964, it was announced that fifteen departmental committees would be established. Membership on these committees was not limited to Socialists but also included members of organizations to the right of the SFIO: members of the *Rassemblement Démocratique*—principally Radicals and members of the UDSR; representatives of student groups—the UNEF and Student Mutual; of unions—members of the CFTC, the *Jeunes Patrons* and *Jeunes Agriculteurs;* of political clubs—especially *Cercle Tocqueville;* and teacher's unions. In addition, a women's "Horizon 80" committee was created, presided over by Jeanne Brutelle (a former head of the *Femmes Socialistes*).[9] Although some assistance in the form of personnel and material came from the SFIO, most of the support for the "Horizon 80" committees appears to have come from the constituent groups.[10]

The function of these groups was to open up access to policy formation by Defferre and his lieutenants to sympathetic groups which normally did not have access to the SFIO. One example of this came from the secretary-general of SGEN-CFDT (*Syndicat Général de l'Education Nationale–Confédération Française Démocratique du Travail*), who justified his membership in a "Horizon 80" committee (which

[9] *Le Monde*, May 22, 1964, January 9 and February 27, 1965.

[10] Parti Socialiste, *Bulletin Intérieur*, no. 135, April, 1965, p. 11.

seemed to violate the principle of syndical independence of political parties) by pointing out that he had been authorized to participate in the elaboration of a "Horizon 80" program dealing with the government's attitude toward unions. He made it clear that the principle of union independence had not been compromised, since the union's national committee would have final authorization over further participation and over endorsement of the "Horizon 80" program.[11]

In one sense, then, the "Horizon 80" committees were a test of the possibility of confederating organizations outside the SFIO with a view toward elaborating a common program. They were also designed to provoke the interest of young people hitherto apathetic toward any activities involving the SFIO or its members. The experiment seems to have been a limited success.

Defferre elaborated his program in two stages. In the first stage he stated his refusal to go into details: "electoral programs or promises have become devalued in the public's eyes." He also based his refusal on Article 5 of the Constitution, which implied that the President was an "arbiter," and on Articles 20 and 21, which say that the government "determines and conducts the policy of the Nation" and that "the Prime Minister directs the action of the government." The problem with this initial position was that it was difficult to distinguish meaningfully between policy and program. What happened was that Defferre frequently refused to state his exact position on certain issues, while, at the same time, he was trying to sketch an outline of his position. By the summer of 1964 he was forced to cede to pressure and to the obvious difficulties of trying to force a distinction:

I had refused to use this term [program] through opposition to a hastily designed catalogue of electoral promises which often were

[11] *Le Monde*, January 9, 1965.

not carried out, although often made. . . . But I realize that this question of vocabulary has led to misunderstandings which are more serious than the terminology. . . . I am not asking for a blank check but for a precise mandate on a program clear enough to eliminate the risk of all equivocation. This is a capital point for me.

Another development in the Defferre presidential campaign related to strategy rather than to program. From the beginning, Defferre had made it quite clear that he would neither negotiate nor discuss a common program or any terms of mutual support with the PCF. He advanced three principal reasons for this attitude. First, he pointed out that the Communist party advocated convening a Constituent Assembly to elaborate a new Constitution to replace that of the Fifth Republic. He thought this both absurd and significant of the Communist desire to return to the Liberation period. Second, he stated that the voyage of the Socialist delegation to Moscow had confirmed the essential differences between the SFIO and PCF over the procedure for assuming power and over the "dictatorship of the proletariat, the single party, and the functioning of democratic institutions." Third, Defferre pointed out that the PCF had absolutely no chance of electing its own candidate to the presidency, since, on the second turn of the ballot, the support of the center-left, center, and right —and even of Communist voters fearful of a popular democracy—would swing to de Gaulle. He also pointed out that if the Communists decided to enter a candidate in competition with himself, their purpose would be not to win the election, but to attempt to blackmail the SFIO into united action. In this event, the PCF would merely assure de Gaulle's election.

On April 13, 1965, after the municipal elections had seen the SFIO and PCF cooperate in many areas of the country in submitting joint lists for the elections, Defferre granted an interview to *Le Monde*. In the course of the interview he clarified some of his thoughts on the problem of cooperation with the PCF. In essence, Defferre said, the primary goal was to reinforce the power of the non-Communist left. Negotiating with the PCF would only make that goal harder to achieve. He added that the best way to influence the PCF to move toward a progressive evolution of both structure and doctrine would be

> To create beside it a more powerful and dynamic formation. From that moment, the equilibrium on the left would be completely modified. The Communist leaders could no longer divide the left or pretend to dominate it, which is to say, to paralyze it. The current toward renovation supported by some militants would then be reinforced and a dialogue would be possible between the non-Communist left and a renovated Communist party.[12]

The guess was, as the *Club Jean Moulin* put it in one of their publications aimed specifically at the SFIO, that a new formation of the left would appeal to that part of the Communist electorate not absolutely opposed to voting for a non-Communist left candidate. Thus arose the idea for a Socialist Democratic Federation.[13]

Although the SFIO, and Defferre's supporters especially, had supported the final resolution of the 54th National Congress calling for a "regrouping of men of Socialist persuasion," Defferre's campaign finally took a serious turn in that direction. In his interview in *Le Monde*, Defferre had commented that, although the SFIO was the axis of any change on the left and had a capital role to play, it could not do this by "remaining what it is and refusing to participate in any federation."[14]

In clarifying the exact form this new federation should

[12] *Le Monde*, January 14, and June 22, 1964.

[13] Club Jean Moulin, *Un Parti pour la Gauche* (Paris, 1965), p. 31.

[14] *Le Monde*, April 13, 1965.

take, Defferre's ideas were remarkably similar to those advanced in *Un Parti pour la Gauche*, the publication of the *Club Jean Moulin.* There the notion of an "action party" was sketched as a model for the new federation. According to the club, the action party differed from the model of a pure and tough party sketched by Guy Mollet. Not only would the action party refuse to claim a monopoly over the elaboration of Socialist doctrine and action, but it would be open and responsive to citizens, party militants, and organizations outside the party.[15] The exact form cooperation between the party and other groups would assume was left open, although, according to Defferre in one of his motions for a party congress, other organizations should be allowed to choose among regular contacts for information and reciprocal consultation, technical representation of the partners in the study commissions of the proposed federations, association in making decisions, and participation as full members.

At the national level the constituent organizations and members would consent to a relinquishing of their authority to a political bureau which would take decisions binding on all members. Decisions would be made by a majority vote. The areas in which the political bureau would be empowered to make decisions would include social and economic policy foreign policy, and the "defense of public liberties," as well as the nomination of common candidates for presidential or legislative elections.

The final goal of the federation would be fusion of the constituent organizations so that, from top to bottom, an entirely new political party would emerge from the initial federative stage. Finally, as possible members of the federation, Defferre had proposed organizations from the Socialists to the MRP.

[15] *Un Parti pour la Gauche*, pp. 70–71.

Objections and Reservations

As the time for the June 3, 1965, National Congress approached, objections were raised to the Defferre campaign. These objections centered primarily on two issues: Defferre's program and his proposals for a Socialist Democratic Federation.

Guy Mollet, Augustin Laurent, and Claude Fuzier voiced objections to the proposals concerning the federation. Their criticisms grew more heated as it became clear that Defferre was proposing to include the MRP in it. Initially, during a National Information Conference held in April, 1965, Assistant Secretary Georges Brutelle had presented a summary report on reforming party structures and on regrouping the parties. The proposed confederation included elements of the left from the PSU to the Radical party, but the MRP was not mentioned. Brutelle had suggested that attempts would be made to find some way to integrate those members of the "Christian Left" who had left the MRP but had not yet attached themselves to another political organization. Mollet took a harder position, declaring that the party was "firmly resolved" to assure the separation of Church and State as well as the *laïcité* of the schools. Mollet also warned against allowing organizations to join the confederation on a collective basis, for this might lead to the inclusion of "Gaullists, Trotskyites, clericals, often general staffs without troops," and often politicians who were anxious to join merely for reasons of ambition rather than out of a sincere commitment to Socialist democracy. Thus Mollet suggested that any new formation include what was called the "little left"—that is, the PSU, the SFIO, and sympathetic elements of the Radical party. Mollet also noted that the ultimate objectives of the SFIO were revolution, democracy, and *laïcité*, objectives on which only Socialists could be agreed.

Moreover, Defferre's complete refusal to countenance any negotiations or contact with the PCF was in complete opposition to Mollet's continuing desire to maintain contact with the PCF through public discussion and debate. Although Mollet reaffirmed the conclusions of the 54th National Congress and noted that "the conditions necessary for a political accord with the PCF . . . have not been filled," he did point out that the PCF had not done well in the municipal elections, that its youth groups were in revolt against party direction, and that, above all, the party militants had "lost their certitude." In view of these facts, Mollet advocated continuing the discussion with the PCF and appealing to youth groups and student groups by demonstrating that their protests against the authoritarianism of the PCF leadership were similar to those advanced by the SFIO. He asked the SFIO also to keep in mind the possibility of concluding defensive alliances with the PCF.[16]

Finally, the resolution of Mollet's Pas-de-Calais federation claimed that, contrary to Defferre's belief, the PCF was more frightened of a strong and united Socialist party than of a new, vast, centrist federation. When Defferre explicitly proposed including the MRP in the federation in the hopes of finally achieving the kind of alliance that had been suggested at the Liberation, he was accused of wanting the SFIO to commit suicide. The federation of Pas-de-Calais said such an alliance would "scuttle" the SFIO and "play the game of the PCF."

The 55th National Congress

The 55th National Congress held at Clichy from June 3 to June 6, 1965, saw Defferre directly confront his opposition. A number of issues were involved in the debates during the

[16] *Bulletin Intérieur*, no. 136, April, 1965; no. 137, May, 1965.

Congress, some of them made explicit, others merely hinted at. They concerned the question of entering a federation that would include the MRP, the manner in which Defferre had conducted his campaign, differing views about the nature of the presidential system, the importance of *laïcité*, the future organization of the new federation, the nature of socialism, and future relations with the PCF. Perhaps the best way to summarize the varying points of view presented at the Congress is to abstract from the debates the major issues and to present the major arguments.

The Defferre Presidential Campaign

The attack against the manner in which the Defferre campaign was conducted was led by Augustin Laurent. He focused on two related points: first, that Defferre had attempted to run his campaign independently of the control of the SFIO—contrary to the spirit of the motion passed at the Extraordinary National Congress in February, 1964; second, that Defferre had lapsed into "presidentialism" by elaborating a detailed program and thereby admitting that he no longer viewed the role of President as one of arbiter. Laurent said Defferre should have left it to the party to prepare the federation and he condemned Defferre's attempt to play the role of the "great reformer" of French political life. Laurent was "not pleased" especially in view of Defferre's tendency toward "presidentialism." Defferre replied in an unusual fashion for a Socialist by pointing to the response his campaign had elicited in the country. Countering the accusation that he had run his campaign independently of party supervision he said he had always acted as a "sincere and disciplined Socialist militant," and he emphasized that he would never change, "no matter what happens." He drove his point home by noting that the Congress was being covered by the entire Parisian press corps as well as by correspondents from papers all over the world:

"Would we prefer to deliberate amidst general indifference as we have done too often in the past?"

Laïcité

The debates once again demonstrated that the question of *laïcité* remained a central concern of many party leaders who tended to judge a man's socialism by his position on this issue. Weill-Raynal maintained that one of the characteristics of the SFIO "is and will continue to be, *laïcité*." Tailleux said he was willing to accept Catholics in the party but only after they understood they should not have their "own schools and their own political organization."

Finally, the authority of Guy Mollet was added to the argument that *laïcité* was "among the fundamental points" that distinguished socialism from other political theories.

Defferre replied by noting that the question of *laïcité* would not enter into the competence of the federation, being one of those questions on which each of the member organizations might define its own position. The following day Defferre noted sardonically: "I belonged to the Guy Mollet government, in the course of which there was never any question of abrogating the Barangé Law." Finally, however, he agreed that although each member of the proposed federation "will be able to hold his own ideas in this area, insofar as a candidate for the Presidency of the Republic I have a conception that is, in fact, that of the SFIO."

Federation with the MRP

The differences over the question of *laïcité* were not the only reasons for some delegates' refusal to look kindly on federating with the MRP. According to Laurent, a "large federation," including the UDSR, part of the Radical party, and all of the MRP, would be only "a heteroclite regrouping [and] your pseudo-Socialist federation will soon look like . . . an opportunistic replastering."

Jules Moch developed another line of argument. First, he pointed out that the SFIO represented a "left of democrats, laics, and collectivists," but that, although some elements in the MRP supported the SFIO in these areas, the entire membership certainly did not. Second, Moch pointed out that the MRP was divided between militants oriented toward the left and an electorate "scarcely distinguishable from that of the Independent Peasants." Third, he noted that the MRP defined itself as being democratic, European, and "social" but not "Socialist." Fourth, he contended that the MRP had postulated as a condition for federation a prior agreement by the constituent members wherein any kind of collaboration with the PCF would be refused. Moch argued that this would throw the federation to the right and lead it to "catastrophe."

According to Guy Mollet, there were four great families in French politics: the PCF, the extreme right—largely antidemocratic—the liberal democrats attached to democracy, and the Socialist democrats.

I am going to be asked where I would place the Christian Democrats. But I am speaking of political families, not religious families. The people who believe in the same God join the same church; I don't see why they should join the same party.

In reply, Defferre simply pointed out that

there are as many, if not more, conservatives on social and economic matters among the Radicals as the MRP. It was with the MRP that we nationalized coal, gas, and electricity. . . . It is with the MRP that we created social security—against the Radicals.

In foreign policy we are as close to the MRP as to the Radicals, notably as concerns Europe. With them we launched the policy of European unification.

Attitudes toward the Communist Party

Although those who supported and those who opposed the proposed federation agreed that the PCF could not be ignored as a major factor in French political life, and although all agreed that someday cooperation between the Socialists and Communists would occur on a regular basis, the methods proposed to attain this goal differed greatly.

According to Laurent, the new federation should be prepared, at the moment of its formation, to address an appeal to all those who accepted the ideas of socialism, including the Communists. Then, according to Laurent, the millions of workers whose power had been "paralyzed" would realize that the true future of democratic socialism depended on the unity of the workers.

Laurent maintained that most of the difficulties encountered by the SFIO came from the PCF, which had, on numerous occasions, obliged the SFIO to come to the defense of the Republic and assume responsibilities that prevented the party from being "itself." But, claimed Laurent, one should never say the Socialist party had renounced its desire to reunify the workers.

Pierre Giraud, municipal councilor in Paris, expressed the fear that Defferre would cut the SFIO off from the workers close to the PCF. Guy Mollet elaborated on this by noting that the PCF had evolved and would probably continue to do so. He warned that Defferre's unwillingness to negotiate with the PCF might reinforce the toughest elements in that party, since the members who leaned toward liberalization and toward future electoral alliances with the SFIO might find themselves isolated.

To these arguments, Defferre answered that only the formation of a more powerful and dynamic federation on the left, incorporating the SFIO and the MRP, would force the Communists to negotiate on a basis of equality.

Organization of the Proposed Federation

As with most of the previous issues, the arguments on the organization of the federation were more or less the same as had been developed prior to the June, 1965, Congress. According to Arthur Notebart, deputy from Nord, the federation proposed by Defferre would lead to the "liquidation of the party." At the April, 1965, National Information Congress, Notebart had objected to proposed structural changes in the SFIO in more specific terms. Then he had noted that reforming party structures in a worker's section would lead to a loss in membership. Opposing the suggestion that local party sections open their ranks to sympathizers and that Socialist militants attempt to become specialists able and willing to discuss various problems with others from different parties, Notebart warned that at the moment when the party was condemning the technocrats in national politics, it should not hand itself over to "certain comrades who take themselves for technocrats but who really are not."[17] Pierre Giraud said that it was an illusion to believe that clubs, mutuals, unions, and cooperatives were ready to join the proposed federation, and he warned that the party was becoming involved in *travaillisme*, but without the workers.[18]

Mollet opened by warning the smaller federations in the SFIO that they should not be such eager supporters of federation if their means were weak. The obvious implication was that SFIO local federations might be swamped in those areas where the Radicals or MRP were very strong. He also opposed Defferre's suggestion that people might join the federa-

[17] *Le Monde*, May 29, June 5 and 6–7, 1965.
[18] *Le Monde*, June 5, 6–7, and 8, 1965.

tion on an individual basis, without having previously joined one of the member organizations. Mollet advocated that the "door be closed" to ambitious people and to those wishing to play an "individual role" by requiring all those wishing to join the federation to first join one of the lower-level federated organizations. Perhaps Mollet was thinking of people joining the federation on an individual basis and then rising immediately to a position of authority, without first having to surmount the obstacles that advancement through one of the constituent parties might pose.

To all these criticisms Defferre responded that federation was the only solution to the ills afflicting the SFIO and he noted that

> the objection to individual membership is that it would lead to the creation of a political party and not a federation. But neither the name nor the juridical term matters to me. . . . What counts is to do something efficacious, to attract toward ourselves, as you yourselves wish, all those who have refused to come until now and who would come if we know how to build a modern force capable of winning the coming political battles.

Finally, on the question of fusion of the constituent members of the federation, Defferre noted that a National Congress would eventually be called to decide this question but that the first step was to organize the federation itself.

When the debates had concluded and no agreement had been reached on a compromise motion, the Congress was asked to designate a resolutions commission. An indicative vote was held, and on the basis of one member on the commission for each one hundred votes or a fraction thereof received, the Defferrists, with 1,302 votes, placed fourteen members on the commission and the Mollet-Laurent group, with 1,270 votes, placed thirteen. Four seats were allotted to the 394 votes from those supporting a compromise motion.

At the opening session of the resolutions committee the Defferre group was immediately attacked on the question of *laïcité*, and tensions ran quite high. Finally, a compromise was reached that provided for the question to figure among the elements of the constitutional charter of the federation with freedom given to potential members to accept it, refuse it, or take no position on it. Other points of discord were raised, including the question of the eventual fusion of the constituent members of the federation, individual membership, and, once again, *laïcité*. Agreement was reached on a compromise motion, although, upon leaving the conference room, Claude Fuzier remarked that "the federation is still-born" and Guy Mollet said that "it is a victory of the party over itself."

On balance, it is difficult to say who won, although subsequent events demonstrated that the final resolution contained points not amenable to compromise when the MRP and SFIO met and that these points were strong factors in the failure of the federative attempt. Certainly the reference in the final resolution to the "reintegration of the PCF" in French political life did not make agreement with the MRP any easier and neither did the proposal to solve "the problem of *laïcité* in teaching by attributing public funds to public schools and [by] the integration into National Education of teachers and private schools receiving public funds."[19]

But the motion made no mention of the revolutionary mission of the SFIO and did not even include the word "socialist." Individual membership in the federation was also to be allowed, and the proposed organization of the federation closely followed that set forth in Defferre's resolution. The final motion was truly a compromise. It was unanimously passed on June 8, 1965. The following day the *New York Times* commented:

[19] *Bulletin Intérieur*, no. 139, June, 1965, p. 7.

This vote represents a triumph for Gaston Defferre. . . . The French Socialists, in attempting to create a coalition of democratic elements composed of moderates from the left and center have gone back to the most popular tradition of French Republican government before the arrival of General de Gaulle.

According to *Le Figaro:*

One formula of Guy Mollet contained in the final text, the "reintegration of the PCF in French political life," is envisioned. Ten days ago, the MRP categorically answered in the negative to any possible agreement with the men of Moscow.

L'Aurore noted:

It was quite an historical turn that SFIO Socialism took yesterday at Clichy. In sum, *finis* the splendid isolation of the "class" party, and its jealous independence in relation to "bourgeois" parties considered as an indistinct bloc.

Le Populaire cautioned:

The Socialist democratic federation is, above all, a political package on which we would like responses and propositions. The party will make a decision in full sovereignty and will say if it thinks that they will permit the creation of a federation.

On June 8, 1965, the 55th National Congress had unanimously voted a motion supporting the party in entering into negotiations on the proposed federation. By June 17, 1965, however, the project for federation had been rejected by the major parties concerned, and by June 25 Gaston Defferre had resigned from the presidential race.

The reaction of the MRP to the results of the 55th National Congress immediately demonstrated that hard bargaining would have to take place between the two parties to bring them together, for on June 11, 1965, the MRP stated its reservations on the Socialist statements concerning the PCF and *laïcité*. But in spite of the seemingly last-minute hesitation on the part of the MRP, preparations for the meetings of the parties and other organizations concerned with federation were completed. Two meetings were finally held, one on June 17, 1965, and the other on June 18, 1965. Attending these meetings were not only representatives of the parties concerned—the UDSR, Radical party, MRP, and SFIO—but also representatives of certain political clubs and important individuals closely associated with the Defferre campaign—men such as Charles Hernu, former Radical deputy and a close associate of Mendès-France, Professor Georges Lavau from the *Ecole de Science Politique*, Georges Vedel from the Law Faculty of the Sorbonne, and Jean-Jacques Servan-Schreiber. Vedel and Servan-Schreiber were also prominent members of the national "Horizon 80" committee.

Conversations at the two meetings disclosed that insurmountable differences existed between the SFIO and the MRP. On the question of the federation's attitude toward the PCF, the representatives of the MRP refused to consider the possibility that the federation might enter into future electoral alliances, and they asked that this permanent refusal be included in the federation charter. The representatives of the SFIO, especially Guy Mollet, opposed this. On the question of *laïcité* the MRP accused Defferre of having diluted his original declarations and refused to consider the possibility that the parliamentary delegates of the federation might be asked to vote against any future legislation granting aid to parochial schools.[20] On the organization of the federation, the MRP leaders asked that it take final shape after the presidential election and that the constituent parties agree on fusion as quickly as possible. The SFIO delegates opposed this also. Finally, no agreement could be reached on the proposed name of the federation, the Socialist delegates demanding and the

[20] *Le Monde*, May 13 and June 11, 1965.

MRP delegates refusing to consider including the word "Socialist" in the name.[21]

At four in the morning of June 19 the meeting broke up in disagreement. The federation was interred. Why did it fail? According to André Philip, "Defferre's error (*felix culpa* to those who helped develop a just idea) was to launch the idea of a federation for the next legislative elections too soon, for it disquieted a number of deputies who would be candidates." But according to Maurice Duverger, "the refusal of the parties to enter into the Socialist Democratic Federation was due to the conservatism of the leaders and to their autocratic domination over the party apparatus, more than to the diversity of the political families to be united."

Duverger claimed that the federation might have succeeded if, instead of the leaders meeting in secret, the parties had held a joint congress where the party members could have listened to a public debate. Finally, Duverger pointed out that the split between the MRP and the SFIO was not based on party lines, since within each party there were those who opposed and those who supported the federation, but rather that the split was between the "ancients" and the "moderns" in each party.[22]

These reasons all have some basis in fact, but there can be little doubt that, once again, the peculiar uncertainty of French political life played a large part in the calculations of the negotiators. For the MRP, de Gaulle's presence only made it more difficult to determine whether its electorate was composed merely of Gaullists of the left or whether sincere MRP militants willing to follow the party into a federation were leaning farther to the left than in the past. Moreover, the

[21] See *Le Monde*, June 17 and 18 on the failure of the meeting; also Jean Ferniot "Le 18 Juin de la Fédération," *L'Express*, June 22, 1965, pp. 19–21.

[22] *Le Monde*, June 20–21, 1965.

MRP had expressed fear it might become a satellite of the SFIO, and this was directly related to the calculations of some leaders that MRP members would desert the party in large numbers in the event it joined with the SFIO. Also, for the MRP, as for the SFIO, the real strength of de Gaulle could not be gauged until de Gaulle had left the scene. No doubt many MRP leaders hoped that this event would lead to an influx of former Gaullists—especially the Gaullists of the left—into the MRP. In addition, the MRP was encountering the same difficulties as the SFIO, for a declining membership and electorate had left it with little influence at the national level, while, at the local level, it still retained possession of a solid base of support in the *mairies* in those regions traditionally MRP. Moreover, there existed within the MRP a right-left split based more on questions of strategy and tactic than on doctrine—although, inevitably, doctrinal justifications were quickly employed to justify the differing positions.[23] Men like Pierre Pflimlin and many parliamentarians were afraid to risk the MRP in the proposed federation. According to Pflimlin, "there is something exceptional in the de Gaulle phenomenon. . . . The MRP can be, one day, a mediator, the great federator of a vast center where all those who are under the influence of Gaullism today, may join one another."[24]

After the breakdown of the federation talks, the president of the MRP, Jean Lecanuet, held a press conference in which he analyzed the reasons for the breakdown and discussed the future of the MRP. His analysis of the reasons for the check in negotiations was not particularly enlightening; he accused the SFIO of clinging to the notion of *laïcité* and of being unwilling to compromise on the issue. He also said that the SFIO would not concede anything on the Socialist nature of

[23] See *Revue Française de Science Politique*, XII (September, 1963), no. 3, 715–727.

[24] *Le Monde*, May 30–31, 1965.

the federation, that Defferre was not the best possible candidate, and that, in any case, a federation flying the Socialist flag was not exactly what the MRP had hoped to join.[25]

On June 25, 1965, Defferre announced his decision to withdraw from the presidential race. As Pierre Viansson-Ponté noted in *Le Monde*, Defferre had been faced with two equally unacceptable choices after the failure of the federation. Either he could continue his campaign for federation by soliciting individual membership in the "Horizon 80" committee and thereby enter into an inevitable conflict with the SFIO hierarchy, or he could remain the SFIO candidate but be put in the position of supporting Guy Mollet's notion of a "little" federation grouping the Radicals, the PSU, and various sympathetic clubs and organizations. Rather than choose between these alternatives, Defferre resigned.[26]

The months following Defferre's resignation saw Guy Mollet reassert control over the party. At the National Council held from July 19 to July 20, 1965, Mollet proposed a motion which reiterated the reasons for the failure of Defferre's federation attempt, and then suggested the modalities of a new kind of federation. Mollet's motion won over a minority motion proposed by Albert Gazier by a vote of 2,028 to 881. At the meeting Mollet played upon the theme of party unity, noting that

> outside our party we have been represented as being divided between innovators and conservatives, between progressives and those who are sclerotic. We are on trial. After this two-day debate, all this must end. We must unite. It is necessary to put an end to these divisive attempts. It is necessary to make people like our party; we must prepare for the coming battles, the presidential and legislative battles.

Mollet then recommended that the SFIO continue to search for partners in a Socialist Democratic federation, but he

[25] *Ibid.*, June 20–21, 1965. [26] *Ibid.*, June 26, 1965.

claimed that the MRP had excluded itself from membership because of its refusal to accept the "Socialist bent" of the federation, because of its refusal to accept the idea of eliminating state aid to church schools, and because of its refusal even to consider the possibility of future electoral alliances with the PCF. Mollet proposed a federation that would include the Radical party, the UDSR, and sympathetic political clubs and organizations.

Talks with the proposed members of the new federation began after the close of the meeting. By September 11, agreement was reached and a new federation was born. At first, its proposed name was the Socialist Democratic Federation (*Fédération Démocrate Socialiste*), but later the name was changed to Federation of the Socialist and Democratic Left (*Fédération de la Gauche Démocrate et Socialiste*) on the demand of the Radical party. The Federation charter included at least two provisions that constituted barriers to the possible inclusion not only of the MRP as a party, but of individual Christian Democrats. The first was the commitment of the federation to seek abolition of state aid for church schools; the second was the desire to someday see the PCF integrated into a regrouping on the left.[27]

On September 9, 1965, François Mitterand, leader of the UDSR, declared himself a candidate for the Presidency of the Fifth Republic. The SFIO was not long in endorsing his candidacy, and the National Council in early November promised him the party's full support during the election campaign. The support of the PCF on September 25, 1965, and of the Radical party on October 23, 1965, served to emphasize the fact that the SFIO had turned—electorally at least—toward the left.

[27] *Bulletin Intérieur*, no. 141, October, 1965, pp. 1 and 12.

11. Dissent, Power, and Organization

"The direction of the party belongs to the party itself, that is, to the National Congress which meets each year" (Article 20, party statutes, 1961). The SFIO is a democratic party. From the lowest to the highest levels of the hierarchy, free elections are held for party secretaries, delegates, and members of the executive committee. The main lines of policy are drawn at the National Congress, and it is here that the preponderant weight of certain large, disciplined federations makes itself felt.[1] The SFIO has always been dominated by its large federations and justly so. Federations are awarded votes proportional to their membership. Each federation gets one vote by right and one additional vote for every twenty-five fully paid-up members. Although during National Council meetings, each federation is represented by only one delegate, at National Congresses every federation with fifteen votes can send two delegates, and a federation is allowed one additional delegate for every fifteen votes after the first fifteen. On this

[1] Congresses were held annually until 1961 and afterward every two years.

basis, then, such large federations as Bouches-du-Rhône and Pas-de-Calais, with over 9,000 members each, frequently send more than twenty delegates to a Congress to cast their 350 or more votes. The efficacy of a federation's vote, however, is determined not only by the number of votes it possesses, but also by the disciplined fashion in which it votes. The federation of Seine, for example, always one of the largest in the party, has tended to split its vote after the Liberation. It has, therefore, not been as effective in influencing policy as the federations of Nord, Pas-de-Calais, and Bouches-du-Rhône. In addition, the number of large federations which, together, have possessed a majority of votes (necessary to pass a motion at Congress or Council meetings) has continued to decline since 1949 (the earliest year for which accurate figures can be obtained). In 1949 the majority of votes was held by fifteen federations, in 1952 by ten federations, in 1956 by eight federations, and in 1966–1967 by five federations. In each case, however, this majority was only potential, since some of the large federations split their vote and other federations voted sometimes with, sometimes against, the majority.[2]

An examination of the votes at party Congress and Council meetings does disclose a definite pattern of voting by certain federations. From 1949 to 1957, for example, the federation of Pas-de-Calais, headed by Guy Mollet, never voted with the minority. The neighboring and even more powerful federation of Nord, headed by Augustin Laurent, mayor of Lille, voted with the majority unanimously thirty-nine times during

[2] A majority-support federation is one which voted by at least a two-thirds majority for the majority motion at party meetings at least 75 per cent of the time during 1949 to 1957. A minority-support federation is one which voted by at least a two-thirds majority for the minority motion at party meetings at least 75 per cent of the time during 1949 to 1957. All statistics on majority and minority-support federations, and on voting at party meetings are based on my calculations obtained from data in the various internal bulletins from 1949 to 1966.

that period and with the minority only once, and it abstained unanimously three times. On other occasions, Nord split its vote, but with by far the largest part of its votes going to the majority. Another powerful federation, Seine-et-Oise, voted unanimously for the minority motion during party meetings only twice and unanimously for the majority fourteen times; on the other occasions, with three exceptions, it went with the majority by a two-thirds vote. Until 1952, a third powerful federation, Haute-Vienne, voted unanimously with the minority ten out of fifty-seven times, and abstained unanimously twice. Beginning in 1952, however, it voted unanimously with the minority only twice, did not take part in one vote, and voted unanimously with the majority on forty-two occasions. In addition to these large majority-support federations, there were three smaller federations (Loire-et-Cher, Basses-Pyrénées, and Deux-Sèvres) which almost always voted with the majority and thereby reinforced the strength of the large federations.

Leaving these smaller federations out of consideration, the percentage of the total vote at party meetings controlled by the large majority-support federations was never below 22 per cent nor above 27 per cent. Including all the majority-support federations, both large and small, the majority-support federations held between 25 per cent and 29 per cent of the *total* vote at party meetings from 1949 to 1957. If one calculates the percentage of the *majority* vote held by all the majority-support federations from 1949 to 1957 it varies between 50 per cent and 58 per cent (see Appendixes E.1 and E.2).

Opposing the majority on most issues which came to a vote were a small number of minority-support federations. These federations, however, had less votes than the majority-support federations. In the middle were the vast majority of federations which voted sometimes with the majority, sometimes with the minority, and frequently split their votes between the two.

Despite the fact that majority- and minority-support federations frequently opposed each other on motions before party meetings, it is important to note that most motions which were presented to the meetings were *motions de synthèse* hammered together in the resolutions committee and presented by a unanimous committee. Of the 61 issues which did come to a divided vote between 1949 and 1958, 9 concerned questions of general policy, 10 questions of party discipline, 11 questions of party structure and organization, 5 questions of participation in government, 7 questions of election tactics, 6 questions of Algerian policy, 6 questions of party policy toward EDC, and 7 questions of amendments to the preceding motions. Thus from 1949 to 1958 the SFIO was primarily unable to agree on questions of organization and of electoral and parliamentary tactics. Algeria and EDC were the most exacerbating issues which confronted it during those years. Only infrequently was the party unable to agree on a general policy orientation, and never did domestic policy questions cause serious debate.

Once agreement among the leaders of the large federations had been reached, however, there was little an opposition could do to defeat the leadership motion. This was due as much to the preponderant weight of the majority-support federations as to the fact that the other federations tended to vote in a more or less random fashion. Other factors also made the task of a minority extremely difficult. As Robert Michels noted early in this century, militants in Socialist parties are often deeply loyal to their leaders, frequently interpreting criticism of the leadership as motivated by personal rather than political reasons. Observers of the SFIO have often used the phrase *patriotisme du parti* to characterize this combination of fierce loyalty and hostility to criticism. *Patriotisme du parti* reached a peak during the period in 1956–1957 when Guy Mollet was Prime Minister.

> As the ideals of socialism have disappeared, they have been replaced by the powerful sentiment of belonging to a collective group which has confidence in the leadership. To those who criticize the government's policy the reply often is that the criticism is reasonable but that one ought not to create difficulties for comrades in positions of responsibility, the criticism might be used against the party by its adversaries. Thus it comes about that actions are no longer judged in themselves, but on the basis of the men who accomplish these actions.[3]

It has also been noted that party members frequently tended to look for a clue as to how they should vote; to look not at the content of the motions submitted to them in the internal bulletin (*Bulletin Intérieur*), but at the names of those who had signed the motions. In addition, some people claim that at Congress meetings typewritten lists were circulated by allies of Mollet or allies of other party leaders, listing those candidates for the CD these leaders wish to see elected.[4]

The Executive Committee

As with any large organization, of course, the executive committee of the Socialist party was the main locus of decision-making power. Throughout party history the composition of, and the mode of electing, the *comité directeur* had been frequently altered and debated. The most important change in the method of electing the CD occurred after the Liberation when, on the advice of Léon Blum, Vincent Auriol, and Daniel Mayer, representation on the CD was allotted

[3] André Philip, *Le Socialisme Trahi* (Paris, 1957), p. 205; see also, *France-Observateur*, July 16, 1959.

[4] Information obtained from interview in Paris, on July 11, 1966, with a member of the Fondation Nationale des Sciences Politiques.

by means of a list system of majority voting rather than by the prewar method of proportional representation. According to Blum, proportional representation crystallized factions; he believed that scrapping it in favor of a list system would facilitate "frank, full, pure democracy . . . which, at the same time, would leave open the possibility of efficacy. . . . The party must find the most direct, efficacious, coherent and logical means giving it force and promptness in action."[5] One of the unforeseen results of the change, however, was that the very same people who had advocated switching from proportional representation were gradually eliminated from the CD as they were gradually reduced to a minority in the party.

Other changes made in the composition of the CD after June, 1956, were also important. Prior to June, 1956, only ten parliamentarians (excluding members of the Assembly of the French Union) could sit on the CD. After the modification twenty parliamentarians were allowed, while the total size of the CD was raised from thirty-one to forty-five members.[6] At the same time, however, the *Bureau*, a smaller committee elected by, and within the CD, and consisting of the secretary-general, assistant secretaries, and the treasurer, was given charge of administrative duties. Elected by a majority of the CD, the *Bureau* could and did represent a stronghold of the party majority.

Party discipline was also tightened in 1956. In reaction against the break in voting discipline by the Socialist group in the National Assembly during the EDC affair (when the group declined to discipline the members who refused, against the decision of the party, to vote for EDC), the National Council was given final disciplinary power. Whereas, prior to 1956, a parliamentarian might appeal to the National Congress

[5] Daniel Ligou, *Histoire du Socialisme en France, 1871–1961* (Paris, 1962), p. 587.

[6] Parti Socialiste, *Bulletin Intérieur*, no. 80, January, 1956, p. 134.

against an adverse decision of the CD, the new statutes made the National Council the court of last resort. Since delegates to the National Council tended to be party administrative personnel (usually federation or section secretaries) the parliamentarian who violated party rules or discipline was likely to get a less sympathetic hearing than if he appeared before the rank-and-file militants at a National Congress. At the same time, control over freedom of dissent was tightened. Article 74 of the revised statutes specifically warned members against "supporting opinions contrary to party decisions in the press."

Although proportional representation had been eliminated as the method for electing the CD after the war, agitation for its reinstitution gathered strength in the early fifties, and in 1953 the question was again submitted to the 45th National Congress. It was rejected by a vote of 2,281 to 811, with 273 abstentions. Only one large federation supported the return to proportional representation, and that was Seine. The minority-support federations also supported a return to the old method. Of the majority-support federations, Haute-Vienne abstained and the others were opposed. Evidently, then, certain federations which tended to vote in the minority saw no other solution to the problem of obtaining a larger voice for their point of view than through a change in the method of representation on the CD.

The question of proportional representation came up again at the 47th National Congress held in 1955. At that time a commission was appointed to study the problem and to submit a motion to a National Council having powers of a National Congress. The commission's report was published in an internal bulletin in May, 1956. The commission rejected the contention of the federations of Seine and Maine-et-Loire that democracy in the party had suffered under the majority-list system of election for the CD. The commission pointed out that proportional representation did come into play in the designation of delegates from the sections to the federations and from the federation to the National Congress. This allowed the minority a voice on the resolutions committees and provided it with an opportunity to vote against motions at party meetings. The commission went on to point out that proportional representation was originally intended to allow for the variegated and divergent doctrinal points of view held by party members prior to the war. The commission held that the need for this had passed, since questions of doctrine and method no longer divided the party as in the past. Moreover, the commission held that the very mechanics of the old method might lead to the creation of previously nonexistent factions because, in order to be represented on the CD, a minority would first have to present minority motions at party meetings. This would give rise to artificial differences as ambitious individuals sought power in the party. The formation of factions would also open the way to "external" influences in the event a minority sought support from allies outside the party. Finally, the commission pointed out that the absence of proportional representation created a climate of compromise within the resolutions committee, an atmosphere which would be destroyed if the old method were reinstituted.[7] Among the members of the commission were Edouard Depreux and Mireille Osmin, both of whom resigned from the SFIO a scant two years later in protest over, among other things, the lack of democracy within the party.

The National Council rejected the motion on proportional representation by a vote of 2,911 to 561, with 33 abstentions. Once again, as in 1953, the vote for the motion came from a number of small federations, including the minority-support federations, and from Seine.

Controversy over election to the CD broke out into the

[7] *Bulletin Intérieur*, no. 84, May, 1956.

open once again in 1960. The quarrel was precipitated when Georges Dardel, mayor of Puteaux and a member of the General Council of the Seine, was not re-elected to the CD in 1960. At the 52nd National Congress held from June 30 to July 3, 1960, Albert Gazier claimed that on three separate occasions after 1958, the number of representatives on the CD who took a dissenting position from that of the majority had declined. He condemned the tendency of the party majority to curtail minority representatives on the CD.[8] As during the period 1956–1958, the question of party democracy was raised again. The results on this occasion, however, were quite different. By the time of the next National Congress a method for representation of minorities on the CD by means of a limited system of proportional representation had been accepted by the party.

What happened was that after Georges Dardel failed to be re-elected, five members of the CD resigned in protest. They were Albert Gazier, Christian Pineau, Claude Fuzier, Etienne Weill-Raynal, and Georges Guille. All refused to take their seats until the mode of election was changed to allow for minority representation. Although both Mollet and Augustin Laurent maintained that Dardel's failure to be re-elected to the executive committee had nothing to do with the fact that Dardel had accepted Communist votes in being re-elected to the presidency of the General Council of the Seine (at that time most party leaders were opposed to any cooperation between the SFIO and the PCF), the dissident members of the CD maintained that this was the real reason for Dardel's not being re-elected. Having a minority group on the CD was opposed by Augustin Laurent, who suggested that it would be much more difficult to arrive at *motions de synthèse* during party congress and council meetings because minorities on the

[8] Parti Socialiste, *Compte Rendu,* 52nd National Congress, 1960.

resolutions committee would then disagree with the majority merely for the sake of being represented on the CD in accordance with the proposed rule changes. But whereas during the 1956–1958 quarrel over exactly the same issue Guy Mollet opposed minority representation on the CD to the end, in the 1960 fight he eventually sided with the dissident minority. Noting that he was in agreement with all the arguments of Laurent, and in disagreement with Gazier *et al.*, he concluded that he would, in the end, still have to side with Gazier against Laurent.

One of the most unhealthy things one can create in a party is an organized tendency [but] we have chosen to be in the same party, we agree on the same objectives, we work in the same sense no matter what our divergencies are, the objective to attain is the same and there is no reason to eliminate from our directing organs the representatives of the minority, whether from the CD or the Bureau, because, in the end, they are the guarantees that the majority decisions are loyally carried out.[9]

But why was this argument not valid in 1956 when Mollet decided in exactly the opposite sense on virtually the same question? Probably the reason for Mollet's change of heart was that in 1960, three of the five dissident members—Fuzier, Weill-Raynal, and Guille—had supported Mollet on most issues in the past. The fight also illustrated the tendency of the party rank and file to censure those leaders who appeared to be diverging from the general party line or to be taking a radical position. Dardel had accepted Communist support at a time when the party majority was adamantly opposed to cooperation with the PCF; Pineau and Gazier had both suggested changes in party organization and opposed the party line during the early part of 1958. It is a testimony to Mollet's shrewd sense of tactics and power that he was able to win

[9] *Ibid.*

victory over the dissident minority in the period before 1958, while, in 1960, he turned aside a possible threat to his leadership and party unity by conceding at a time when the threat was less serious. For it should be remembered that the 1960 threat did not directly impugn Mollet's leadership and that three of the dissident members of the CD were allies of Mollet on other issues, while in the pre-1958 controversy the threat did not come from within the party oligarchy—that is, from the leaders who enjoyed prestige within the party or the leaders of top federations.

In addition, the possible support for changing the party statutes was fairly large in terms of votes, for Fuzier was the leader of the Seine federation with 228 votes and Defferre's Bouches-du-Rhône—certain to support a change as it had in the 1956–1958 battle—held 376 votes. Thus Mollet probably decided that both circumstance and tactics required concessions to the dissidents and support for the proposed change. When the votes were finally counted at the 53rd National Congress, only the large federation of Nord among the top four voted with the minority in opposing the change, and its 330 votes (89 votes from Nord were abstentions) made up nearly half the total minority vote of 723.

Under the changed rules for election, any minority which won 20 per cent of the vote during a party Congress on a motion of general policy or party orientation was entitled to two-thirds of the seats it would have obtained by direct proportional representation based on the number of votes received for its motion. In addition, in 1963, the 54th National Congress voted to create the post of honorary member of the CD. This gave seats on the CD to members with ten years of service on it since 1944, or on the clandestine wartime CD or the prewar CAP, and to those who had been party members for thirty years and had sat on the CD for at least seven years.

Honorary members of the CD were not, however, given the right to participate in votes or to be elected to the Bureau.

Ancillary Organizations

Although the SFIO had lost votes and members since the Liberation, it was after 1958 that the decline in party fortunes seriously began to disturb party leaders. Under the parliamentary system of the Fourth Republic, where coalition politics was the rule, it was possible for a minority party like the SFIO to obtain control of the government—as from February, 1956, to May, 1957, with the Mollet government—or to participate in government. Under the presidential system of the Fifth Republic, however, with the growing strength of the Gaullists in the National Assembly and the immense powers, real and potential, of the presidential office, the SFIO was forced to play a minor role in national politics. Thus the party was subjected for the first time to the same kind of pressures that had led other European Socialist parties to reform their doctrine and organization in response to party reformers tired of years of failure at the polls and of playing a secondary role in national parliaments.

It was only during the Defferre interregnum from February, 1964, to June, 1965, however, that a serious attempt was made to reform party doctrine and organization and to change the image of the SFIO. One of the main explanations for the weakness of the reform element is the departure before 1958 of a large dissident minority which included such major party figures as Daniel Mayer, André Philip, and Edouard Depreux. During the latter part of 1962, Guy Mollet emerged as the leader of the left camp in the SFIO, resuming a role he had had briefly in 1946, when, carrying the banners of orthodox socialism, he played upon party militants' resentment of the *travailliste* Mayer-Blum leadership to win the post of party secretary-general from Daniel Mayer. During 1963, however, Gaston Defferre, a long-time supporter of *travaillisme* (the notion of a French Labor party grouping the SFIO and moderate elements to its right, including the MRP, under one roof) emerged as the leader of the moderate tendency.[10] Both men differed on points of doctrine, strategy, and party organization, and both had their allies within the party—although it has been pointed out that Defferre drew a good deal of outside support from academics, political clubs, and some elements of the press, particularly *L'Express*.

In making himself the champion of the *parti pur et dur*, Mollet criticized those who backed Defferre for their attempts to de-emphasize the radical aspects of Socialist doctrine in order to attract support from the right. "It isn't less socialism that we need to arm ourselves with in order to succeed Gaullism," he said; "it is more socialism."[11] To suggestions that the SFIO open its organization by permitting trade unions, political clubs, and other independent organizations to join on a collective basis and to open party meetings to debates in which members of other parties could present their points of view, one of Mollet's allies replied:

> To reform its structures, break up the party and share it among specialists of all kinds, it was not for that men once became Socialists. . . . In reality, working-class militants have come to our sections out of a sentiment of injustice they feel toward the regime, they come from an instinct of revolt, in order to fight, in order to transform society and not to be present at academic discussions no matter how interesting they might be.[12]

[10] See *Le Monde*, June 5, 1965, where Defferre states he had been one of those favoring the creation of a French "Labor party" when the issue arose during the Resistance years.

[11] *Bulletin Intérieur*, no. 136, April, 1965, p. 204.

[12] *Ibid*., p. 92, statement by Arthur Notebart, deputy from Nord.

Much of the debate in the SFIO in 1964 and 1965 seemed to center more around questions of party organization, tactics, and personalities than of doctrine. But it was difficult to criticize any one aspect of party activity without calling into question all the others. That is why those who opposed suggestions emanating from the Defferre camp that the SFIO open its organization to indirect membership from trade unions, political clubs, and other independent organizations rightly felt this would inevitably lead to a dilution of Socialist doctrine and to a greater emphasis on short-term goals. In one sense, however, the quarrel was deceiving, for the question of whether the party should radically alter its organization was not completely open to debate. The reason for this was simply that the SFIO had long ceased to fit the image of a *parti pur et dur*—that is, a party sparked by the efforts of devoted militants acting through numerous specialized party organizations such as youth groups, workers' circles, and study groups. If the SFIO ever was an instrument for recruiting workers into the party community, by the 1950's and 1960's it had certainly ceased to perform this function.

The postwar history of the SFIO demonstrates the profound changes that have taken place in French politics with the growing proliferation and independence of voluntary organizations. Like other European Socialist parties, the SFIO found itself unable to dominate the activities of trade unions, interest groups, and other similar organizations, and it was forced to the position where, in order to elaborate policies in many areas, it had to solicit the advice and occasional participation of independent organizations in the policy-making process. Even more frequently, the top levels of the party organization devoted themselves to supplying information on the activities and claims of these independent organizations, whereas in the past it was hoped the party itself would be able to process these claims as they arrived from party militants active in voluntary or party-dominated organizations. This general inability of the SFIO to maintain a network of dependent organizations had serious implications for its structure and doctrine.

After the Liberation, the SFIO attempted to launch a number of specialized organizations, hoping thereby to recruit new members and to extend the party's influence. By 1966, however, most of these organizations had disappeared and those remaining were more paper constructs than living, functioning bodies. The decline of these organizations and their failure to perform most of the tasks for which they were established had a profound effect on all aspects of party activity.[13]

When the SFIO created a large number of specialized organizations after the Liberation, party membership had swollen to a record high. According to Léon Blum, socialism was the "master of the hour," and throughout the SFIO morale was extraordinarily high as members were convinced the party would occupy the center of the French political stage.[14] In creating or resuscitating various specialized organizations, the party hoped to achieve a number of goals. To a greater or lesser extent, depending on its characteristics, the organizations were expected to: (1) recruit new party members, (2) extend the party's influence to interest groups, trade unions, and other independent organizations, (3) propagandize for the party by distributing information on party policies, (4) assist the party during election campaigns, (5) provide a pool of potential party leaders skilled in the area of concern of the specialized organization, (6) reinforce party cohesion, (7) educate party members and sympathizers in the tenets of

[13] Maurice Duverger, *Political Parties* (New York, 1962), pp. 106 and 109.

[14] *L'Oeuvre de Léon Blum, 1945–47* (Paris, 1958), p. 77.

Socialist doctrine, and (8) provide the party with information on the policy demands of independent organizations.

During the ambitious period in the late 1940's, the specialized organizations included a Socialist and Workers' Music and Choral Group (*Fédération Nationale des Musiques et Chorales Ouvrières et Socialistes*), a traveling theater and variety group, a camping association, and an itinerant cinema group.[15] Most of the specialized organizations whose primary intent was to entertain and to provide leisure-time activities for the party members or sympathizers failed to get off the ground. The competition from the mass media and the declining party membership made them among the first casualties in the complex of organizations. The party did very little to rescue them, since, in its scale of priorities, recruitment from and propagandizing among the working class took precedence over other activities. Thus the party diverted scarce funds from more peripheral specialized organizations to those considered more essential. One of these important specialized organizations was the Socialist Enterprise Group (*Groupes Socialistes d'Entreprises*, or GSE).

THE SOCIALIST ENTERPRISE GROUP

The GSE was a specialized organization somewhat similar to Communist workplace cells, except that the latter are an integral part of party organization and the former are not. According to Socialist party statutes (Article 12), party sections are required to establish a GSE whenever possible in a concern, and Socialist party members are required to participate in its activities. Political control is exercised by the Socialist federation and the party executive committee. The GSE is not allowed to participate in the deliberation, activities, or direction of the SFIO. The SFIO has, at various times,

[15] *Bulletin Intérieur*, no. 42, May, 1949, p. 97.

set forth the goals of the GSE. It conceived of them as "groups for propaganda and political action," and they were given the task of "propagandizing, informing the party about activities in the factory, and educating militants and sympathizers." Soon after their creation, however, it was discovered that rather than being used for party purposes, the GSE's were being used by their members as a "refuge and rallying center" for those who wished to defend the independence of the *Confédération Générale du Travail* (CGT) against growing Communist domination. Once the CGT split and the *Force Ouvrière* was formed, the GSE rapidly lapsed into desuetude. It was this, rather than lack of financial support, that caused them to fail.

Despite the early setback to the GSE's, the party continued to work for their re-establishment. It was difficult for the party to admit that the average Socialist worker had only a limited amount of time to devote to party activities and that many felt activity on behalf of a trade union was more effective than party work. In 1954, the annual report noted that

> for our party, the party of the working class, [it is] an essential task to organize the dozens of thousands of our adherents working in the factories and offices and to regroup them around the hundreds of thousands of workers faithful to the cause of socialism.[16]

By 1966, however, no mention was made of the GSE's in the party's annual report, and it is likely that they have ceased to have any real importance.

CENTRAL WORKER'S COMMISSION

Originally, the GSE's were linked to the party by a Central Worker's Commission (*Commission Centrale Ouvrière* until 1950, afterward *Commission Nationale Ouvrière*, or CNO).

[16] *Bulletin Intérieur* no. 42, May, 1949, p. 45; no. 53, April, 1951, p. 40; no. 72, May, 1954, p. 29.

The CNO was one of a number of national commissions established in 1944 at suggestion of Jules Moch.[17] In some cases these commissions merely served as study and propaganda-disseminating groups and were composed of parliamentarians, party officials from the national headquarters, and party specialists. In the case of the GSE and other mixed specialized organizations, the national commission provided the liaison between the party headquarters and the various branches of the specialized organizations. As the GSE declined, the activity of the CNO was restricted to diffusing party propaganda on economic and social questions to the working class through party correspondents, usually Socialist militants employed in large factories, and to organizing meetings where Socialist workers would be informed of party policy on social and economic affairs. At the same time the CNO attempted to garner information on the policy demands of the workers and their unions through the occasional Socialist union members who participated in regional or national meetings of the CNO. By the 1960's the CNO was restricted to an information gathering and policy elaboration function. The annual report for 1961 noted that the CNO had

> devoted itself above all to becoming as competent as possible and thereby rendering more complete and precise the studies on the current situation as concerns the worker, a situation it followed and clarified so as to enlighten the directing organs of the party —the bureau and executive committee.
>
> Toward this end, on the initiative of the Secretariat, an effort was made to have all professional branches represented on the Commission by one of the important representatives of the large union federations.

In 1966, the regional conferences organized by the CNO were characterized in the party's annual report as having met with a "disappointing" response.

[17] Ligou, *Histoire du Socialisme*, p. 589.

JEAN JAURÈS CIRCLES

Another example of a specialized organization with a drastically reduced field of activity is provided by the Commission for National Education and Laïcité (*Commission Nationale de Défense Laïque* until 1957, and then integrated into the National Study Commission as *Section Education Nationale-Laïcité*). Originally the CNEL was expected to serve as an administrative link between a mixed specialized organization, the Jean Jaurès Circles (*Cercles Jean Jaurès*) and party headquarters. In 1948 the CNDL was assigned the task of ensuring "laic unity" by backing the activities of the Jean Jaurès Circles in the Cartel for Laic Action (*Cartel d'Action Laïque*), an independent organization which grouped a number of laic groups in France at the departmental and national level. The Jean Jaurès Circles included both party members and sympathizers interested in the problems of education and *laïcité*, and were intended to recruit members to the SFIO from the teaching profession and to coordinate party policies on education with the demands of those in the profession.

In 1952 the Cartel for Laic Action collapsed under the strains of internal dissension caused mainly by Communist agitation. At this time the Jean Jaurès Circles became independent of the CNDL and were directly linked to the party through federal and national officials responsible for their activities. In 1958, the CNDL became part of the larger National Study Commission (*Commission Nationale d'Etudes*) where, as the Section for National Education and Laïcité (*Section Education Nationale et de la Laïcité*), it functioned mainly as a study group for parliamentarians interested in its area of concern.

The Jean Jaurès Circles, however, seem to have met with a certain brief success. The profound commitment of the SFIO to *laïcité* led it to devote a great deal of attention to animating the circles. By 1953 federal officials responsible for activating and supervising the circles had been named in seventy-three departments, but only fifty of these responded to party appeals for a list of party members and sympathizers in the teaching profession. Eventually the circles seem to have focused on ensuring cohesion among party members and sympathizers, providing information on teacher's policy demands to the party, and, during election periods, providing a locus for Socialist campaign activity among members of the teaching profession. The continued interest of the SFIO in the Jean Jaurès Circles was not only due to the party's commitment to *laïcité* but also to the fact that the party valued recruits from the teaching profession. The annual report for 1959 noted that "to attempt to recruit workers is an excellent thing, but to recruit a teacher or a professor is no less so, their particular qualifications making them very efficient in the sections."

This statement might be interpreted in more than one way. It is possible that, in 1958, party leaders felt that the teaching profession was more susceptible to recruitment than other professions or groups because the teachers' unions were weak and the SFIO was considered a traditional friend of the teaching profession. It is also possible that the party had so lost faith in its ability to recruit working-class members that it felt obliged to turn toward a milieu sympathetic with its aims. Or it might have been that teachers were particularly well equipped to deal with the increasingly specialized tasks required of party cadres as well as being excellent "propagandists" for the party. A party annual report noted that "the problems to be studied are increasingly complex, and they often spill over departmental borders. Contacts with specialists, 'technocrats' outside our ranks, imply a profound study of dossiers." The report went on to observe that the federation secretaries were in dire need of militants who could assist in coping with the multifarious tasks they were called upon to perform. Whatever the reason for the party's continued and energetic attempts to recruit among teachers, the Jean Jaurès Circles devoted themselves primarily to "making a census of and regrouping the members or sympathizers of the party in the teaching profession."[18]

The Jean Jaurès Circles were, however, allotted one seat on the executive committee of the Federation of the Democratic and Socialist Left, which was formed in 1965.

THE YOUNG SOCIALISTS

Perhaps the most striking example of the party's inability to energize a specialized organization is provided by the decline of the Young Socialists (*Jeunesses Socialistes*, or JS).

Before the Second World War, the Young Socialists had grown steadily from a membership of 1,100 in 1925 to a high of 54,641 in 1947, the year before they were forced to disband.[19] The postwar period saw the party encounter both recruitment and political problems in its dealings with the JS. In 1947 the party executive committee was forced to disband the National Bureau of the JS because the movement had been captured by left-wing leaders highly critical of the party's policies and intent on joining the Fourth International.[20] In 1948 the JS was reorganized and the new statutes stated explicitly:

> The movement does not constitute a party elaborating a doctrine and a line of political action, but has for its mission to spread among young people the policies decided upon by the party

[18] *Bulletin Intérieur*, no. 42, May, 1949, p. 37; no. 48, April, 1950, p. 30; no. 66, June, 1953, p. 29; no. 102, May, 1958, pp. 65 and 69; no. 110, May, 1959, p. 46; no. 115, May, 1960, p. 46; no. 120, March, 1961, p. 32; no. 135, April, 1965, pp. 10 and 30–31.

[19] Georges Lefranc, *Le Mouvement Socialiste sous la Troisième République, 1875–1940* (Paris, 1963), p. 436.

[20] Ligou, *Histoire du Socialisme*, p. 588.

during its regular meetings. The Young Socialists will, in no case, discuss the decisions and actions of the party in their movement.

Anyone from fourteen to twenty-five years of age could join the JS, although members might remain until the age of thirty if they joined before the age of twenty-five. The organization of the JS paralleled that of the party, with local, federal, and national organizations. Initially after the Liberation, the National Committee (*Comité National*) included twenty members of the JS elected at the Annual Conference and eleven adult members designated by the party executive committee on the suggestion of the JS National Committee. The National Committee, which was the directing organization of the JS, elected a National Bureau composed of five adult members and five Young Socialists. The bureau was the permanent executive body of the JS.

The purpose of the JS was defined as "the formation of cadres and militants who will enter the party in possession of qualities of discipline and organization." Above all, the *raison d'être* of the movement was to educate its members so that they might become "skilled propagandists." In spite of early attempts to found a Socialist school, the party depended on occasional federal, national, and international meetings and conferences to socialize the younger members into the party community. But these meetings were available only to the top leaders, and most members were socialized only in a haphazard fashion. This was implicitly admitted by the party in 1954 when the annual report stated that "it is by participating in the life of the Movement that the best political and civic education can be obtained by our young people."[21]

From the very beginning, however, the revamped JS encountered recruitment difficulties. Membership hovered around 5,000 until 1956, when, after a brief rise while Guy

[21] *Bulletin Intérieur*, no. 72, May, 1954, p. 49.

Mollet was Prime Minister, it once again declined. Not only did the party find it difficult to attract young people, but the attitude of adult members created additional problems. In many cases the adults were unwilling to let the Young Socialists assume responsible tasks in the organization, and they frequently took advantage of the young members by using them to perform menial secretarial tasks.

Although the ostensible goals of the JS movement remained the same—to recruit and mold potential militants and leaders—the party has in recent years been forced to recognize that it cannot build a mass movement endowed with an extensive organization engaged in numerous activities. By 1960 the party annual report explicitly stated that the JS could not be expected to develop into a mass movement and that its most important function was to develop and train cadres. The education of Young Socialists was given top priority for the movement. In 1963 the annual report stated that the JS had been assigned two tasks, to educate militants and to propagandize among young people. "Propagandizing" here was defined not as attempting to recruit as many new members as possible but rather to keep young people informed of the party's position and to "detect elements likely to join the ranks of the Young Socialists, especially among your people already occupying positions of responsibility in mass organizations."

Thus, having been defeated in its effort to build a large youth movement involved in numerous activities and realizing that independent youth groups and organizations were better adapted to recruit members on a mass basis, the party attempted both to recruit the top members of these organizations—especially the UNEF (*Union Nationale des Etudiants de France*)—and to establish direct links with their leaders. In addition, the party called upon the Young Socialists to join other youth organizations and there to act as antennae for the party.

Rather than toward massive recruitment it is toward a geographical distribution of members as well as toward increasing specialization of action among the different groups of young people (workers, students, farmers, women) that we intend to orient ourselves.

The party also made a deliberate effort to establish schools for cadres and to ensure larger participation by Young Socialists in their activities.

THE FÉDÉRATION NATIONALE LÉO LAGRANGE

If most of the ancillary organizations of the SFIO declined to the point where they existed primarily on paper in Paris, one of these organizations, the *Fédération Nationale Léo Lagrange* (FNLL), from very small beginnings, blossomed into one of the most important ancillary organizations associated with the SFIO. Named after Léo Lagrange, the Undersecretary of State for Leisure in the Léon Blum government of 1936, the FNLL was originally an adjunct to the Socialist youth and student groups in the 1940's. While these latter groups failed to elicit any widespread support, however, the Léo Lagrange clubs were able to "attract and retain elements that we no longer attract solely because of our political position, especially since, for many years now, young people have been turning away from politics in distrust."[22]

Thus, whereas membership in 1951 was approximately 4,000, by 1965 it had jumped to almost 40,000 with 15,000 members subscribing to the club's monthly review, *Jeunesse*. Also, by 1966, the FNLL had expanded to the point where there were more than 350 Léo Lagrange centers and groups involved in myriad leisure and sporting activities such as running cinema clubs, vacation resorts, youth hostels, credit co-

[22] *Bulletin Intérieur*, no. 42, May, 1949, p. 62; no. 48, April, 1950, p. 59; no. 53, April, 1951, p. 58; no. 115, May, 1960, p. 58; no. 127, March, 1963, pp. 51–52; no. 135, April, 1965, pp. 57 and 70.

operatives, and holding frequent meetings and exchanges with youth groups from other European and African countries.[23] The Léo Lagrange clubs were given a tremendous boost in 1958, when they were recognized as being organizations of *utilité publique* and thus eligible for public aid, and again in 1961, when, under the provisions of the Fourth Plan, communes could apply for government subsidies to construct youth clubs as well as receiving 50 per cent of the salary of the directors of these clubs from the government. The FNLL was also made legally eligible to provide directors; thus Socialist mayors took advantage of the existence of the network of Léo Lagrange clubs and of government subsidies to construct and staff Léo Lagrange youth clubs.[24]

When the original discussions about expanding the FNLL took place in the Socialist party in the early 1950's, people like Pierre Mauroy, assistant secretary-general of the SFIO and a founding member of the FNLL, and Maurice Deixonne, former Deputy from Tarn and president of the Socialist parliamentary group, realized that the initial popularity of the clubs was due to their minimizing Socialist doctrine and policies and to the emphasis they put on providing a place where young people could meet and engage in social and sporting activities. Thus the individual clubs came to play a small but important role in national and local politics since the directors of these clubs, and the national committees, were staffed almost wholly by members of the Socialist party. The executive committee of the FNLL in 1966, for example, counted five current or former members of the executive committee of the SFIO among its eleven members.[25] One of the officials of the FNLL pointed out in an interview that the clubs con-

[23] Interview, Paris, summer, 1966.

[24] Socialist Party, *Agir*, no. 3 (October–November, 1964), p. 9.

[25] Fédération Nationale Léo Lagrange, VIIth Congress, mimeo, April 16–19, 1965.

tributed mainly to enhancing the prestige of socialism and the SFIO for young people through the activities of the clubs and of their staff, and that they were especially influential in forming Socialist voters, for often a young voter who might not otherwise vote Socialist did so if the candidate happened to have been an official of the local Léo Lagrange Club. In addition, the monthly review *Jeunesse*, edited by Pierre Mauroy, was highly professional, well written and illustrated, and certainly did not resemble the fusty literature usually associated with the SFIO. One edition of the review, for example, was taken up with film and theater reviews and articles of the type, "Yes, Other Inhabited Planets Exist," but there were also articles in the same issue on "Group Medicine" and "For a Short and Voluntary Military Service" that closely followed the Socialist party policy on these issues.[26]

The FNLL was also represented indirectly on the executive committee of the *Fédération de la Gauche Démocrate et Socialiste* through the *Centre National d'Etudes et de Promotion* (CEDEP), whose three seats on the executive committee of the FGDS were held by Pierre Mauroy, a member of the executive committee of both the Socialist party and the FNLL, and Guy Marty and Jacques Mellick, members, respectively, of the executive committee and national council of the FNLL and of the SFIO.[27]

MISCELLANEOUS ORGANIZATIONS

Two other organizations are also worthy of note, the Socialist student organization, *Etudiants Socialistes* (ES), and the Socialist women's group, *Femmes Socialistes*. The student group was a small one. In 1956 its membership was reported to be 2,000; by 1960 it did not number more than 200 mem-

[26] Socialist Party, *Jeunesse*, no. 43 (June, 1965).
[27] *Le Populaire*, May 26, 1966.

bers and in 1966 it had approximately 800 members.[28] The ES was handicapped not only because of the comparatively short time students spend in school and by lack of funds and time available to French students, but also because the movement was prey to the radicalism many student groups seem peculiarly subject to.

Created in 1947, the ES constantly threatened to disappear, and party annual reports throughout the years testify to the difficulties faced in supporting the organization. Most of the time it was merely a skeleton organization with a staff that represented it at international conferences, published bulletins, and held occasional meetings. The ES encountered difficulties during the period 1956–1957 when the policies of the Mollet government in Algeria became increasingly unpopular among students.[29] In 1957 the national bureau of the ES was suspended after the ES had voted its disagreement with the policy of the Socialist-led government in Algeria. Revision of the ES statutes by the SFIO led to the packing of the organization by admitting students from *lycées*—thus diluting the university and anti-Mollet representation.[30] By 1966 the party still had not been able to launch a stable and growing student organization, and aside from the fact that some Socialist students were elected to the national bureau of the *Union Nationale des Etudiants de France* (UNEF), the ES remained small and unimportant.[31]

The women's group in the SFIO never played a very important role in the party.[32] One of the reasons may have been the small number of women in the SFIO. In 1956 only 12 per cent of the members were women, and only 10 per cent in

[28] *Le Monde*, June 4, 1965.
[29] *Bulletin Intérieur*, no. 42, May, 1949, p. 74; no. 72, May, 1954, p. 53.
[30] *France-Observateur*, April 4, 1957.
[31] *Bulletin Intérieur*, no. 102, May, 1958, p. 57.
[32] Ligou, *Histoire du Socialisme*, pp. 372 and 588.

1963.[33] By contrast, the German Social Democratic Party membership in 1965 included 33 per cent women and the Austrian Socialist party 45 per cent. In a country like France where women make up more than half the electorate (53.8 per cent in 1961), this should be considered a severe handicap. Moreover, the Socialist women's group met with either indifference or lack of comprehension from many of the male members who thought the National Commission of Socialist Women was an organization devoted primarily to charitable activities. The annual party report for 1959 stated that the goal of the organization was to provide information on party activities to the female electorate and to recruit women into the party—not to function as sisters of charity.[34] Aside from organizing meetings where questions of interest to women are discussed, representing the SFIO at various international congresses, and campaigning during electoral periods, the activity of the women's organization has been limited. Its journal, *Femmes Socialistes*, disappeared in 1959 and was replaced by a new journal entitled *Femmes*, which appeared only every two months. The conclusion to the annual party report for 1966 sadly noted that the party still refused to take seriously the need for propagandizing among women. The attitude of the male members was characterized by Jeanne Brutelle in 1963 when, using the same phraseology as Léon Blum, she noted that "you have the same nostalgia for the past, the mistrust and even disdain vis-à-vis women and young people. You do not place women on the electoral lists, and you consider young people only as raw recruits."[35]

[33] On 1956 figure see Pierre Rimbert, "Le Parti Socialiste SFIO," in Association Française de Science Politique, *Partis Politiques et Classes Sociales en France* (Paris: Armand Colin, 1955), pp. 195–207. On 1963 figure see *Bulletin Intérieur*, no. 120, March, 1961, p. 63.

[34] *Bulletin Intérieur*, no. 120, March, 1961, p. 63; no. 110, May, 1959, p. 64.

[35] *Le Populaire*, June 1–2, 1963.

The examples discussed above merely illustrate a general decline in the number, membership, and extent of party ancillary organizations. In the 1949 annual report more than thirty separate organizations were mentioned, in the 1966 report only fifteen. By 1966 the party's activities in many areas had been restricted to information gathering and study in the various sections of the National Studies Commission (*Commission Nationale d'Etudes*). Whereas in 1948 the party attempted to launch camping, tourist, and theater organizations, for example, activities in these areas were limited to discussions in the Tourist and Information sections of the National Studies Commission. This commission was divided into fifteen sections roughly paralleling the permanent and *ad hoc* committees of the National Assembly. It grouped Socialist parliamentarians, members of the executive organs of the SFIO, and specialists for the purpose of study and for the elaboration of *propositions de loi.* It was at this level that contacts took place between interest-group and union representatives, and the party.[36] The work of the National Studies Commission had increased vastly from 1949, when the annual report devoted two pages to recounting its activities, to 1966, when twelve pages in the annual report were needed to summarize these activities.

The decline of specialized organizations is not peculiar to the SFIO, but is a result of the growing power and independence in France of trade unions, interest groups, and professional organizations of various kinds. In addition, the decline of parliament in the Fifth Republic and the ever-increasing involvement of the government in the economy has led to a proliferation of alternate decision-making centers and access

[36] See *Bulletin Intérieur*, no. 135, April, 1965, pp. 68 and 70, where it is noted that representatives of student, theater, and veterans organizations participated in discussions in the various relevant sections of the National Studies Commission during 1964–65.

points for interest groups. The creation of Regional Economic Development Commissions (*Commissions de Développement Economique Régional*, or CODER) in France in 1964, and the presence on these commissions of representatives from groups such as the *Fédération Nationale des Syndicats d'Exploitants Agricoles* (FNSEA), the *Centre National des Jeunes Agriculteurs* (CNJA), and from the three major trade unions, the CGT, the FO and the CFDT, attest to this fact. Moreover, given the technical nature of many decisions and the unwillingness of governmental and administrative organizations to arouse violent reactions from interest groups and unions, their representatives are solicited to join consultative committees and participate directly in the decision-making process. Government officials often find interest groups easier to deal with than the parties because of the limited aims of the former and their consequent willingness to keep policy demands narrowly focused.[37]

The SFIO found that its own specialized organizations could neither compete with nor greatly influence trade unions, interest groups, and other organizations of more limited scope and ambition. Implicit in the attempt to launch these specialized organizations dominated by the party after the war was the belief that the SFIO was a primary instrument for the achievement of socialism and that only insofar as other organizations were linked to the party could they be said to participate fully in the struggle.[38] For those who maintained that the mission of the SFIO was essentially revolutionary—to abolish the capitalist system of property and substitute community ownership of the means of production and exchange—there

[37] Club Jean Moulin, *L'Etat et le Citoyen* (Paris, 1961), pp. 168–9.

[38] *Bulletin Intérieur*, no. 66, June, 1953, p. 151. A party motion states that "it is an essential task for the SFIO to lead the workers toward a comprehension of their class duty and to show them the road toward true syndicalism."

was, therefore, an unwillingness to risk sacrificing doctrinal purity by opening the party organizations to members who did not believe in the party doctrine.[39] Moreover, since the SFIO emphasized the democratic nature of its organization, there could never be a concerted attempt to use the ancillary organizations as "transmission belts" for the party in the same way as, for example, the PCF did. In addition, and again unlike the Communist party, the SFIO lacked a coherent doctrine that could be used for missionary purposes through these organizations, and Socialist militants in them were constantly being placed in the very difficult position of having to defend Socialist participation in government at a time when the Fourth Republic was slowly losing support in the country.

[39] See the speech of Guy Mollet in *Bulletin Intérieur*, no. 136, April, 1965, p. 203, where he quotes from the party declaration of principles on this point.

12. Elites and Styles

Elites

The party Guy Mollet had led since his elevation to the post of secretary-general seemed to be dominated by a particularly homogeneous elite. One of the most striking characteristics of the this elite was the extensive experience its members had in both local and national politics. Of the 110 executive committee members for whom information could be obtained elected from 1945 to 1966, only 25 (22 per cent) had never held elective office during their careers, while 69 (62 per cent) had been deputies or had also held office as mayor or as municipal or general councillor. The same extent of experience held for party deputies. Of the 278 deputies who held seats in the four legislatures surveyed, 198 (71 per cent) had been elected mayor at one time or another during their career, while the percentage of those who were mayors at the time of their election to the National Assembly rose from 35 per cent in 1956 to 68 per cent in 1958, then to 72 per cent in 1962 and 71 per cent in 1967 (see Appendixes F.1 and G.1). The sharp increase from 1956 to 1958 and thereafter can be accounted for by the change from the modified list system of proportional representation of the Fourth Republic to the single member two-ballot system of the Fifth Republic. Under the first system the party federation executives drew up the party lists, and although some attention was paid to local reputation in placing candidates on the list, in strongly Socialist areas whoever was first on the list was bound to win a seat. In 1958, however, due to the drastic reduction in the size of the electoral districts and the increase in number from 90 to 465 in Metropolitan France, local reputation began to assume increased importance in nominations and elections.

Another striking characteristic of the SFIO elite, and one that has been frequently remarked upon, is the extent to which the party recruits its leaders from the teaching profession. Of all Socialist deputies from 1956 on, 33 per cent began their careers as teachers and another 29 per cent began as doctors, journalists, or lawyers; 78 per cent were college educated. Of the one hundred members of the executive committee for whom information could be obtained, 39 per cent began as teachers and another 29 per cent were recruited from journalism, medicine, pharmacy, or law; 75 per cent held college degrees (See Appendixes F.2 and G.2).

Since the halcyon days after the Liberation, the executive committee has aged. In 1945 the average age of committee members was 43.7 years; by 1965 it was about 54 years. Of course, it should be recalled that the Resistance period eliminated a number of older party leaders and opened the ranks to younger blood, but like most mass parties the SFIO continued to elect the same leaders to office as time passed. By 1967, for example, the average length of time a member served on the executive committee was more than seven years.[1] Despite the

[1] In a study of the party elite, information was obtained for most of the members of the CD (*comité directeur*) from 1945 to 1966, while information was obtained for party deputies elected in 1956, 1958, 1962, and 1967. Information was obtained from various sources including *Who's Who in France*, numerous biographical dictionaries and from

aging of the leadership, a large number of members were elected for one- or two-year periods (see Appendixes G.4, G.5, G.6, and G.7). Since there was no guarantee of re-election, Mollet frequently dealt with dissenters and thus had to change his policies to maintain the support of the CD. He could not exercise dictatorial power, since his power was the power of persuasion. Certainly experience, friendship, and loyalty are important tools for the party leader. In the end, however, Mollet's success or failure depended on his own talents, his own ability to win the support of the party delegates and the members of the CD. The presence of people like Edouard Depreux, André Philip, Tanguy-Prigent, and Gaston Defferre at various times on the *comité directeur* testified to the fact that the CD was not a handmaiden of the leader, but rather a lever whose fulcrum he had to find by seeking the support of his fellow members and then bending the CD in the desired direction. Finally, in interviews, more than one party delegate mentioned that he voted, deliberately, both for Mollet and for certain opposition candidates to the CD in an attempt to prevent the majority from completely dominating the party and suffocating minority opinion. This is important, for the formal democratic procedures of the SFIO mean that the delegates do have ultimate power to elect or defeat the party leadership when they wish.

In the light of this information certain characteristic modes of thought and action within the SFIO may be better understood. The SFIO has often been criticized by intellectuals on both sides of the Atlantic for countenancing an apparently yawning gap between Socialist doctrine and Socialist practice. Critics have always called attention to this seemingly glaring defect in the SFIO and have explicitly or implicitly suggested

---

data kindly supplied by SFIO headquarters in Paris. See Appendixes F.1–3 and G.1–7 for statistical information on Socialist deputies and CD members.

that the Socialists might well attempt to bring either the practice in line with the doctrine or the doctrine in line with the practice, and that, in any case, consistency would bring the results a political party aims for—increased votes, larger membership, and, perhaps, power. But the difference between party doctrine and practice, between the ideal goals of socialism and the everyday demands of politics did not shock most party members simply because they were quite able to keep the two distinct. Most Socialist parties have long-term goals and short-range policies. Party members and, especially, the leaders were quite aware of the difference between the two and took pride in the ideals of a doctrine which distinguished the SFIO from the more practical and nondoctrinal parties of the center and right in French politics. After all, as the figures indicate, the party elite was an elite of political veterans—men with broad experience in local and national politics. Indeed, the SFIO often boastingly referred to the 60,000 Socialist officeholders in local and national political positions throughout France as its "60,000 *élus*." In addition, from 1949 on, the percentage of the total party membership that conceivably might have been serving as municipal councillors ranged between 57 per cent and 70 per cent (see Appendix D.4).

Given their backgrounds, it becomes easier to understand how the SFIO was able to forgive and justify the extraordinary twists and turns taken by the party under both the Fourth and Fifth Republics. For the party elite was both an elite of political veterans and an elite in terms of educational achievement. They were not rigid ideologues, nor intellectuals devoid of experience in, or contact with, the realities of practical politics. Nor, on the other hand, were they simply bread-and-butter Socialists willing to abandon party doctrine or ideals as soon as the achievement of political power was close at hand.

In addition, those who wonder at the ability of Guy Mollet to dominate the party for a period of over twenty years, impelling it first toward the center and then to the left on the French political spectrum might do well to consider not only the background of the party elite sketched here, but also the history of the SFIO since Mollet assumed leadership.

After the Liberation the SFIO was broadly divided into three groups. There were those who wished to see the SFIO cooperate with the PCF even to the point of considering organizational integration; there were those who, with Mayer and Blum, wanted the SFIO to retain its essential tradition and doctrine but wished to see some opening to the right; and there were those who, with Guy Mollet, felt that the SFIO should re-emphasize its Marxist revolutionary heritage and make every effort to distinguish the party from both the MRP and the PCF. Mollet took control of the party in 1946 and consistently followed an independent line. In France—where the vagaries of the electoral system and the complicated process of contracting alliance frequently allow a party to win seats in parliament far out of proportion to the national vote it receives (and where some parties like the PCF are consistently disadvantaged by the electoral and alliance system)—it is easily understandable that ability to maneuver within and to gain the best advantage from the system is a paramount quality for a party leader. This helps to explain the continued dominance of Guy Mollet in the SFIO, for in a party in which so many of the members make their living in politics, the reformer or innovator is not likely to win broad support. He is even less likely to be popular if, in a situation where the political system is unstable and where the future of the entire system is unclear, he calls for reforms on the basis of his own predictions of what is durable and what is tenuous in the system. This reforming zeal was not Mollet's style.

Leadership Styles

Since its foundation the SFIO has usually been dominated by one man for extended periods of time. Until his assassination on July 31, 1914, Jean Jaurès was the most powerful and important of the Socialist leaders. Although his conflict with Jules Guesde was important because of the vital nature of the issues dividing them, Jaurès' influence was deeper and more lasting than that of Guesde. During the war of 1914–1918, Guesde shared leadership with other party figures, but gradually, during the immediate postwar period, Léon Blum emerged as the successor to Jaurès. Blum remained spiritual leader of the SFIO until his death, although, during the years of the German occupation, Daniel Mayer played a key role in reorganizing the party and directing its participation in the Resistance. But it was not until 1946, when Guy Mollet assumed the post of secretary-general, that, for the first time in its history, the SFIO was led by a man who owed his power both to his position in the party bureaucracy and to his own personal qualities. Neither Blum nor Jaurès ever held important posts in the extraparliamentary party, although Blum did exercise tremendous influence as editor and columnist for *Le Populaire*. They imposed themselves on the party through the sheer force of their intellect and personalities, using the party press and the tribune of the Chamber of Deputies to capture the attention of the party as well as the entire French nation. At the same time, however, both Jaurès and Blum were continually faced with opposition within the SFIO. They were almost always able to prevail, but many people were troubled by the constant tendency to factionalization in the party, and they put part of the blame on the system of proportional representation used to elect party leaders at all levels of the organizational hierarchy. Only a few years after the 1905 unification Congress, for example, Vaillant proposed doing away with proportional representation. In criticizing the number of tendencies represented in the executive organs he noted that

> new ones are always being created, even temporary ones, in order to play some role. . . . In order, for example, to get elected to the administrative commission [CAP], motions are suggested, propositions advanced not in the interest of Socialism, but in the interest of a coterie. . . . Someday we will see a faction which will propose that we walk on our heads because we are in the habit of walking on our feet, and, by virtue of this proposition it will demand a place on the CAP.[2]

This problem remained severe throughout the period of the Third Republic. Finally, after the Liberation, Mayer and Blum were able to convince the members that the party would gain in effectiveness if the old system of proportional representation were replaced with a majority system. The intent of this change was to reinforce the powers of the executive committee, now called the *comité directeur*, and to centralize power in the higher reaches of the bureaucracy thereby divesting the federations of a good deal of their prewar authority and independence.[3] When Mollet assumed the post of secretary-general, therefore, he did no violence to the intentions of Blum and Mayer by taking the party firmly in hand and attempting to impose stricter discipline and reinforce cohesion.

In many ways Mollet's career paralleled that of many Socialist militants. Born in 1905 in the department of Orne, he earned a degree in English and became a professor at a *lycée* in Arras. He entered the Resistance during the Second World War and later emerged a captain in the FFI. In 1945 he was

[2] Daniel Ligou, *Histoire du Socialisme en France, 1871–1961* (Paris, 1962), p. 182.

[3] B. D. Graham, *The French Socialists and Tripartisme, 1944–47* (Toronto, 1965), p. 45.

elected mayor of Arras. A forceful, incisive, and lucid speaker, he soon became a leading figure in the powerful Pas-de-Calais federation, and during the famous 38th National Congress held in late summer of 1946 he presented a resolution condemning the "revisionism" of Mayer and Blum. He won a seat on the *comité directeur* and, on September 4, 1946, he was elected secretary-general.

Although he had been frequently accused of using his position as secretary-general to suffocate minority opposition, there is little proof of this, and probably Mollet was able to celebrate his twentieth anniversary as secretary-general in 1966 simply because he had almost always been supported by a majority of party members. Not even his enemies denied his consummate abilities as parliamentarian and his uncanny sense of what party members would and would not tolerate.

His method was not autocratic; rather it combined a certain flexibility and willingness to compromise in the face of overwhelming opposition with an ability to put his point across in a convincing and simple fashion. Time after time in interviews, party militants, leaders, and officials used almost the same adjectives to describe the qualities that helped maintain Mollet in office. One young official commented:

He is a good professor, he explains things quite clearly and has the interest of the party at heart. He is quite sincere and the militants really feel he expresses their own feelings when he speaks at congresses. When I first joined the party I was prepared to dislike Mollet because I differed with him over Algeria, but when I met him I was very impressed and I've grown to respect him since then.

A Socialist mayor noted that "Mollet is a formidable debater, very honest and hardworking," and a French political scientist said, "Mollet is a very intelligent man and a wonderful debater. He has great sincerity even though his position on questions may frequently change."

Not all people were quite so laudatory. One high official who broke with the Mollet leadership after holding a high post in the party during most of the 1950's said:

Guy Mollet dominated the party through his abilities, he is adept at implying that his enemies wish to sabotage the party, and frequently he will change tack when his position is menaced, thus reattaching old opponents to his new position. . . . He will always go to the limit of deforming other people's opinions to keep himself in power.

Other Socialist officials also commented on the strong personal ties that bound Mollet to Augustin Laurent, the leader of the powerful Nord federation. Most of those interviewed felt that Laurent was a highly competent mayor, but that Mollet had gained ascendency over the party mainly because Laurent limited his interest to the affairs of Lille, leaving Mollet to take major decisions in other areas of party activity. One former Socialist who was a high official in the youth group but has since resigned from the party observed:

Guy Mollet and Augustin Laurent usually agreed on general policy before meetings on the *comité directeur* and elsewhere. Of course, Nord and Pas-de-Calais are both worker's federations, they are next to each other, but informal discussions on policy questions did take place between the two.[4]

Time and again, Mollet used the *patriotisme du parti* and the feeling of community that seemed to suffuse many militants to reinforce party discipline. He made it quite clear on many occasions that he had been forced to publicly defend decisions with which he was not in agreement, but he always maintained that discipline was necessary to party unity: "This party is only an instrument—but an instrument that we have tried to make effective—and it can be so only if we all speak

[4] Interviews, Paris, summer, 1966.

the same language. . . . I am ready, no matter when, to fight for policies that are not mine."[5]

But rarely was Mollet forced to defend policies he personally opposed; in most cases the party majority seemed to endorse precisely those policies that Mollet himself backed. Only during the debate over altering the method of election to the executive committee and during the Defferre campaign was Mollet in obvious opposition to policies backed by the party majority. Yet, in the case of the debate over elections to the CD, Mollet gave ground and, in fact, voted with the majority, while in the case of the Defferre campaign, he did not oppose Defferre once the party had nominated him, although some observers accused him of subtle sabotage by giving Defferre only lukewarm support during the period from the fall, 1963, to June, 1965.

Moreover, Mollet imposed himself on the party because of his ability to present the issues facing it in such a way that his own talents as parliamentarian and strategist extraordinary could be fully exercised. During the chaotic days of May and June, 1958, for example, Mollet presented the case for supporting de Gaulle as Prime Minister and then for the Fifth Republic referendum by claiming that to vote against de Gaulle was to completely undermine the Republic. In 1962, between the two ballots of the legislative elections, he was able implicitly to seek Communist voting support for the SFIO by emphasizing the primary danger to the Republic that seemed to emanate from the UNR, and to minimize the Communist threat by "realistically" calculating their possible numbers in the new National Assembly at a very low figure. It is significant that Mollet was outmaneuvered during Defferre's campaign for the SFIO nomination because Mollet was unprepared to respond to the questions and issues raised by

[5] *Bulletin Intérieur,* no. 101, April, 1958.

Defferre and his supporters. And Mollet was unprepared because he was convinced that the presidential system had not taken, and indeed should not take, deep roots in the political culture of France. By underestimating the popular response aroused by the Defferre campaign and the tremendous pressure that could be brought to bear on the SFIO by journalists, academics, former SFIO members, and the innumerable, talented, frustrated spiritual Socialists who have always hovered on the fringes of the SFIO, repelled by the party but imbued with the doctrine, Mollet demonstrated that, for once, he seemed to have lost touch with political reality. But he emerged from what looked like the beginning of the end of his reign to reassume control over the party once the MRP had scuttled Defferre's plan for a federation.

Although the route he followed to leadership in the SFIO was roughly similar to that followed by Guy Mollet, Gaston Defferre incarnated a quite different political style from that of Guy Mollet.[6] Defferre was born in 1910 to a Protestant family of moderate means in Marseille. After graduating from law school he practiced law in Marseille until the fall of France, when he became active in the SFIO southern Resistance movement. After the end of the war he was elected a municipal councillor and then was elected mayor in 1944. Except during the period 1947–1953, when the RPF tidal wave overwhelmed France, Defferre has been mayor of Marseille. A staunch anti-Communist, he always tended to rely for support on the Moderates on the municipal council and always refused to make any deals with the Communists during legislative elections. A moderate on the Algerian question during the Fourth Republic, he was frequently in the minority during party meetings on this problem and on the problem

[6] For an excellent summary of Defferre's career, see Colette Ysmal, *La Carrière Politique de Gaston Defferre* (Foundation Nationale des Sciences Politiques, Série: Recherches, no. 3; Paris, 1965).

of party democracy. Until 1963, however, Defferre seemed content to devote himself to running Marseille, to carry out his duties as deputy, and to leave the management of the SFIO to Mollet and the other leaders. But after 1963, Defferre developed a style and a view of politics that differed markedly not only from that of most Socialist politicians, but from most French politicians. First, and most important, Defferre appealed for support outside the party community. By winning the support of *L'Express* and *Le Monde* for his campaign for the SFIO presidential nomination, he offended many SFIO members who remembered that *L'Express* had been harshly critical of the Mollet government and the SFIO during the latter part of the Fourth Republic, and that *Le Monde*, although more temperate, had also expressed serious reservations about the Mollet government during that tense period.

Second, not even the SFIO dissidents during 1956–1958 had appealed to outsiders for support in their fight against the party leadership but had restricted their appeals to party members and to the few sympathizers that fill the political space between the PCF and SFIO. By campaigning for the presidency and for federation with the MRP, Defferre broke with Socialist tradition, for the party had always opposed a strong presidential system, and the suggestion of organizational as opposed to electoral or parliamentary alliance with the MRP was certain to arouse the resistance of party members. In proposing that the SFIO open its organization to Socialists and non-Socialists alike and in suggesting that the party simplify its vocabulary, Defferre was implicitly opening the door to new members who would be much less inclined to become emotional about either the traditional symbols or personalities that dominate the SFIO. Finally, by running his Horizon 80 campaign with the assistance of personalities and organizations outside the SFIO, he was demonstrating that there were situations in which an SFIO leader might well have to be responsive to suggestions and pressures emanating from outside the party.

In addition, the relations that Defferre entertained with members of certain political clubs, mainly from the *Club Jean Moulin* and *Citoyens 60*, prior to and after declaring his candidacy for the Socialist nomination for President put him into contact with people who were working for the renovation of the Socialist party outside the party itself. This was important because, unlike other would-be reformers in the SFIO, Defferre headed one of the most powerful federations in the party. This position guaranteed him a certain minimum support within the party during congress and council meetings and also ensured that whatever position he took would be duly noted and reported by the press—especially by papers hostile to Guy Mollet and his supporters. Moreover, Defferre's absolute devotion to the party, his consistent refusal to contemplate leaving it over one or another issue as had some of the dissidents in 1958, weakened the case of party militants who might otherwise have accused Defferre of undermining party discipline or of being a splitter. In this sense, then, Defferre showed the way to the rest of the party. In his contacts with the clubs and with *L'Express* during the "X" campaign, and in his later efforts to involve the SFIO in a federation with the MRP, his early failures paved the way for acceptance of the successful formation of the *Fédération de la Gauche Démocrate et Socialiste*, which merely formalized what had been informally taking place prior to 1965—namely, increased contact and discussion among the leaders of the various political parties of the non-Communist left and the elite of sympathetic clubs and unions. The significant difference, however, was that the FGDS was built on a foundation that deliberately excluded one of the key participants in Defferre's proposed federation, the MRP.

Obviously, Defferre felt responsible to more than just the

party community in his campaign for President. In the end, however, his campaign raised an interesting question that remains to be answered by the SFIO. How can the party maintain its control over a leader who undertakes the task of running for President? As the Defferre campaign demonstrated, once the leader begins to appeal to the community outside the party, he is forced to confront issues and to develop policies that are not necessarily those the party in interested in. Realizing this fully, Defferre made explicit the implications of his campaign for a party like the SFIO in *Un Nouvel Horizon.* There he explained that the presidential election provided an opportunity for reforming the old parties on the left if a large number of hitherto uninvolved but sympathetic citizens could be convinced that political participation was both necessary and worthwhile. To do so, however, Defferre suggested that a new "majority of action" be recruited within a "party of movement." Defferre noted that both Socialists and non-Socialists would be welcomed into this new party and that the old slogans and structures would be cast away. In effect, what Defferre stated in circumspect but clear language was that the presidential election offered the first real chance to smash the old parties and to construct a larger, majoritarian party composed of the reformist elements from within and of interested citizens previously outside the traditional parties.

For the first time, the renewal of these structures depends less on the executive committees than on the French people itself. One factor could unleash them, carry them to victory much more quickly than one believes, that is the arrival on the theater of operations of a powerful reserve army: those who in France are the men who have remained outside political life but are not indifferent to the fate of their country.

It is in order to respond to their expectations that we have decided to fight the presidential battle.

For Defferre, then, only a radically reformed and revised socialism and Socialist party could hope to recruit the necessary members to compete successfully in the presidential arena. Party boundaries only served to separate many individuals who were in basic agreement on the important issues and to keep alive moribund political issues such as *laïcité*.

It is necessary to understand that the persistance of this division [over *laïcité* in the schools] forces the defense of certain causes in the economic and social realms to take second place even though they are of primary importance.[7]

Thus, the nature of the division between Defferre and Mollet was quite clear. For Mollet the preservation of the organizational, doctrinal, and personal *status quo* in the SFIO was of the highest priority. Although Mollet sensed the wave of support for some restructuring of alliances growing within the party since 1963, he had made certain that, in supporting Mitterand and in discussing issues with the PCF, no real steps were taken to radically change the SFIO in any important respect. For Defferre, the opposite was true. He was primarily interested in radical reform, in reshaping the SFIO and, indeed, the entire party system on the left. Defferre seemed inclined to transfer from local to national politics the tactic of cooperation between the Socialist and sympathetic center parties. Certainly electoral cooperation between Socialists, the MRP, and independent parties during municipal elections and on numerous municipal councils was hardly rare in France, but the unique characteristic of Defferre's proposal was to extend this to the national level, and, most important, to build a new party on this kind of alliance. As befitted a man whose administrative capabilities and nondoctrinaire approach had transformed Marseille into a showpiece city, Defferre, the reformist administrator, ran up against Guy Mollet, the

[7] Gaston Defferre, *Un Nouvel Horizon* (Paris, 1965), pp. 181–3.

militant *par excellence*. And this was the crucial difference between the two: Mollet, faithful to the working-class doctrinaire tradition of the North, putting preservation of party doctrine and traditional structures at the top of his scale of priorities; Defferre, pragmatic, flexible, putting the achievement of concrete policy goals and electoral success before traditional values and structures.

13. Against Revisionism

In 1951, Jules Moch, one of the motivating forces behind doctrinal revision had advanced the idea that Socialist doctrine needed re-examination. Aside from the 1905 declaration of unity, and the Declaration of Principles drafted by Léon Blum in 1946, the SFIO had never elaborated any fundamental statement of principles. In 1958, a new impulse to draft such a statement came when Jules Moch and Roger Quilliot —both leading party theorists—were able to win the support of other members interested in questions of doctrine. These people began to pressure the party's executive committee to give them an opportunity to organize study groups.[1] By 1959, the executive committee had given permission for study groups to be organized and to focus on six general areas: doctrine, planning and management in business, problems of peace and socialism, religion, education, and Socialist conceptions of national defense. Most of the work of these study groups was published in *La Revue Socialiste* over the next two years. Despite energetic attempts to interest party mem-

[1] See R. Quilliot, "Pierre Bonnel," *La Revue Socialiste,* no. 163 (May, 1963), pp. 489–492, where details on the chronology of development of the study groups is provided.

bers in the activities of the commissions, the majority of members appear to have been indifferent. The continued low circulation of *La Revue Socialiste* tended to confirm this.

Although the process of discussion and debate took place over at least a two-year period, the drafting and passage of the Fundamental Program had minimal effect on the party. As Jules Moch pointed out, unlike the Bad Godesburg program of the German SPD, the SFIO Program was not a fundamental revision of party doctrine. And even Guy Mollet admitted: "I say to you that in the beginning some people, and I was among them, feared for a moment . . . that our party was moving toward revisionism. . . . But our party has realized a synthesis and it is necessary to preserve it."[2] Mollet also pointed out that the Declaration of Principles of 1946 was not affected by the new Fundamental Program and that the latter should be considered something between a declaration of principles and a program.

Whereas in the SPD the drafting of a new program was a traumatic event that was part of a process whereby the old party and parliamentary leadership was replaced by reformers, in the SFIO such traditional leaders as Guy Mollet greeted the new program with approval.[3] Some people, such as Pierre Bonnel, a frequent contributor to *La Revue Socialiste*, complained that the Fundamental Program did not seriously depart from the 1946 Declaration of Principles, and thus the impact of the new program was hardly noticeable.[4] Bonnel claimed that the study groups had merely reformulated traditional Socialist principles in a new vocabulary and had

[2] *Bulletin Intérieur*, no. 108, January, 1959, pp. 16 and 20; no. 118, January, 1961, pp. 10 and 24.

[3] See Douglas A. Chalmers, *The Social Democratic Party of Germany* (New Haven, 1964), p. 64.

[4] Pierre Bonnel "Programme Fondamental et Doctrine au-delà de l'avant-projet," *La Revue Socialiste*, no. 142 (April, 1961), pp. 420–438.

done nothing to descend from the rarified atmosphere of doctrinal debate to elaborate, specific, long-term (ten or fifteen years) policy recommendations explaining exactly how the party hoped to achieve the goals set forth in the Fundamental Program.[5] Bonnel suggested that party doctrine functioned mainly as a tactical weapon in the hands of party leaders, providing ideological justifications for blocking undesired policies or alliances, but was frequently ignored or reinterpreted when necessary.

When unanimously ratified by a party National Congress in May, 1962, the Fundamental Program was divided into five sections. It elaborated upon and expanded some of the themes touched upon by Léon Blum in the 1946 Declaration, while at the same time briefly discussing such issues as nationalism, disarmament, and the Soviet Union.

In vocabulary the Fundamental Program was toned down as compared with the Declaration. There was no direct reference to phrases that appeared in 1946, such as the one stating Socialist intentions to "abolish the capitalist property system," or the one defining the SFIO as a party of "class struggle." Nor was the party defined as "essentially a revolutionary party" as in 1946, but rather as "at the same time both reformist and revolutionary."

The Fundamental Program was also careful to qualify the 1946 statement that Socialists intended to transfer the means of production and exchange to the community, by noting that a system of Socialist planning would not necessarily mean transferring all the means of production and exchange, but rather that such transferral would take place only when economic oppression was present. Moreover, the Program explicitly excluded from communal appropriation "important sectors of agriculture, small productive industries, artisans and

[5] "Restauration ou Novation? Notes en vue d'un congrès," by Pierre Bonnel in *La Revue Socialiste*, no. 161 (March, 1963), pp. 493–501.

distribution." This section had given rise to some debate because in 1960 Jules Moch accused Socialist parliamentarians of wishing, for electoral reasons, to exclude the "little people" from the purview of Socialist appropriation, even though, in his words, "capitalist exploitation is no less unjust when it is a question of two or three people than of 100 or 1,000 people." Interestingly enough, the final draft added a phrase not present in an earlier one suggesting that "the necessary modernization [of 'les petites'] will take the form of common purchases, creation of sellers, buyers and development cooperatives."

As Moch had pointed out in the 1960 debates, the Fundamental Program was supposed to take account of the changes that had occurred in capitalist society since 1946. Thus the study groups which prepared the Program had gone into the questions of worker participation, government bureaucracy, planning, and the development of modern capitalism. They had also discussed the Soviet Union, disarmament, and foreign relations. On the whole, though, the Program produced no new ideas or suggestions for reform. In a simplistic fashion it attacked the unjust, inefficient though admittedly durable French capitalist system, contrasting its inequities and defects with the virtues of socialism. Except for one section where Socialist efforts to ameliorate the situation of the workers was mentioned, there was little to suggest that the SFIO would have to work within the French economic system for the foreseeable future. Most of the Program, therefore, consisted in briefly outlining some of the steps the party would take to achieve its final goal of a democratic, classless society where each would "produce according to his means and receive according to his needs."

Wherever "economic oppression" was found to exist, property in the means of production or exchange would be transferred to the community. In addition, the program promised to democratize the French Economic Plan by elaborating procedures for the participation of people working in all areas of the economy. In sum, the SFIO explicitly recognized that capitalism was not about to collapse, that large industries were oriented toward expansion and increased production and did not milk the workers merely to provide increased stock benefits to shareholders, that the tertiary sector of the economy was increasingly important, and that the working class was becoming more rather than less wealthy. But these events had not passed completely unnoticed in the West since the war, and the party was, therefore, merely catching up on some long overdue economic homework. Bonnel was right, the SFIO still had not thoroughly explored the difficult terrain that lay between the pristine goals of traditional Socialist doctrine and the sticky day-to-day policy-making that is necessary for any moderate Socialist party.

Given the general atmosphere of consensus in which it was elaborated, and the apathy of most members toward the debate and discussions leading to its passage, the Fundamental Program apparently did little to revitalize interest in Socialist doctrine either within or without the party. Those who had always been interested in these questions, notably those who contributed articles to *La Revue Socialiste*, were the main participants in the discussions that preceded its passage. It may be speculated that the very consensus surrounding its drafting and ultimate passage also worked to eliminate whatever interest might have arisen if the program had become the focus of serious debate within the party. In one sense the elaboration of the program, its explication of current economic trends, and its statement of vague goals for the SFIO—planning, nationalization of certain industries, internationalism, disarmament—were beneficial in that, formally, it seemed to bring the party up to date. For, as Jules Moch unconsciously implied, it was the thing to do among Socialist parties: "Why this study? It is an international need. You have noticed, those of you who follow the life of other parties, that all or almost all have engaged in studies of this kind."[6]

In many ways, of course, the acceptance of the Fundamental Program was an ironic commentary on the distance the SFIO had traveled since those days in 1946 when Guy Mollet had led the "orthodox" Marxists against Léon Blum's attempt to round off some of the radical edges of party doctrine. It was Mollet who had presented a resolution at the 38th National Congress condemning "all attempts at revisionism, notably those inspired by a false humanism whose true intention is to mask that fundamental reality, the class struggle." That same resolution attacked the party for concentrating on "parliamentary and ministerial activities" and observed that "the goal of our party is not the exercise of power in the framework of the current system, but the suppression of that system." In 1961, however, Mollet was to remark that the SFIO was a "revolutionary" party in the sense that "to change an economic system is a revolution . . . it isn't synonymous with bloody revolt." And in the Fundamental Program the word "revolution" was watered down in much the same fashion, for there it was defined as being a "social transformation abolishing classes, assuring to all . . . the full value of work and guaranteeing equality of rights." Almost twenty years after his victory over Blum at the 38th Congress in 1946, Guy Mollet found himself defending a position that Blum had fought for so passionately many years before. By admitting that the SFIO was both "reformist and revolutionary" the Socialists only made explicit what had been obvious to anyone who had followed their activities since the Liberation. Yet the irony was that by clinging to the vocabulary of the two traditions that are characteristic of European socialism—while

[6] *Bulletin Intérieur*, no. 127, March, 1963, p. 213; no. 118, January, 1961, pp. 10–12.

at the same time defining "reform" and "revolution" in an ambiguous fashion—the party gave no evidence that it was interested in a serious re-examination of party doctrine and vocabulary.

Of course, many party members do feel a deep commitment to party doctrine. There exists in the SFIO a strong feeling that the party is "different from the others," that it is basically a revolutionary party. If the exact meaning of the word "revolution" is frequently ambiguous when employed by French Socialists, SFIO members still feel that their tradition and aims differ from those of the British Labor party or the German SPD. The SFIO still differentiates between a system called "capitalism" and a system called "socialism," and in recent years party leaders like Mollet have reaffirmed Socialist goals as aiming at serious structural changes in France and the creation of a Socialist society.

The fact that the SFIO has preserved at least a *pro forma* belief in revolution, however vaguely defined, has two consequences. First, the party remains open to proposals for radical reform of the economic system and is less divided than moderate Socialist parties over such questions as the nationalization of key industries. Second, the continued obeisance to a revolutionary tradition keeps the Socialist party within a doctrinal framework that includes the Communist party and even implies certain common goals.

After all, both the PCF and the SFIO have a common heritage that dates back to the French Revolution. Since the traumatic split of 1920, both parties have often reiterated their desire to see the Left reunited in the future. And many Socialists still recall Blum's famous remarks uttered during the Tours Congress of 1920: "Even separated let us remain Socialists; despite everything, let us remain brothers, brothers who have separated after a cruel quarrel, but a family quarrel in a family that may someday reunite in a common home."

14. *The Socialist Dream and the French Reality*

The dream of the Socialist party has always been to form a homogeneous Socialist government, or barring that to be the main element in a loyal opposition. The Socialist dream has always been an escape from the French nightmare, however, for the realities of the French multiparty system have effectively prevented the Socialists from realizing either alternative. The Socialists had accepted this fact before World War II, when, under the leadership of Léon Blum, they abandoned their opposition to governmental participation and agreed to accept the responsibilities and risks that went with participation in coalition government. Léon Blum characterized this role of the SFIO as the "exercise of power," and he observed that while in this position the SFIO would have to work with its partners in government for the general interest of the nation, acting as "honest, loyal managers of the capitalist system." He also promised that the SFIO would not undermine the system while participating in coalition government, but would merely "orient its evolution" so as to ease the way for a future transition to socialism. He said that the SFIO would demand agreement on a minimum program as its price for support or participation, but he observed that, once it was in government, the SFIO should attempt to obtain for the workers "some counterpart, some compensation to balance the inevitable disadvantages" of living in a capitalist system.[1] Blum predicted that the compensations of the Fourth Republic would come in the form of the increased power of international organizations and an emphasis on peace.

Exactly the opposite of what Blum had expected occurred during the Fourth Republic. The Cold War began a period of severe international tension that tested the United Nations. In the case of Algeria and Suez, the Socialist-led government of 1956–1957 acted in a way that many sympathizers thought completely alien to the ideals and historic practices of the SFIO and of the Socialist movement.

The difficulties encountered by the SFIO under the Fourth Republic had a number of reasons. In choosing the road of parliamentarianism, reform, and coalition politics, the SFIO was always forced to compromise a good deal more than it might have otherwise done if it were acting within a two- or three-party system. In addition, the Socialists came to power during a time when the Algerian problem had just begun to assume serious proportions. The Socialists did not find themselves confronted with a purely anticolonial uprising led by an exploited and deprived native population who had suffered decades of repression. Rather, Algeria had been part of France since the middle of the nineteenth century. One out of every nine Algerians was of French or European origin. The class structure of Algerian society was not characterized by the presence of a tiny colonial elite, a small middle class, and a large but powerless native proletariat, but was complicated by

[1] Léon Blum, *L'Oeuvre de Léon Blum, 1945–47* (Paris, 1958) pp. 282–84.

the presence of a non-Moslem working class whose standard of living, although higher than that of the native Moslem population, was still lower than that of the French Algerian middle and upper classes.

The majority of SFIO members also tended to view the Algerian rebel movement in the light of postwar events in developing areas where nationalist elites had frequently installed single-party dictatorships in countries abandoned by the colonial powers. Many Socialists sincerely believed that only a French presence in Algeria could save that country from the ruthless suppression of political liberties, as well as the economic hardship that ensued when a revolutionary native elite assumed power. Thus the SFIO tried to counter the nationalist appeal of the FLN with the principles of democratic socialism—that is, by offering the Moslem Algerians the possibility that economic, social, and political development might take place within the framework of a democratic state if, and only if, the French retained their ties with Algeria and the rebels negotiated with the French. Independence was considered out of the question.

Perhaps one of the reasons for the stubbornness with which many Socialists—and others too—insisted that the Algerian standard of living could be quickly raised while retaining democratic procedures was based on certain similarities some people saw between the FLN and certain Communist movements. It is one of the characteristics of Communist movements in developing areas that the mystique of nationalism is combined with the promise of rapid modernization, all to take place within the framework of a "Socialist" state. Since the French Socialists had traditionally been staunch anti-Communists, more particularly anti-Stalinists, to have handed Algeria over to the nondemocratic modernizers of the FLN would have been explicitly to concede that rapid economic and social development had to take precedence over the maintenance of democratic political procedures. But the French Socialists are democratic Socialists, and for a long time they have claimed that socialism and democracy are inseparable. For many in the SFIO, however, the FLN was simply a nationalist movement, and they felt nothing in Socialist doctrine or experience should lead them to look favorably on movements of that kind.

Although the Socialists reacted with antipathy toward the rebels from their very first appearance in Algeria, still, in late 1955 and early 1956, the Socialists hoped to undermine the FLN through economic, social, and political reforms. Even when Mollet accepted Catroux's resignation after the events of 1956, Robert Lacoste was chosen Minister for Algeria only after two days of searching and after Gaston Defferre had refused the post. During early February, *L'Express* stated its faith in the government's intentions and even the PCF supported the government's activities in Algeria. Guy Mollet and the other government leaders had few preconceived ideas about Algeria but, as time passed, found themselves increasingly committed to the use of force to crush a rebel movement that seemed deaf to all appeals for negotiation on the government's terms.

At the same time, as Mendès-France left the government and as dissent grew within the ranks of the SFIO, the party majority increased its commitment to the policy of military repression. The Socialists continued to lead the government during the sixteen months from February, 1956, to May, 1957, despite the apparent failure of their Algerian policy, simply because the party was deeply committed to enacting a program of domestic social and economic reform. Throughout its entire term, the Socialist-led government concentrated on passing and on preparing to pass measures of this kind, and when the government fell on May 21, 1957, Albert Gazier was pushing for the passage of a law whereby the government would pay 80 per cent of doctor's fees through the social security program. And that same day Mollet waved his Socialist membership card and spoke of increasing the power of workers' committees in industry.

If there were limits beyond which the Socialist-led government would not go in attempting to retain power therefore, these limits seem to have been set by the desire for domestic reform, not by Algerian policy. The sixth of February, the Ben Bella incident, the Algerian pacification campaign, all illustrate cases where the government quickly retreated before those who flouted its authority in Algeria. In the case of Suez, party editorialists writing in *Le Populaire* went to extraordinary lengths to justify the Suez invasion in terms of Socialist doctrine rather than as an example of the *Realpolitik* it was.

The Mollet government's Algerian policy did win the support of the Independents, however, and after the departure of the Communists to opposition in July, 1956, the support of the Independents was essential for the government's survival. Most likely, if the SFIO leaders had attempted to discipline the recalcitrant administration or army in Algeria, and to institute social and economic reforms for the Moslem population, the Independents would have withdrawn their support. Thus the government, if it had wished to remain in power to put through a liberal Algerian policy, would have been forced to seek Communist support in the National Assembly. This the Socialists did not want to do. Alternately, the Mollet government might have pushed for a reform policy in Algeria and won the support of the center and center-right, including the Independents—but the price would have been sacrifice of the SFIO's program of domestic reforms. The most frequently heard complaint from the Independents was that France's inflation was aggravated because of Socialist reform measures such as the Old Age Fund. In any case, it would have been political suicide for any Socialist leader to have tried to convince the party that domestic reform measures would have to wait until the miserably low standard of living of the Moslem population was raised to the point where the rebel appeal would be blunted. The SFIO had to compromise on Algerian policy to remain in the government. It could not sacrifice its program of domestic reform for a liberal Algerian policy unless it were willing to solicit Communist support. It chose domestic reform.

With the 1958 election the political situation became confused. It was true that the UNR had achieved a sudden and surprising success; but, if the durability of the UNR was open to question, then the desirability of regrouping the opposition parties was also disputable. As a delegate from Alpes-Maritime said at the SFIO Extraordinary National Congress in December, 1958, the UNR did not have a program and it was impossible to predict in which direction it was heading. Many people felt that, given the heteroclite composition of the UNR, governmental responsibilities and time would inevitably sap the new party's unity.[2]

On this thesis then, many party members thought it advisable to await the inevitable collapse of the UNR and to profit from the situation as best as possible. Attempts to regroup or unite the opposition parties would be wasted energy and the result might well be to enfeeble the opposition at the very moment when all energies should be directed toward strengthening the SFIO. Other people drew different lessons from the election. Albert Gazier saw the need to regroup the forces of the left, including cooperative and trade union movements, in the heart of a confederation of the left. This confederation would allow the constituent units—parties, unions, movements—a large degree of autonomy. Guy Mollet agreed on the necessity for some regrouping of the forces of the left.

The general sentiment at the 1958 Congress was one of

[2] *Le Monde*, February 27, 1957.

hostility toward de Gaulle and the UNR. The SFIO was obviously not happy about continued Socialist participation in the government, especially in view of the fact that a Gaullist majority in the National Assembly was likely to be formed. According to Guy Mollet, however:

> We envisage governmental participation in very precise cases: to remain on the defense when it is a question of saving the Republic or the country. We have done that. . . .
>
> In other cases, when on the offensive, it is in order to save something, to contribute something. We have a permanent tactic and I do not propose to modify it, it is to assume responsibilities only when there is a chance of making some progress in the sense of democratic Socialism.[3]

One month after the close of the Extraordinary National Congress, however, the Socialist ministers decided to resign from the government in protest against the government's financial policies. Once again, the Socialist party had returned to opposition.

During the last years of the Fourth Republic, the party's internal situation deteriorated. Although the schism of September, 1958, did not lead to massive defections, the loss of individuals like Edouard Depreux, André Philip, Daniel Mayer, and Alain Savary damaged the party. The Algerian policies of these people, their fight for increased party democracy and for a re-examination of party doctrine had attracted the support of many young militants and their departure seemed to indicate that the SFIO would not tolerate energetic internal criticism.

Despite these difficulties, Guy Mollet continued to dominate the party. It is true that Mollet's power was limited by

[3] *Le Populaire*, December 5, 1958. In an interview with a high Socialist official in the summer of 1966, it was pointed out that many people in and out of the SFIO thought Mollet might become de Gaulle's *dauphin* during the period before the fall of 1958.

the willingness of other party leaders, specifically Augustin Laurent from Nord and Gaston Defferre from Bouches-du-Rhône, to support him, but, in normal circumstances, even the opposition of Defferre was not enough to overturn the party majority led by Mollet. This was evidenced in the debates on Algerian policy and party democracy. When the issues confronting the party were minor, then the votes of Nord and Pas-de-Calais combined with scattered votes from some of the smaller federations to ensure Mollet's dominance. When, however, the party was sharply and evenly divided, as in September, 1958, when the question of supporting the Constitutional referendum arose, then the vote of a federation like Bouches-du-Rhône was of crucial importance. But this unique crisis found Defferre eventually siding with Mollet, thus ensuring party unity.

The minority had hoped that the majority might be converted if the minority were allowed to express itself more freely and more systematically. Whether the party minority would ever have attained this goal is doubtful. The last revolt of the militants had occurred in 1946 when Guy Mollet ousted Daniel Mayer as secretary-general. At that time party membership was 354,878, the number having been swollen during the post-Liberation years by the SFIO's real accomplishments during the Resistance, by the disrepute of the right, and by the desire to see the SFIO participate in working radical changes in the French economic, social, and political system. It was a period of movement and change for the SFIO. Argument and debate within the party centered on the burning issues of unity on the left, the SFIO's attitude toward the MRP, and the nature of party organization. But as these questions were resolved, as it became clear that the SFIO would not, or could not, reach agreement on closer cooperation with the PCF or the MRP, that it was fated to participate in or support the inevitable coalition governments which once again characterized a parliamentary system reminiscent of the Third Republic, then the party began to suffer a sharp decline in membership. At the same time consensus within the party increased as the possibilities of party action became circumscribed. From 1950 to 1957, for example, the vast majority of issues which gave rise to a vote in party meetings concerned party organization, discipline, or electoral strategy. No wonder then, that the minority faction found it so difficult to recruit support and to overturn the party majority. The opportunities to shake consensus were few indeed. Moreover, the minority was hindered by the leadership's monopoly of the party press and information facilities and by its domination of the executive committee. The reluctance of the majority to agree to reinstitution of a system of proportional representation for elections to the executive committee and to the opening of a free tribune in the party press was understandable in view of the fact that such concessions might well have allowed the minority to obtain a foothold in party organization from whence it would always constitute a potential threat to the majority.

The inability of the minority to win support to its cause was also due to the background of party members, which must have affected their attitude toward the minority. During the years 1956–1958 there were approximately 58,000 municipal councillors throughout France who called themselves Socialists. It is likely that many of them were members of the SFIO. On the assumption that all belonged to the party, then 61 per cent of the party membership during these years was made up of municipal councillors. In addition, a famous study of party members and cadres undertaken by Pierre Rimbert in 1951, and perhaps still approximately correct in 1966, found that 25 per cent of a sample of party members were civil servants. The presence in the party of such a large proportion of individuals whose profession was bound up directly or indirectly with government service might help to explain the abnegation of party members before the leadership, especially during that period when the SFIO led the government.

It is true that Mollet's position on the Algerian problem changed from 1956 to 1958, but it is difficult to say whether it was minority pressure—especially from Defferre—repeated criticism from the Socialist International, or merely changing circumstances that motivated this change. Probably it was a combination of all three. On the whole, though, the majority remained defensive and unwilling to change the *status quo* in the party. When critics noted the declining popularity or vitality of the SFIO, the leadership usually ascribed party difficulties to a lack of motivation on the part of some members; to the PCF, which, it was said, had deceived the working class; to the difficult political position of the SFIO, forced as it was to defend the Republic by participating in unpopular and non-Socialist governments; or to internal dissension. At the September, 1958, National Congress, Guy Mollet noted that he had attended party meetings where

> one can still find those 'types' who devote themselves during the entire evening to explaining that the party is nothing at all, that it was deceiving itself . . . and that everything was going badly. And all this in a long and devious discourse delivered with signs of joy as disagreeable to behold as the content of the speech was to hear.
>
> But how can this be possible? How can you expect the comrades to believe in anything after that? How do you expect them to retain their confidence when you yourselves demoralize them![4]

After having failed to obtain a free tribune in the party press or the restoration of proportional representation in elections for the executive committee, the minority could offer

[4] Parti Socialiste, *Compte Rendu*, 50th National Congress, 1958.

little in the way of constructive solutions for the party's difficulties. After Defferre demonstrated his solidarity with the party leadership and his support for de Gaulle, the only possible course for the minority, as they saw it, was to leave the SFIO.

In creating the PSA they hoped to rally disaffected Socialists as well as Communists to a party free from bureaucratic domination and open to all currents of thought. The initial spurt in membership and the adherence of twenty-one former SFIO parliamentarians seemed to augur well for the new party. By 1959, however, when the PSA had reached a total membership of approximately 15,000, it ceased to grow. Later, after the PSA had been integrated into the Unified Socialist party, dissension and quarreling seriously affected recruitment and damaged its prestige. In part, the quarrels were the result of party democracy which allowed proportional representation of currents of thought at all levels of party organization. The variegated membership was unable to agree on so many occasions, however, that the profoundly democratic structure of the party hindered its effectiveness.

In spite of the vicissitudes of party action, in spite of a major schism and the growth of friction among party leaders, the SFIO survived the fall of the Fourth Republic, not unscathed, but vital enough to constitute the principal non-Communist leftist party in France. Those who expected the SFIO to collapse under the combined blows of Gaullism and internal dissension were deceived. Having salvaged its electoral following from the wreckage of the Fourth Republic, the SFIO was then confronted with the task of coping with an entirely new constitutional system and with the phenomenon of de Gaulle.

Assured of widespread local support because of its heavy representation in local government, safely ensconced in certain industrial departments such as Pas-de-Calais, Nord, and

Bouches-du-Rhône, the party assumed that, like the phoenix, it could rise again on the national level given a certain concatenation of circumstances—namely, the eventual disappearence of Gaullism along with the resolution of the Algerian problem. Thus many wished to see the party exert itself in order to retain its membership and enter into discussions with other democratic parties concerning regroupment, but delay radical changes in party doctrine or structure until the political situation was clarified. These measures were woven of the same cloth as Socialist strategy in the Fourth Republic in that they were essentially defensive. They were designed to prepare the party for the moment when the SFIO could once again play a key role in parliamentary politics.

Before the Second World War and for a time after the war, debate in the SFIO focused on questions of participation versus nonparticipation on and the proper role of the extraparliamentary party. After Guy Mollet acceded to the leadership in 1946, however, these questions became academic. In spite of this, during the last years of the Fourth Republic, there again arose within the party a nostalgia for the opposition, a feeling that the party was somehow betraying Socialist principles by continued participation in power. Although everyone paid obeisance to the revolutionary goals of the SFIO, party tradition and practice seemed to belie this belief. Yet there were some who took the belief seriously, or, rather, abstracted from it a basic differentiation between the party's day-to-day activity and its ultimate goals. Whereas the leadership glossed over the ambiguities of the Socialist ideology, the minority began to agitate for a real differentiation in the roles of the parliamentary and extraparliamentary parties. Having failed in their attempt, they left the party only to confront the problems posed by allowing freedom of expression to take precedence over the harsh necessity of making occasionally unpopular decisions.

When the party went into opposition in 1959, then, what remained was an amorphous doctrine, a sentiment of loyalty toward an aging leadership, possession of the mayor's seat in a number of small and large cities, and a tradition. Within the SFIO there seemed to be either confusion or outright apathy. Although Jules Moch, Roger Quilliot, and others exerted themselves to discuss and then draft the Fundamental Program, the fact that the elaboration of the Program gave rise to such little conflict and was passed in an atmosphere of consensus was testimony to the absence of an effective opposition to the Mollet leadership or to the party line. Perhaps one of the main reasons for this apparent consensus was simply that those who might have used the Program as a base from which to attack Mollet and demand basic reforms in the party had already left the party before or during September, 1958. Critics such as André Philip, Edouard Depreux, and Daniel Mayer —all of whom had been harshly critical of Socialist policies during the Algerian years of the Fourth Republic and of Mollet's leadership—had ended whatever real chance they might have had for reforming the SFIO by leaving, rather than waiting for the chance to turn the flank of the leadership when an opportune moment presented itself.

The inability of the Socialists to deal with the changed realities of the Fifth Republic's electoral and constitutional system was also demonstrated in 1962 when the party turned from the *Cartel des Non* on the first ballot to tacit cooperation with the Communists on the second. What was most remarkable about this maneuver was not necessarily that the party endorsed it ex post facto, but that a large part of the Socialist electorate seemed to follow the SFIO in its reasoning. For so long had the SFIO defined itself by what it was against—communism, fascism, clericalism—that it appeared as if both members and voters almost automatically responded to party pleas whenever some "menace," be it de Gaulle or the PCF or the right, threatened the Republic. Thus the SFIO found it relatively easy to agree on what it was against, but much less easy to agree on what positive steps it should take to remedy its steadily deteriorating situation.

In 1963, when the question of regrouping the parties came up, a difference of opinion seemed to be brewing between Mollet and his allies, and Defferre and his supporters. On the one hand, Mollet came down on the side of a "pure and tough party," a party that would advocate a radical transformation in the structure of society—but one to be achieved by peaceful, democratic, parliamentary means. Mollet defended this view by noting that even de Gaulle could enact "reformist" policies within the French context. Thus Mollet suggested a rather unspecific return to the revolutionary tradition of the SFIO—perhaps the only really specific point of his appeal was that closer relations between the SFIO and the PCF should be envisaged in the future. On the other hand, Defferre and others attempted to point out that revolutionary slogans were meaningless in contemporary France, not only because the basic political style had changed but, more important, because the SFIO had already demonstrated that it was above all a reformist, comprising and bargaining party whose revolutionary vocabulary was not taken seriously by anybody. Moreover, they pointed out that since basic doctrinal disagreement over such issues as *laïcité* or revolution had never prevented the SFIO from cooperating or collaborating with the Radicals, the MRP, or the Moderates in the past, there was no reason to assume these points of doctrine would or should constitute obstacles to future agreement. Quilliot in particular suggested that the SFIO might reach agreement with other democratic parties on specific policy questions and that interest groups, unions, and other voluntary organizations might also be brought into a discussion when elaborating a common program.[5]

Even Mollet's proposals for a return to Socialist revolutionary traditions must have sounded hollow to many members and certainly to many people who were not party members. It appeared that Mollet was merely attempting to prepare the party for closer relations with the PCF rather than actually taking a stand in favor of the radical theoretical and organizational reform that was implied by his notion of a *parti pur et dur*. For so long had every tactical and strategic move taken by the SFIO been justified in doctrinal terms that it had become second nature to party leaders to use this fashion of speaking.

At the 54th National Congress held in late May and early June, 1963, Mollet dropped from tenth to twenty-sixth place in the elections to the CD, while the first five places went to A. Laurent, Emile Muller, André Cluzeau, Kléber Loustau, and Maurice Pic, none of them particularly controversial figures, all of them current or former parliamentarians. Laurent, the symbol of party unity, moved from eleventh to first place. Obviously, most delegates preferred to vote for men who took no clear stand on the question of regrouping the parties or changing party structures.

Another significant development in the SFIO was the fact that a majority of the federation votes was held by the top four federations in 1966–1967. The number of federations which held a majority of votes at national congress and council meetings had steadily decreased since at least 1949 when the top fifteen held a majority. The top four in 1966–1967 were Bouches-du-Rhône, Pas-de-Calais, Nord, and Seine. Thus by 1967 not only was the party vote shrinking to within a few large departments, but the party membership was in-

[5] Roger Quilliot, "Rénovation et Regroupement," *La Revue Socialiste*, no. 161 (March, 1963), pp. 267–287.

creasingly being grouped within the large and powerful federations of the industrial north and the Mediterranean littoral (see Appendixes E.1 and E.2). If the party were to extend its influence and voting support something radical would have to be done in the near future, for the old method of contracting advantageous electoral alliances seemed to be of increasingly limited value.

The problem posed by the question of regrouping the parties was seen in different ways, however, depending upon one's view of the organizational health and stability of the SFIO. Moreover, there was still the sticky problem of determining the direction of such regrouping. Should a new unified party be constituted on the left? And, if so, with what parties should the SFIO consider merging? With the PSU? With the PCF? Or should the SFIO look to its right, toward its traditional parliamentary allies, the Radicals and perhaps the MRP? Or, rather, should a confederation of parties be attempted with gradual unification taking place in a number of stages? Or, finally, should the party merely attempt to elaborate closer ties with other sympathetic parties with a view toward electoral cooperation but little else?

The debate that began in the SFIO in the 1960's over the question of regrouping the parties and over organizational reform took place against a background of growing public disillusionment with, and a declining interest in, political parties. Late in 1960 the French Political Science Association held a round-table discussion on the subject of "depolitization." The individual reports and discussions were later collated and published in a volume entitled *La Dépolitisation.*[6] Although the general conclusion of the participants was that there had not been a general decline of interest in politics, as the word depolitization implied, still there had apparently

[6] Association Française de Science Politique, *La Dépolitisation: Mythe ou Réalité* (Paris, 1962).

been a clear decline in interest and participation in political parties and especially in the parties of the left. Moreover, the discussants noted, the style of participation also seemed to have undergone change since at least the Liberation. The discussants noted there had been not only a decline in militant activity but also a change in interest from party meetings toward parapolitical subjects and increased emphasis on the leading personalities in the life of the party.

One of the interesting results of the declining interest in political parties was the consequent increase in the prestige and influence of political clubs.[7] Particularly important in the politics of the French Socialist party during the period when Defferre was running for the SFIO presidential nomination, and then later during the campaign, were the *Club Jean Moulin*, the *Cercle Tocqueville*, the *Club des Jacobins*, *Citoyens 60*, and *Démocratie Nouvelle*. The April, 1964, convention of these and other clubs held at Vichy attracted 1,100 members from all over France. The *Club Jean Moulin* attracted academics like Georges Lavau, Maurice Duverger, and Georges Vedel, and men like José Bidegain, president of the *Centre des Jeunes Patrons*, and Pierre Gaudez, former president of the *Union Nationale des Etudiants Français*. The rising influence of the clubs on the left was due mainly to the inability of the non-Communist left to develop a coherent strategy in the face of Gaullist successes and to growing discontent among party members with the rigid structures of the traditional left-wing parties. The clubs were also fortunate in obtaining the membership of numerous high civil servants who, especially those in the *Club Jean Moulin*, thought they saw in the clubs a means for expressing their political opinions

[7] See Jean-André Faucher, *Les Clubs Politiques en France* (Paris, 1965). Also see section on "Les Forces Politiques en France," in *Revue Française de Science Politique*, XV, no. 1 (February, 1965), 103–13, and XV, no. 3 (June 1965), 555–569.

in the best way they knew how, without getting involved in the details and frustrations of party politics.

None of the major political clubs originally intended to replace the political parties on the non-Communist left. Their goals were generally to provide a forum for political discussion and publication for all those generally sympathetic to the club. According to one of the founders of the *Club Jean Moulin*, for example, the original aim of the club, founded on June 18, 1958, was to constitute a sort of "shadow Parliament, an Assembly . . . whose executive committee would correspond to a shadow cabinet." The only common viewpoint would be opposition to the regime.[8] With the formation of the *Fédération de la Gauche Démocrate et Socialiste*, however, a number of clubs, including *Club Jean Moulin* and *Citoyens 60*, joined the federation in one way or another. Of course, political clubs of the kind just mentioned should be differentiated from clubs like the *Cercles Jean Jaurès*—the former having been created independent of any political party and with nonpartisan intentions, the latter being an emanation of the SFIO, created and dominated by the party and devoted to extending its influence into sympathetic teaching and laic circles. Moreover, the nonpartisan independent clubs served as a channel of access for people interested in politics who otherwise would not have been able to participate in decision-making at high levels of the political hierarchy. The presence of people like Michel Crozier and jurists like René-William Thorp sitting side by side with people like Guy Mollet and François Mitterand on the executive committee of the FGDS testified to the variegated and flexible nature of the arrangement.[9] The integration of the clubs into the FGDS also allowed such former members of the SFIO as Alain Savary to participate in decision-making along

[8] *Le Monde*, letter from Francis Dumont, March 31, 1966.
[9] *Le Populaire*, June 30–July 1, 1966.

with Socialist leaders without having to return to the SFIO and face the impossible task of winning a seat on the CD in the face of the almost certain hostility of those members resentful of Savary's departure in 1958.

In the 1960's, the SFIO seemed to be on the verge of a profound evolution. Not only was an effort made to cope with the changed constitutional system of the Fifth Republic, but, internally, the party seemed to be ready to engage in the reformist-traditionalist battle that had occurred in other European Socialist parties in the postwar period.

Initially, however, as the presidential election began to loom in the background, the SFIO appeared unable to respond. In 1963 the party seemed to be governed by the same kind of strategy that had characterized its actions under the Fourth Republic, namely to seek the most advantageous electoral alliance possible. The discussions about regrouping the parties and the opening of the dialogue with the PCF have to be viewed in this light. There was no real evidence to suggest that party leaders—aside from Defferre and some of his allies such as Albert Gazier and Gérard Jaquet—were willing to examine the implications that a serious regrouping would have on the organization and doctrine of the SFIO. When the rumors about de Gaulle's resignation began to circulate in the early fall of 1963, the party seemed totally unprepared. Mollet was opposed to the presidential system, but the party was uncertain, and the country was interested in the "X" campaign. Thus, when Defferre and his supporters stepped into the breach they swept the party majority with them. The Defferre campaign for the SFIO nomination and his subsequent campaign for the presidency were conducted in a style unique in French politics—except perhaps for that of Mendès-France. For Defferre deliberately played down the major doctrinal points that distinguished the SFIO from the MRP or, indeed, from parties on the center-left in general. He did not make an issue of *laïcité*, and he deliberately attempted to elaborate a political program based on short-term policy commitments and grounded in reformist Socialist doctrine. In previous years the SFIO had never been loath to enter electoral or parliamentary alliances on the basis of a minimum program quite similar in its limited aims to the one advanced by Defferre; now, for the first time, Defferre attempted to use the program as the basis for a permanent alliance among the non-Communist parties of the left. Whereas the SFIO could always claim a distinction between its minimum and maximum programs by observing that the necessities of political life demanded compromises but that the existence of the party itself guaranteed that the maximum program would remain as an ideal against which day-to-day proposals and activities could be measured, Defferre's radical proposals seemed to many party members to threaten the essence of the party—and, therefore, to threaten the achievement of socialism itself.

The style of the Defferre campaign may throw some light on the debate over the "decline" or "end" of ideology in the West. Ideology usually refers to a comprehensive explanation of socioeconomic phenomena allowing for the formulation and prescription of solutions to socioeconomic problems. Thus it is both a world view and a program of action, the latter justified and explained by the former. It is interesting to note that the argument over ideology frequently uses political parties or party personalities as terms of reference. When it is claimed there has been a decline or end of ideology this usually means that something has disappeared from the political discourse of parties or party personalities.

But in examining the question it might be simpler and more enlightening to discard the word "ideology" and substitute two terms in its place: "doctrine" and "program." This does not do violence to the reality, for all political parties have some doctrinal or philosophical preconceptions that inform their action—and even the most pragmatic of parties, or the most pragmatic of party spokesmen, can provide some philosophical or doctrinal justification for action. In this case, it would be absurd to talk about the decline of doctrine, or of philosophy. But since it is safe to assume that most parties and most party spokesmen attempt to be consistent and that they would strive very hard indeed to justify program and actions in terms of a coherent framework of ideas and values, then to talk as if these justifications have disappeared or declined is to confuse the issue—for obviously they have not. They may be concealed, or the party spokesmen may be reticent or inarticulate, but they exist nonetheless. Mendès-France said, "To govern is to choose"; but in choosing one must justify. And it is the manner in which such justification takes place that differs from culture to culture, from country to country, and from political party to political party. Particularly on the left in Europe there has always been an elaborate doctrinal justification available to support most choices. Sometimes it is presented in a contentious or flamboyant style, as when terms like "*laïcité*" or "anticlerical" or "socialism" or "revolution" are used by a party like the SFIO; sometimes these terms may be avoided and the doctrine kept well hidden; sometimes the doctrine may even be unconscious. But this does not mean it is absent. Even the most reformist of Socialists can probably cite Marx, or Jaurès, or Léon Blum to prove the authentically Socialist nature of the moderate reforms he advocates. Indeed, during the Suez crisis Socialist spokesmen attempted to attack Nasser's nationalization of the Suez Canal on the basis of Marx's teachings. Thus the rhetoric of political discourse may be inflammatory or anodyne, but the world view certainly remains and there is still the link between this world view and the particular action or policy. The question is, therefore, not whether ideology does or does not inform the action or program but whether it is explicit or implicit, meant to arouse or sooth passions, to excite the party community by referring back to party traditions and doctrine, or to seduce a larger community which may be stranger to and offended by the language of the party community.

It is only in this context that Defferre's campaign can be understood. In a country where the language of political discourse on the left usually contains explicit reference to party doctrine or tradition, Defferre chose to avoid reliance on the traditional style of discourse in order to appeal to something broader than the party community. But in suggesting a re-examination of Socialist doctrine, and in proposing moderate reforms, he was not implying that the SFIO forsake its doctrine or that its policy proposals should no longer be informed by reference to this doctrine. To interpret Defferre as a harbinger of the decline of ideology in the SFIO is, therefore, to misconstrue the problem and to miss the point of his campaign.

The implications of the Defferre campaign for intraparty politics were also important. For a long time Defferre and his Bouches-du-Rhône federation could not be counted on as stable supporters of the party majority led by Pas-de-Calais and Nord. During 1957, especially, Defferre voted consistently against the majority on questions of party democracy and on the Algerian issue. At one point there had been some hope that Defferre would vote against supporting the Constitution of the Fifth Republic, thus providing an opening wedge for the minority faction led by Depreux, Mayer, Verdier, and others. But Defferre's swing to de Gaulle and the Fifth Republic temporarily obscured the fact that he and his federation were in basic opposition to Mollet and Laurent on substantive issues. As Defferre pointed out during the Congress of June, 1965, Bouches-du-Rhône was the only large federation that had increased its membership since the Liberation in a consistent fashion. He also noted that he had always been in favor of creating a great "French Labor party," and had been in favor of doing so during the Resistance but that, at the time, he was defeated by Daniel Mayer, who wanted to preserve the SFIO at all costs.

Once again, therefore, the debate in the SFIO revolved around issues as old as the party itself, although somewhat changed since the days of Jaurès and Guesde. Mollet and Laurent seemed to have made themselves the spokesmen for the revolutionary tradition of the party, while Defferre had become the spokesman for the reformers. But whereas in the days of Guesde and Jaurès the substantive issue of debate was the question of participation versus nonparticipation, in the Fifth Republic the issue was alliance with the left or with the center-left, whether to try to "reunite the workers' movement" or to work with the center. And implicit in the debate was the question of whether the SFIO should content itself with being a regional party unlikely to extend the borders of its support by its own efforts and therefore dependent on electoral or parliamentary alliances as a means for achieving national power, or whether the SFIO should make a concerted attempt to change both its vocabulary and its organization in the hopes of attracting new support and preparing the ground for a fusion with the neighbors to its right on the political spectrum.

The SFIO had become less, not more important in the French system after the Liberation. All parties found that interest groups, labor unions, and other independent organizations frequently preferred to negotiate directly with the administration or with government officials rather than to work through the largely ineffective political parties. Under the Fourth Republic, the moribund nature of the SFIO organization was hidden from view by the dominant role the party played in the National Assembly during much of the period from 1946 to 1958. With the coming of the Fifth Republic, of de Gaulle and the majority UNR, however, it soon became apparent that the SFIO organization was not functioning well in certain traditional areas of party activity. It did not recruit many new members, nor did it "educate" the new members in the ways of the party and in Socialist doctrine as it had done before the war. The functions of interest articulation and aggregation were performed to a certain degree by the party, but mainly at the national level rather than through local organizations.

The SFIO was a party in flux. It was certainly not a mass political party with a highly diversified and vital organization inspired by the energies of numerous devoted militants active in many areas of party and political life. But it was also not an amorphous electoral party which functioned solely during election periods, highly permeable and held together only by the members' ambition for political office or a low level of consensus on most elements in the party program. Formally the SFIO had the organizational structure and doctrine of a traditional working-class mass party; actually its shrinking membership was active only periodically and then, most important, at the top levels of the party organization. Although party doctrine and traditions were ancient, providing a strong cement for party cohesion, the rhetoric derived from this doctrine was frequently used in an emotional rather than a meaningful way.

Thus the French Socialist party was in search of a role. Its leaders seemed to realize that, unless the balance of power shifted away from the Gaullists, or the party was finally able to bridge the hitherto impossible gap that separated it from both the PCF to its left and the MRP to its right, it was probably doomed to play a minor role in French politics for quite some time.

The political realities of the Fourth and Fifth Republics never allowed the SFIO to make consistent decisions. Under the Fourth Republic, as a minority party during election periods and then in the National Assembly, the SFIO tried to win allies wherever it could. Of course the Socialists might have chosen perpetual opposition, as did the Communist party, but this choice had already been rejected under the Third Republic when the SFIO decided that the road to socialism was paved with piecemeal reforms, not with unsullied election programs. In the case of the 1962 legislative election, when Guy Mollet made his famous statement opening the way to a haphazard alliance between Socialists and Communists on the second ballot, the SFIO was severely criticized by its partners in the *Cartel des Non.* In a multiparty system, however, it is perfectly natural that parties near the middle of the political spectrum try to compromise their differences so as to increase their representation in the legislature. The frequent changes in alliance by the SFIO could be defended as the natural result of the highly temporary and limited nature of these alliances. They were not expected to last beyond the election, but simply to allow the parties involved to take advantage of the vagaries of the French election system so as to win adequate representation in the National Assembly.

Moreover, it is hard to see how shifting alliances could compromise party principles or goals—unless a consistent election strategy was part of the party doctrine—for party goals could only be achieved once the party had won some representation in the National Assembly. Furthermore, the Socialists, like other parties in 1958, were confused and divided about the nature and future of the system. In 1958, for example, the SFIO sought halfheartedly to carve out a place as the left-wing loyal opposition to de Gaulle, and it ran under the slogan, *Le Parti Socialiste dans l'Avant Garde de la Cinquième République.* In a burst of enthusiasm Guy Mollet predicted that the SFIO might win 150 seats in the new assembly. The party won 40.[10] By 1962, with de Gaulle interpreting and revising the Constitution so as to develop a strong presidential system, the Socialists and Communists concluded implicit alliances between the turns of the legislative election, with the PCF increasing from 10 to 41 seats and the Socialists from 40 to 64. By 1967, an explicit alliance was concluded between the Federation of the Democratic and Socialist Left (*Fédération de la Gauche Démocrate et Socialiste*) and the PCF, again to their mutual benefit as the Communists won 73 seats and the Federation 116, of which 76 were held by Socialists.

Party leaders often used phrases from the Marxist lexicon during their party meetings and referred to the "revolutionary" heritage and mission of the SFIO. But it was also true that this style of discourse was used more for sentimental and evocative reasons than for political purposes. In their public statements and actions, Socialist politicians avoided talking or acting in terms of orthodox ideological pretensions. Thus there were two vocabularies, one for internal, the other for external consumption. Internally, the SFIO was obviously bound by more than simple policy agreements, and so reference to Socialist traditions, symbols, and vocabulary served to reinforce party cohesion. It should be remembered that the SFIO had lost members steadily after the Liberation. It is likely that many new members were lukewarm in their attachment to party traditions and principles and as the years passed and the membership declined, those who remained were probably the most militant and committed of members. Thus it is perfectly understandable that a party increasingly dependent on hard-core members should use a vocabulary and refer to symbols that were foreign to the nonparty community. In addition, under the Fourth Republic there was little

[10] *L'Année Politique, 1958*, p. 140.

reason for the party to engage in the kind of revisionism most prominently illustrated in the SPD's acceptance of the Bad Godesburg program. In Germany, and in Great Britain as well, Socialist parties moderated the radical provisions in their programs and toned down revolutionary doctrine so as to appeal to the large uncommitted vote that held the balance of power in the middle of the political spectrum. This mass of uncommitted voters did not exist in France; at least it did not exist on the left. To have engaged in revisionism under the Fourth Republic might have lost the SFIO much of the support it had. The SFIO was hemmed in by the PCF on one side, and the MRP and Radical Socialists on the other. What the party might have gained in members and voters by moving to one side might have been lost on the other. It was natural, therefore, that the SFIO devote its energies to winning the votes of those already committed to the party or to recapturing those who had formerly voted Socialist. Rather than trying to elaborate a radical strategy for winning new votes from either the PCF or the MRP and Radical Socialists, the SFIO depended on the electoral alliance game to maintain its electoral positions.

It was only under the Fifth Republic, when a Gaullist majority party emerged from the amorphous right and the fulcrum of political power shifted to the presidential office that the SFIO was forced to consider new methods for expanding its power and influence. Although the elaboration and final acceptance of the 1962 Fundamental Program was a cautious attempt to eliminate some of the more objectionable and anachronistic features of party doctrine, most party leaders were aware of its anodyne nature. Moreover, some Socialist officials emphasized that the very distinctiveness of Socialist doctrine, the use of words like "revolution," "class struggle," and "socialism," was a source of attraction for the party serving to differentiate the SFIO from its neighbors to the right and left. In this sense then, one might make an unemotional, unsentimental *political* argument for the retention of some Marxist phraseology in SFIO doctrine. The widespread opposition in the SFIO to German-style revisionism was motivated not only by sentimental and emotional attachments to party doctrine and tradition but also by cold calculations of the probable political consequences that might follow upon stripping the SFIO of its distinctive doctrinal character. As Guy Mollet noted under the Fifth Republic, even the most reactionary mayors could, given government financial support, devote resources to social welfare programs, and de Gaulle himself supported many social and economic reform measures also favored by the SFIO.[11]

Despite a continued decline in members and voters, the SFIO had been able to survive the vicissitudes of postwar French politics so successfully that in 1967 it was the second largest party in France in terms of paid-up members, and one of the top parties in the National Assembly. In 1945, party membership stood at 335,705, while figures of paid-up members in 1964–1965 showed slightly less than 70,000 paid-up members. It is also true that the SFIO lost votes steadily from the first postwar election of October 21, 1945, its share dropping from about 23 per cent to between 12 per cent and 15 per cent in the elections held under the Fifth Republic. The number of Socialist deputies has also fluctuated since the Liberation; for example, in the first postwar elections the SFIO sent 139 deputies to the National Assembly, while by 1962 the number had declined to 40. In the 1967 elections, however, the party increased its representation in the parliament by almost 80 per cent by winning 76 seats. On the national scene, therefore, there has been an apparent decline in Socialist members, votes, and deputies if one uses the Liberation as the base

[11] *Le Populaire*, December 17, 1962.

point for comparison. But this is only half the picture, for it is necessary to plunge below the surface and estimate the concealed portion of the Socialist iceberg as it moves slowly through the troubled waters of French politics. In local politics, especially in comparison with its closest rival, the PCF, the SFIO has not fared too badly since the Liberation. In 1965, for example, the Socialists counted 40,029 municipal councillors—more than any other party. In cities with populations of 20,000 or more in 1965, the Socialists counted 975 municipal councillors, only 21 fewer than the 996 Communist municipal councillors in cities of the same size. In addition, in 1965, Socialist mayors headed 33 cities of populations of more than 30,000, with Communist mayors heading 34 cities of the same size. At the department level, in 1964, the SFIO outstripped the Radicals and the RGR, with 557 Socialist general councillors as compared with 410 for the Radicals.[12] These figures illuminate the fact that the SFIO has developed deep and extensive roots in French local politics over the years (see Appendix D.4). A party like the SFIO was therefore, not likely to be swept away by an electoral ill-wind that blew through France, and the possession of a large number of municipal or general councillor's seats and the numerous mayors' posts meant that party members and militants could develop ties in their cities and towns that might later help the SFIO in legislative elections. Moreover, in the case of a party like the SFIO where organizational and doctrinal traditions are fairly strong, the activities of local Socialist officials tend to reflect on the reputation of the party as a whole—although some French mayors claimed that voters remained loyal to the local party even when they opposed the SFIO's actions in the National Assembly.[13] The enormous number of local Socialist officials also provided the SFIO with a reserve army of experi-

[12] *Le Monde*, March 24, 1965.
[13] Interview with Socialist mayor, summer, 1966.

enced and energetic members available for a myriad of tasks. Thus the establishment of local and departmental committees of the FGDS in 1967 was facilitated by the presence of Socialist party members willing and able to build local organizational structures. Even if it is true that all parties in France have suffered from a general decline of interest in party politics during the postwar period, the activities of numerous Socialist officials in communes across France have helped to keep the party in the public eye.

The importance of the deep roots sunk in local politics by the SFIO has been discussed in previous chapters, but it is worth repeating in this context that the extensive political experience of Socialist party members, and especially of the elite, is one of the best reasons for assuming that, even if the SFIO should suffer major defeats on the national level, it will not be mortally wounded until its numerous mayors and municipal and general councillors have been turned out of office once and for all.

One criticism that has been leveled against the SFIO elite refers to its age. The SFIO has been called a "sclerotic" party —a term that refers both to the aging leadership and to the hardening of organizational arteries that prevents freer circulation of elites. The implied assumption of such criticism is that there is something wrong with age. But what? and why? Some people assume that old age and conservatism are synonymous—forgetting the large number of aging radicals who pass their days twitting their younger and frequently more cautious colleagues. Moreover, since the days of Michels, writers have noted that frequently the more democratic a political party's organization, the older its leaders. This is especially true of Socialist parties where sentiment and tradition are important factors of cohesion. Thus, in one sense, the continued reign of traditional Socialist leaders like Guy Mollet is testimony not only to the sentimentality of the members, but also to the democratic procedures of the organization. Moreover, it should be noted that the SFIO leadership was quite young in 1945, since the Liberation had provided an unnatural break in party organization opening up channels for younger leaders. These leaders certainly grew older in office, but since many of them were still in their middle and late fifties in the 1960's, it was natural for them to reject the implication that they had suffered any severe loss of vitality simply by virtue of their long tenure in power (See Appendix G.5).

The French Socialist party neither acted in a vacuum during the postwar period, nor were decisions made in terms of a North American or Anglo-Saxon scale of priorities. Rather, the SFIO acted in terms of party tradition and experience as interpreted by party members integrated into the French political culture and choosing within the French political context.

What were their priorities?

First, the SFIO always maintained that preservation of the republican form of government was a top priority, for, if the Republic fell, then the very basis for democratic socialism would be destroyed. As Guy Mollet put it: "The Socialists, democrats, have always been among the best defenders of their country. In order that France remain republican . . . in order that tomorrow it become Socialist it is necessary that France exist. The national interest is identical with Socialism."[14]

Second, party leaders all seemed agreed that the SFIO would have to remain a *Socialist* party. The definition of socialism was always open to controversy, of course, but even during the difficult years when Mollet was heading the government, both those who supported Mollet and those who

[14] *Le Populaire*, September 24, 1956.

opposed him in the party tried to prove that their position was best in keeping with Socialist traditions and principles.

Third, all party members bent their efforts toward winning as many seats as possible in the National Assembly, in local politics, and in the Senate.

Fourth, ever since the 1930's, the party had been willing to choose participation as opposed to nonparticipation when participation opened the possibility of passing Socialist-sponsored reforms.

Fifth, the SFIO emphasized recruiting new members and retaining old ones.

This is a rough order of priorities in that, during the postwar period at least, whenever it appeared that achieving one priority might necessarily exclude achieving another, the priority highest on the scale took precedence. Thus in June, 1958, when Guy Mollet and other party leaders were faced with the question of supporting de Gaulle as Prime Minister, and then later of supporting the Fifth Republic Constitutional referendum, despite the fact that de Gaulle had come to power by a rather devious route, Mollet and others defended their support by claiming that only de Gaulle could save Republican forms and preserve French democracy. In addition, despite the fact that the constant shift of Socialist electoral and parliamentary alliances offended many party members, it was apparent that the party majority preferred the perquisites of office and the possibility that increased representation in the National Assembly offered for the achievement of the Socialist program, to the loss of prestige the party might have suffered in the nation or the resignation of members who were offended by the party's seeming lack of consistency.

Viewing party activities in terms of this scale might also help to explain how the SFIO majority was able to master the party's minority opposition during the period after 1956. Not only did the Socialist leaders in government defend their Algerian policies in terms of Socialist doctrine, but by following a hard line in Algeria, by backing the use of military force to crush the rebellion, they were able to obtain the support or neutrality of a large number of deputies on the center right—especially from those in the Independent and Peasant group—on votes for Socialist economic and social reform legislation. The dissident Socialist minority, led by Edouard Depreux, André Philip, and others, demanded that the Socialists in government devote more resources to nonmilitary measures while also attempting to reach some negotiated agreement with the Algerian rebels. But since the center-right in 1956–1957 provided crucial voting support for the Mollet-led government, the Socialist minority decided not to risk alienating these supporters by liberalizing its Algerian policy. Thus the SFIO seemed to choose passage of domestic reform legislation over a more liberal policy toward Algeria during 1956–1957.

In the case of the 1962 Fundamental Program, it appears the party's resistance to revisionism was motivated not only by a much stronger devotion to "orthodox" Socialist doctrine than seemed to be the case with the German SPD, but was also reinforced by the belief that revisionism might blur the characteristic image that served to distinguish the SFIO from competing parties in France. This was further illustrated in 1965 during SFIO–MRP negotiations concerning a proposed federation when the MRP categorically refused to agree to the inclusion of the word "Socialist" in the title of the proposed federation. This was certainly not the main reason for the collapse of the negotiations, but the adamant refusal of the SFIO negotiators to drop the word "Socialist" from the title shows how seriously some SFIO leaders felt about maintaining the party's image. During those same negotiations, the SFIO and the MRP disagreed over future election alliances, with the MRP demanding and the SFIO refusing to include a prohibition against election alliances with the PCF in the federation charter. By the same token, the formation of the *Fédération de la Gauche Démocrate et Socialiste* was made all the easier since the inclusion of the Radicals and clubs neither threatened the "Socialist" nature of the new federation nor put any limitation on future electoral alliances.

One might even explain the "opportunism" of the SFIO (or of other parties, for that matter) as simply the rapid movement of a party up and down its scale of priorities as party leaders discover that decisions made in terms of one priority suddenly threaten other, more important, priorities. Thus the switch in the 1962 legislative elections from alliance with the center in the *Cartel des Non* to implicit electoral alliances with the Communists was defended by Guy Mollet when he realized that an increase in the number of UNR-UDT seats (which might have occurred had the SFIO remained true to the spirit of the agreement) might threaten the very existence of the Republic, while agreement with the Communists might well preserve the Republic by reducing the size of the UNR representation. One might also claim the SFIO changed alliances in midstream simply because it became apparent that the party might lose heavily without Communist support. In this case, so long as changing alliances did not threaten other, higher priorities, the SFIO was acting consistently within its own frame of values.

In all aspects of party activity—in its structure, its style of decision-making, its view of authority—the SFIO changed very little during the Fourth Republic and the first few years of the Fifth Republic simply because, given Socialist priorities and the French context, there was little reason to change. Unlike Socialist parties in stable two- or three-party systems, the French Socialists could expect little from organizational or doctrinal reform. All parties were losing members during the

Fourth Republic, and the SFIO had little reason to expect that it would find a simple solution to a problem that was afflicting other French parties. In addition, the loss of members and voters may have looked bad on paper, but party representation in the National Assembly was increased or decreased almost as much by the ability of party leaders to conclude shrewd and profitable election alliances as by the number of votes the party won in each election (from 1951 to 1956, the SFIO lost approximately half a million votes, but dropped only 8 seats in the National Assembly, while from 1958 to 1962 the party lost 800,000 votes and increased its representation from 40 to 64 seats). In the National Assembly during the period of a Socialist-led government from February, 1956, to May, 1957, the Socialists put through a number of reform programs (increases in old-age pensions, extension of paid vacations, agricultural reform bills) well in keeping with Socialists traditions, while their hard-line policy of military repression in Algeria kept the support of the center. As a minority party, the SFIO would have faced a herculean task had it tried to win Assembly support for a more conciliatory policy toward the Algerian FLN in the early stages of the rebellion—although there were some who felt that it was only in the early years of the rebellion that a French government might have reached some arrangement with the rebels prior to a hardening of policy lines on both sides.

In any case, it is no wonder that it first took the decline of the National Assembly in the Fifth Republic, and then the formalization of the change from a parliamentary to a presidential system in the 1962 referendum, to shock the party into action. Under the Fourth Republic most party values could be preserved without doing very much more than maintaining party positions and acting according to the traditional scale of priorities. Under the Fifth Republic's strong presidential system the old priorities seemed somewhat beside the point. The

Republic seemed secure after 1962 and the "socialism" of the SFIO was never really put in jeopardy, while the number of seats won in the National Assembly, election alliances and the question of participation, all seemed to pale beside the simple fact that the SFIO, like the other opposition parties, seemed doomed to play a minority role unless some new and radical strategy could be elaborated to reduce the powers of the presidency or somehow unify the left against the overwhelming weight of the Gaullists.

Fidelity to party doctrine, suspicion about the stability of the political system, satisfaction with the local positions of power occupied by party members, and sentimental attachment to party leaders and organization all militated against change in the SFIO. Those who opposed change in the party did so in the belief that the presidential system and the presence of the Gaullist majority in the legislature were temporary deviations from the normal condition of French politics where a multiplicity of parties competed and compromised in an all-powerful legislature. Those who tried to lead the party toward doctrinal and organizational reform tended to view the presidential system and the phenomenon (if not the political coloration) of a majority party with widespread electoral support as responding to the real needs of the French electorate and as structurally appropriate developments in a political system badly in need of modernization. Thus those who opposed and those who supported change in the party both based their opinions on hypotheses about the future of the French political system. But because it is always difficult to define what is "normal" or "permanent" in a political system as unstable as that of France, equally compelling arguments could be advanced by both sides. Thus the French Socialist party was a party in search of a role, a party torn by debate over a question which can only be answered by history.

Postscript, 1969

A Party Metamorphosed

"The Socialist party is dead, long live the Socialist party." So might have been the cry on July 12, 1969, when the SFIO, the *Parti Socialiste–Section Française de l'Internationale Ouvrière*, immolated itself at a party congress to be reborn once again simply as the *Parti Socialiste*, the Socialist party. The new party is composed of the former SFIO and of elements from a number of French political clubs. Absent from the two founding meetings in May and July, however, was the largest federation of French political clubs, the *Convention des Institutions Républicaines*, the CIR.

The founding congresses were the conclusion of more than three years of confused wrangling and sudden changes of fortune on the French non-Communist left. The reason for this confusion must be sought in the period following the withdrawal of Gaston Defferre from the 1965 presidential race. Immediately after Defferre withdrew, Guy Mollet was able to swing the SFIO to the support of François Mitterand, who declared his candidacy for the race. At the same time the SFIO decided to enter a new political party federation called the *Fédération de la Gauche Démocrate et Socialiste*, the FGDS. Composed of elements from the Radical party, the

CIR, and the SFIO, the new federation was intended to widen the appeal of the non-Communist left and to symbolize the desire of its members for renovation of the party system. The preamble to the charter of the FGDS stated, "This Federation is considered a step toward the goal of a Socialist Democratic Federation of a new type, corresponding to the needs of our time."

With Mollet's assent, and presided over by Mitterand, the Federation concluded an election alliance with the French Communist party for the 1965 presidential election. When Mitterand forced de Gaulle to a second ballot during the election, finally winning 45 per cent of the votes cast on the second ballot, the Federation partners were encouraged. Based on its showing during the presidential election, the Federation again concluded an election alliance with the Communist party for the 1967 legislative election. Once again the alliance was a resounding success, as the Federation won 18 per cent of the vote, sending 116 deputies to the National Assembly, including 76 Socialists. But then, little more than a year later, disaster struck. First came the student revolt and general strike in the spring of 1968, followed by the disastrous legislative election of June, 1968, when, despite the election alliance with the Communist party, the Federation lost half its seats, dropping to 57 seats in the Assembly, including 42 Socialists. Within the Federation, the decline of the SFIO continued. In 1967 the SFIO received 10.6 per cent of the votes cast, in 1968 8.4 per cent. The electoral fortunes of the SFIO had never been lower.

The summer of 1968 also brought with it a sharp decline in the prestige of Mitterand. The turning point in Mitterand's career came on May 28, 1968. On that day, at the height of the student revolt and the general strike, Mitterand held a maladroit press conference whose central theme was based on the highly questionable assumption that de Gaulle would be forced to resign from the presidency because of his inability to handle the crisis. Analyzing the situation in France, Mitterand drew some unfortunate parallels with the chaotic days of 1944, then went on to suggest that after de Gaulle resigned, the interim president appoint himself or Mendès-France to head a "provisory" government. Then Mitterand peremptorily announced his candidacy for the presidential election. But the irony was that de Gaulle had not in fact resigned and did not resign until a year later. Thus Mitterand's statements about assuming the leadership of the government, his analogizing 1944 with 1968, and his talk about a provisory government were used to great effect by the Gaullists who pointed out that Mitterand's statement implied a willingness to use illegal means in order to come to power. Even worse, Mitterand had not bothered to discuss his statement with the other leaders of the Federation prior to holding the news conference.

After the June, 1968, election debacle, therefore, many Socialist deputies tried to pin part of the blame for the decline in seats on Mitterand, and some deputies suggested that Mitterand resign from the presidency of the Federation. Since Mitterand also symbolized the new policy of election cooperation with the Communists, he also became the target of anti-Communist Socialists who added their voices to others who saw in him one of the leading personalities dedicated to the dismantlement of the "vielle maison."

If the events of the spring and summer of 1968 dealt a severe blow to the unity of the Federation, the surprising defeat of de Gaulle's referendum on April 28, 1969, followed by his resignation, created chaos in the ranks of the Federation. The Federation had scheduled a congress for early May when unification of the Federation partners in a new party was to take place. Before any of the Federation partners had a chance to react to de Gaulle's resignation, however, and to discuss the effect this might have on the creation of the new party, Gaston Defferre declared his willingness to run for the presidency as the candidate of the new party. Although the Federation's parliamentary group approved, followed almost immediately by the executive committee of the SFIO, some party leaders including Guy Mollet expressed grave reservations about Defferre's move. Defferre's quick action put the SFIO and the Federation in a very awkward position and also prejudiced the freedom of action of the new party which, at the moment of its birth, was to be faced with nominating a presidential candidate. Moreover, since the Communist party had always been hostile toward Defferre, it was immediately apparent that if the new party did in fact endorse Defferre's candidacy, an election alliance with the PCF would be extremely difficult to achieve. Finally, Defferre's declaration led the Federation leaders to move up the scheduled founding congress of the new party from May 9–11 as originally planned, to May 4–6. But the CIR had scheduled its own congress during that first week in May, and Claude Estier, secretary of the CIR, protested to Pierre Mauroy of the Federation that the Defferre candidacy and the rescheduling of the meeting simply confronted the CIR with a *fait accompli.*

With the stage set for comedy, the first meeting of the new party held in Alfortville degenerated into farce. Called for the purpose of founding the new party and to decide on Defferre's candidacy, the meeting was so disorganized that at one point when the delegates had apparently voted for a motion which would have denied the party's endorsement to Defferre, a second vote had to be called to reverse the original decision. When Defferre was finally nominated it was not unanimously, as in 1963, but by a two to one margin.

The subsequent resounding defeat of Defferre in the presidential election certainly helped to diminish his influence within the new party, although his presence, like that of Mollet, at the head of a powerful federation still gives him an important power base within the party. In any case, the second founding congress of the new party was held July 11–13,

1969. With the CIR still refusing to attend, the new party unanimously decided to call itself the Socialist party. It also voted a motion on strategy and orientation, chose an executive committee, a bureau, and a first secretary, Alain Savary. For the first time in more than twenty years Guy Mollet was absent from all the executive organs.

Principles

At the July, 1969, meetings, the new Socialist party voted by a two-thirds majority for a motion which was both a condemnation of the past and a commitment for the future. In the first part of the motion the party rejected the strategy of the SFIO as it had evolved during the postwar period. In the past, the SFIO had justified participation in government on a number of grounds, but "defense of the Republic" and the desirability of passing Socialist-sponsored reform legislation were two of the most favored excuses. The 1969 motion, however, declared quite explicitly, "Outside of exceptional cases when this tactic is justified, participation in power by the Socialist party is conceivable only to the degree that it helps advance the country toward socialism. This excludes any alliance with the political representatives of capitalism, including the search for a centrist combination." This, of course, referred to the fact that the SFIO had rarely hesitated to form a coalition government with elements from the center when it suited its purposes.

This rejection of alliance with the center was also extended to election strategy. The motion stated, "In order to avert the dangers of opportunism, the party must equip itself with a rigorous strategy and subordinate itself to the decisions that it makes. . . . The union of the left constitutes the normal axis of Socialist strategy." Reorientation toward the left was also confirmed by the statement that the party should enter into a "public debate with the Communist party concerning the modalities of the fight against capitalist forces, the roads to socialism, and the foundations of socialist society." The dialogue would be intended to help lay the basis for a policy agreement.

This motion was intended to reorder the traditional priorities of the SFIO. In the past, questions of election strategy and government participation had been decided mainly on the basis of whether or not the SFIO would thereby increase its representation in the National Assembly. By reversing the order of priorities, so that the alliance on the left must now take precedence over other considerations, the new party has definitely broken with previous habits. A reorientation of this kind also means the new party will have to engage in a much more serious quest for new recruits than did the SFIO. Under the Fourth Republic and early in the Fifth, the search for new members in the SFIO was not successful for two main reasons. First, the organizational rigidity and doctrinal simplicity of the party repelled many potential recruits, especially young people. Second, since the party leadership knew that the SFIO's electoral fortunes were governed more by the skillful conclusion of election alliances than by the number of party members, there was no real urgency in the task of recruiting new members or retaining old ones. But if the new party remains faithful to its declared intention of searching for union on the left, then prudence would demand that it be in as strong a position as possible for negotiations with the much larger and more powerful Communist party. This will require a massive effort aimed not only at recruiting new members (as well as keeping some of the older Socialists who might now be tempted to abandon the new party) but also at winning the adherence of the CIR and the Unified Socialist party, the PSU.

The second part of the motion voted at the July meeting was unanimously approved. Entitled a "Socialist Plan of Action," it dealt with principles, with the characteristics of capitalism and collectivism, and with the Socialists and Europe.

In the part devoted to principles the motion simply stated the party's desire to reduce to "the strict minimum compatible with social efficiency all inequalities of power, wealth and dignity, and, in the first place, the inequalities transmitted by ignorance." Emphasizing also the need to give priority to "collective social needs," the motion deliberately avoided any mention of the means that might be used to achieve these goals. The section on capitalism admits that in the developed countries capitalism has attained a high degree of "efficiency and complexity," while taking account of the fact that if the Socialists should arrive in power great skill would be required to make necessary reforms while ensuring continued stability.

The motion is also interesting because it sets forth an incremental approach to the creation of a Socialist system. Thus the motion states that a sudden change in the socioeconomic system might well lead to a decline in the economy and a lowering in the standard of living. This is something few people would consider to be an acceptable price for the creation of Socialism. Thus the motion speaks of changing the basis of economic power in the system without at the same time seriously affecting its productive or distributive capacities. In addition, it is interesting that the language of class and class conflict has completely disappeared to be replaced with a vocabulary that simply speaks of "inequalities" of various kinds, thereby freeing the party from identification with any one socioeconomic group while at the same time implying that society is divided along lines other than class.

A New Party?

How "new" is the new party? At both founding congresses of the new party, observers remarked on the number of young people present, a rare occurrence at SFIO meetings. At the May meeting the treasurer, Victor Provo of the SFIO, stated that the new party counted 87,654 members. But two months later at the July meeting he noted that the party had

74,230 members. Whether there had been a drastic decline over the two months because of Defferre's crushing defeat, or whether the marked difference was due simply to difficulties in keeping track of the members in the still nascent party organization, is unclear. Of the sixty members of the new party's executive committee, twenty-eight were newcomers in the sense of not having ever been previously elected to the committee, but of these twenty-eight, at least five were current or former members of the SFIO. Even the newly elected first secretary, Alain Savary, had been a member of the Guy Mollet government, but had resigned from the government over the Ben Bella affair, and then had left the SFIO to join the short-lived *Parti Socialiste Autonome*.

In one sense, therefore, the creation of the new party is more a regrouping than a renovation or rejuvenation of the non-Communist left. In another sense, in terms of doctrine, strategy, and organization, the new party seems much more clearly oriented toward the left than was the SFIO. This orientation takes the form of a willingness to deepen and widen the scope of discussion with the PCF. It is also apparent in the explicit condemnation of the SFIO's opportunism and the tough line the new party is taking on the question of participation.

In the past, the secret to understanding the SFIO lay in understanding its organization. This will be equally true of the new party. Although the exact form its organization will take will not be clear for some time to come, unless some radically new method is found for counting and weighing votes, it would appear that the large party federations will continue to be dominant. As in the past these federations are Pas-de-Calais, headed by Guy Mollet; Nord, headed now by Pierre Mauroy; and Gaston Defferre's Bouches-du-Rhône. Of the three, the first two are favorable toward an opening to the left, while Defferre is still very reserved in his attitude toward the Communist party. Mauroy was one of the founders of the highly successful Léo Lagrange clubs, and has also been the head of CEDEP (*Centre National d'Etudes et de Promotion*) an organization of political clubs within the federation. Mauroy is sympathetic to the demands of the younger members of the SFIO and the Federation, and many expected him to become the leader of the new party. Although he lost to Alain Savary by one vote in the leadership election he will continue to play a vital role in the party both because of his leadership of the Federation of Nord as well as his skill in discerning and responding to the needs of the younger members of the SFIO.

A party in search of a role is also a party struggling for survival. There is nothing in law or nature that says that a political party is eternal, although the history of Western Europe does indicate that Socialist parties are tenacious and long-lived. One of the prerequisites for survival, however, is the willingness to change, and to change in the right direction. It is not enough for a political party to alter its doctrine, organization, or election strategy if the party loses seats in the legislature and is unable to recruit new members. Although there have been party members who resisted almost any changes, the problem the Socialists faced was to correctly estimate the future pattern of French politics and to make the best changes in view of their assessment.

The difficulty here, however, is that the French political system has been notoriously unstable. Thus it is quite understandable that the party clung to traditional patterns of behavior and thought during the postwar period. Measuring success in terms of the number of elected local and national offices the party held, and balancing that reality against the very grave risks the party would run if it undertook serious reforms, the party majority almost always chose to avoid adventure.

Paradoxically, however, the party began to make serious changes in the Fifth Republic because two conditions held.

First, the French political system was more stable under the Fifth Republic than at any time since the postwar period. The resignation of de Gaulle and Pompidou's accession to the presidency took place in an atmosphere of calm, bordering on indifference. The apparent stability of the presidential system, therefore, has meant that discussions about the future of the SFIO were not complicated and exacerbated by differing estimates of the future of the French political system. In this sense, those in the SFIO who might otherwise have desperately clung to traditional forms as security in a rapidly changing situation could no longer claim that the unpredictability of the system increased the risks involved in reforming the party. Also, the legislative elections of 1968 and the presidential election of 1969 demonstrated more sharply than ever before that the SFIO had declined to minor-party status.

Thus, in the spring and summer of 1969 a new Socialist party emerged from the SFIO. The leaders of the new party, both those who came from the SFIO and those who have risen through the clubs, are obviously interested in working serious changes in all aspects of party activity. In the long run, however, their enterprise will succeed or fail only to the extent that they can revitalize the appeal of socialism in France. No amount of organizational reform or strategic ingenuity will preserve a political party that has ceased to kindle the fires of political passion. The SFIO survived as long as it did because its doctrine, however denatured, still evoked the loyalties and energies of Frenchmen. The thousands of locally elected Socialist officials not only reflected these loyalties, but helped to keep them alive. But the electoral decline of the SFIO over the years was a sign of its shrinking support. Parties may continue to function long after the heat has dissipated from the crucible where they were forged. Lacking this generative heat, however, they grow cold and rigid, and eventually they die. The creation of the new Socialist party is an attempt to rekindle the dying flames of French socialism.

Appendix A

The Voting Population

1. Characteristics of the voting population in 1956

Status	PCF (%)	SFIO (%)	Radials RGR (%)	MRP (%)	Independ- ents (%)	Voting Popula- tion (%)
Sex						
Men	49	65	58	38	49	47.2
Women	51	35	42	62	51	52.8
Age						
21–29	17	8	10	9	6	19.0
30–44	21	29	21	30	26	27.5
45–54	26	24	21	24	25	19.6
55–64	22	20	26	19	16	16.6
65 and older	14	19	22	18	27	17.3
City or town						
Under 2,000	51	26	34	32	40	37.4
2,000–4,999	8	14	19	19	15	12.8
5,000–19,999	22	26	13	16	15	16.4
20,000–99,999	17	15	20	24	12	16.4
100,000 and over	2	19	14	9	18	17.0

Education						
None	0	0	0	0	0	
Primary	86	78	68	70	70	79
Advanced primary	7	14	19	18	13	
Incomplete secondary	5	3	6	4	4	
Baccalaureate						16
(completed secondary)	2	3	1	4	6	
College or university	0	2	6	4	7	5
Occupation						
Farmers	0	4	7	6	19	22.5
Agricultural laborers	5	4	1	1	3	
Executives and professionals	3	3	8	6	13	13.7
Self-employed	7	7	13	10	18	
White-collar workers	17	23	23	20	11	13.4
Blue-collar workers	49	39	28	31	16	35.2
Retired and *rentiers*	19	20	20	26	20	15.2

Source: Sondages, 1960, no. 4, p. 18.

2. Characteristics of the voting population in 1958

Status	PCF (%)	SFIO (%)	MRP (%)	UNR (%)	Independents (%)	Voting Population (%)
Sex						
Men	51	55	32	45	40	47
Women	49	45	68	55	60	53
Age						
21–29	23	11	21	12	10	13
30–44	17	30	18	36	21	29
45–54	20	23	32	17	28	22
55–64	17	17	14	14	13	17
65 and older	23	17	14	20	28	19
City or town						
Under 2,000	51	26	36	36	41	38
2,000–5,000	6	7	28	12	2	13
5,000–20,000	26	22	11	17	7	17
20,000–99,999	14	28	18	13	29	15
100,000 and over	3	17	7	22	21	16
Education						
None	3	1	3	3	3	2
Primary	83	71	61	68	74	71
Advanced primary	5	20	21	13	9	13
Baccalaureat (completed secondary)	9	7	14	11	9	9
College or university	0	0	0	5	5	5

Occupation						
Farmers	0	4	7	5	14	8
Agricultural laborers	6	0	4	1	1	2
Executives and professionals	6	3	7	7	12	7
Self-employed	8	4	0	17	14	15
White-collar workers	20	29	36	20	17	19
Blue-collar workers	43	35	25	30	28	29
Retired and *rentiers*	17	25	21	19	14	20

Source: Elections, 1958, p. 158.

3. Characteristics of the voting population in 1962

Status	PCF (%)	PSU (%)	SFIO (%)	Radical Social-ist (%)	MRP (%)	UNR-UDT (%)	Independ-ents (%)	Absten-tions (%)	Voting Popula-tion (%)
Sex									
Men	65	85	58	60	50	49	51	35	48
Women	35	15	42	40	50	51	49	65	52
Age									
21–34	35	35	26	21	32	28	26	38	31
35–49	31	27	32	26	35	24	30	25	26
50–64	24	31	27	28	20	28	29	21	26
65 and older	10	8	15	24	12	20	15	16	17
City or town									
Under 2,000	40	30	39	57	51	41	48	37	37
2,000–4,999	11	10	10	15	17	10	13	11	13
5,000–19,999	8	7	16	2	9	10	10	15	17
20,000–99,999	18	7	10	12	17	14	12	20	16
100,000 and over	18	45	23	12	5	23	16	15	17
Education									
None	2	0	0	0	0	1	1	3	
Primary	77	42	70	71	70	59	53	62	70
Advanced primary	5	19	10	7	8	13	10	7	
Technical, commercial	9	12	8	3	10	7	9	12	
Secondary	4	12	9	15	8	14	18	11	26
College or university	**3**	**15**	**3**	**2**	**4**	**6**	**9**	**5**	**4**

Occupation							
Farmers	5	17	22	16	13	21	9	23
Executives and professionals	3	2	2	3	4	9	6	4
Self-employed	3	4	19	11	8	8	5	9
White-collar workers	13	18	10	13	16	13	16	14
Blue-collar workers	38	20	12	20	15	9	15	35
Manual laborers	13	7	9	6	6	7	10	
Retired	7	15	13	7	17	14	10	15
Housewives	18	17	13	24	21	19	29	

Source: Elections, 1962, pp. 230, 233, 239.

Appendix B
Votes on Questions of Confidence, 1956

1. October 25, 1956, ballot number 254, question of confidence on government's general policy

Party	For	Against	Abstain
SFIO	99	—	1
PCF	—	140	9
Independent and Peasant	66	—	16
Others	165	—	22
Total	330	140	48

2. December 10, 1956, ballot number 362, question of confidence on a government finance bill.

Party	For	Against	Abstain
SFIO	84	—	16
PCF	—	133	—
Independent and Peasant	31	8	38
Others	127	52	79
Total	242	193	133

Appendix C

Votes of the Various Parties in the 1956 and 1958 Legislative Elections in the Department of Ardennes

Parties	1956	1958
Republican Front (SFIO, Radicals, etc.)	46,463	
PCF	38,252	
MRP	20,711	
Independents, Peasants, and Social Republicans	14,881	
Poujadists	13,320	
UNR		30,030
Independents		25,575
PCF		24,023
MRP		18,133
SFIO		17,036
PSA (Desson)		7,219
Radical Socialists		4,774
UGS-UFD		2,751
Registered voters	164,654	166,616
Votes cast	138,539	113,143
Valid votes	135,442	127,966

Appendix D
Socialist Party Membership and Election Results

1. Socialist party membership from 1945 to 1966

Year	Membership	Year	Membership
1945	335,705	1955	91,062
1946	354,878	1956	95,946
1947	278,762	1957	96,401
1948	131,621	1958	84,834
1949	99,664	1959	83,260
1950	98,141	1960	78,721
1951	95,322	1961–1962	77,683
1952	82,945	1963–1964	73,996
1953	84,379	1965–1966	69,968
1954	88,106		

Source: Figures from 1945 and 1946 obtained from M. Duverger, *Political Parties*, p. 68. Figures from 1947 through 1966 obtained from reports of annual congresses of SFIO.

After 1961, the party held congresses every two years and membership figures were averaged over the two-year period.

2. *SFIO vote in the legislative elections of 1956, 1958, 1962, and 1967*

	1956	*1958*	*1962*	*1967*
Number of seats contested	527	423	365	211
Seats contested as a percentage of total number of seats	96.8%	90.9%	70%	44.9%
Registered voters in districts where party presented candidates	25,988,559	25,549,028	19,460,915	13,167,518
Registered voters in districts where party presented candidates as a percentage of total registered voters	97%	90.1%	70%	46.54%
First ballot				
Total vote received by SFIO	3,247,431	3,193,786	2,298,729	2,425,773
SFIO vote as a percentage of total registered voters	12.1%	11.7%	8.03%	8.57%
SFIO vote as a percentage of all votes cast	14.8%	15.5%	12.54%	10.59%
Registered vote where party presented candidates	20,985,074	15,579,055	12,661,923	11,415,801
SFIO vote as a percentage of number of registered voters in districts where party presented candidates	12.4%	13%	11.8%	18.42%
SFIO vote as a percentage of all votes cast in districts where party presented candidates	15%	20.3%	18.3%	21.2%
Second ballot				
Total vote received by SFIO	—	2,574,606	2,264,011	2,763,725
SFIO vote as a percentage of all votes cast	—	13.8%	14.83%	14.8%
Number of Socialist deputies elected	93	40	64	76

3. *Composition of the 1956 National Assembly*

Communists	150
Communist group (144)	
Group of Republican progressives (*apparenté* to Communist group (5)	
Other *apparenté* (1)	
Socialists, total	95
Radical Republicans and Radical Socialists	58
Radical Republican and Radical Socialist group (54)	
Apparenté (4)	
UDSR-RDA	19
UDSR-RDA group (18)	
Apparenté (1)	
MRP	83
MRP group (70)	
Apparenté (3)	
Group of Overseas Independents (10)	
Social Republicans	21
Social Republican group (20)	
Apparenté (1)	
RGR and Republican Centrists	14
RGR and Republican Center group (10)	
Apparenté (4)	
Independents and Peasant groups	95
Independents and Peasants of Social Action (80)	
Apparenté (3)	
Peasant Group (12)	
UFF	52
UFF group (Poujadists) (51)	
Apparenté (1)	
Deputies not belonging to any group	7
Deputies not authorized to sit	2
Unfilled seats (Algerian departments)	32
Total membership	596

4. *The SFIO in local politics*

Year	No.	% of total party membership
Socialist municipal councillors elected:		
1947	66,548	23
1949		66
1953	58,772	70
1959	52,145	62
1962		67
1965	40,029	57
Socialist municipal councillors elected in cities of 20,000 or more inhabitants:		
1958	984	
1965	975	
Socialist mayors elected in cities of 30,000–99,999 inhabitants:		
1959	41	
1965	33	
Socialist mayors elected in cities of 100,000 or more inhabitants:		
1959	12	
1965	8	

Appendix E

Socialist Federations

*1. Top fifteen federations ranked by voting strength and majority support from 1949 to 1967**

Federation	1949	1950	1951	1952	1953	1954	1955	1956	1957	1958	1959	1960	1961	1963	1965	1967
Nord	1	1	1	1	1	1	1	1	1	1	1	1	1	3	3	3
Pas-de-Calais	2	2	2	2	2	2	2	2	2	2	2	2	2	2	2	2
Seine	3	3	3	5	4	3	4	4	4	4	4	4	4	4	4	4
Bouches-du Rhône	4	5	4	4	3	3	3	3	3	3	3	3	3	1	1	1
Haute-Vienne	5	6	6	6	6	5	5	5	6	8	7	5	5	5	7	8
Seine-et-Oise	6	4	7	7	7	6	6	6	8	7	8	10	8	9	—	—
Hérault	6	8	—	—	—	8	—	—	—	10	—	—	—	—	10	10
Dordogne	7	—	9	10	—	—	—	—	—	—	—	—	—	—	—	—
Aude	8	—	—	—	—	9	—	—	10	—	10	8	6	7	6	5
Senegal†	9	7	5	3	5	—	7	7								
Landes	10	—	—	—	—	—	—	—	—	—	—	—	—	—	—	—
Gard	—	9	10	8	9	10	9	10	9	—	—	—	10	—	—	—
Gironde	—	—	8	9	10	—	10	8	7	6	6	7	10	10	9	7
Haute-Garonne	—	10	—	—	8	7	8	9	5	5	5	6	7	6	5	6
Var	—	—	—	—	—	—	—	—	—	9	9	9	9	8	8	9
No. of federations whose total vote constituted a majority	15	11	12	10	10	10	12	8	10	10	8	7	7	6	5	5

* After 1961 congresses met once every two years instead of annually.
† Senegal was no longer represented at party meetings when it gained its independence in 1956.

2. *Top socialist federations by vote and rank, 1949–1967*

Federation	1949	1950	1951	1952	1953	1954	1955	1956	1957	1958	1959	1960	1961	1963	1965	1967
Nord																
Vote	293	428	391	438	377	399	409	408	409	429	461	443	419	409	387	350
Rank	1	1	1	1	1	1	1	1	1	1	1	1	1	3	3	3
Pas-de-Calais																
Vote	201	355	344	344	374	371	378	328	398	419	434	434	411	415	418	424
Rank	2	2	2	2	2	2	2	2	2	2	2	2	2	2	2	2
Seine																
Vote	149	223	225	224	229	246	249	254	270	286	283	221	228	250	204	121
Rank	3	3	3	5	4	3	4	4	4	4	4	4	4	4	4	4
Bouches-du-Rhône																
Vote	123	132	221	230	234	246	302	336	347	366	391	374	376	419	470	465
Rank	4	5	4	4	3	3	3	3	3	3	3	3	3	1	1	1
Votes of Nord and Pas-de-Calais as percentage of majority vote	.33	.41	.36	.39	.44	.44	.43	.39	.41	.42	.41	.51	.48	.50	.51	.53

Appendix F
Socialist Deputies

1. Political experience of Socialist deputies in 1956, 1958, 1962, and 1967

Position	1956	1958	1962	1967
At time of election:				
Mayor of city with under 20,000 inhabitants	19	16	25	30
Mayor of city with 20,000–39,999 inhabitants	6	8	11	14
Mayor of city with 40,000–59,999 inhabitants	2	4	6	7
Mayor of city with 60,000–79,999 inhabitants	1	0	1	2
Mayor of city with 80,000–99,999 inhabitants	1	0	0	0
Mayor of city with 100,000–119,999 inhabitants	3	1	1	0
Mayor of city with 120,000–139,999 inhabitants	0	1	0	1
Mayor of city with 140,000 or more inhabitants	1	0	2	1
Total	33	30	46	55
Total number of Socialist deputies in legislature	93	44	64	77
Percentage of all deputies	35%	68%	72%	71%
Previous to election:				
Mayor	49	36	54	59
Minister in the Fourth Republic	20	3	5	5
Secretary or under-secretary of state in the Fourth Republic	21	3	7	4
Member of a ministerial cabinet or similar official in the Fourth Republic	9	5	9	3

2. Socioprofessional origins of Socialist deputies, 1956, 1958, 1962, and 1967

	1956		1958		1962		1967		All years	
Occupation	No.	%	No.	%	No.	%	No.	%	No.	% of Socialist deputies
Workers	4	4	1	2	3	5	4	6	12	4
White-collar Employees	3	3	1	2	2	3	2	3	8	3
Minor civil servants	9	10	2	4	6	9	6	9	23	9
Farmers	3	3	0	0	3	5	4	6	10	4
School teachers	16	17	7	16	9	14	14	21	46	17
Professors (in *lycée* or college)	15	16	7	16	9	14	11	17	42	16
Journalists	7	7	2	4	3	5	5	7	17	6
Doctors and pharmacists	9	10	9	20	8	12	6	9	32	12
Lawyers	13	14	4	9	5	8	7	10	29	11
High government officials	4	4	2	4	7	11	2	3	15	6
Engineers and architects	1	1	3	7	3	5	2	3	9	3
Executives	5	5	5	11	4	6	0	0	14	5
Merchants	4	4	1	2	1	1	3	4	9	3
Industrialists	0	0	0	0	1	1	0	0	1	0
No information							11			
Total	93		44		64		77			

3. Educational background of Socialist deputies, 1956, 1958, 1962, and 1967

Education	No. in 1956	No. in 1958	No. in 1962	No. in 1967	All years No.	All years % of Soc. deputies
University degree:						
Law	21	9	10	8	48	23
Letters	14	5	4	22	45	22
Medicine	9	8	8	2	27	13
Science	3	1	4	5	13	6
Field unknown	18	1	8	2	29	14
Training college	1	8	8	6	23	11
Secondary or trade school	2	6	0	0	8	4
Primary school	3	3	5	2	13	6
No information	23	3	17	30	73	

Source: Who's Who in France (Paris: Editions Jacques Lafitte, 1953–1968), various election studies published by the Fondation Nationale des Sciences Politiques, and data obtained from SFIO library.

Appendix G
Executive Committee Members of the Socialist Party

1. Political experience of executive committee members, 1945–1966

Highest elective office attained	No.	%
Deputy	69	63
Senator	6	5
Mayor	3	3
Assistant mayor	1	1
Municipal councillor	2	2
French union member	4	3
No elective office	25	23
No information	12	

Source: Who's Who in France and data obtained from SFIO library.

*2. Socioprofessional origins of executive committee members, 1945–1966**

Workers	7%
White-collar employees	4%
Minor civil servants	6%
Farmers	1%
School teachers	16%
Professors (in *lycée* or college)	23%
Journalists	13%
Doctors and pharmacists	3%
Lawyers	13%
High government officials	5%
Engineers and architects	2%
Executives	3%
Industrialists	4%

* Figures derived from *Who's Who in France;* Assemblée Nationale, *Notices et Portraits* (Paris: Imprimerie de l'Assemblée Nationale, 1956–1967); and data obtained from SFIO library. Total number of executive committee members considered was 122, and there was no information for 22 of them.

3. Educational background of executive committee members, 1945–1966

Education	No.	%
University degree:		
Law	20	27
Letters	18	24
Medicine	3	4
Science	5	7
Field unknown	10	13
Training college	6	8
Secondary or trade school	7	9
Primary school	6	8
Total members for whom information was available	75	
No information	47	

Source: Who's Who in France and data obtained from SFIO library.

4. *Average age of executive committee members, 1945–1966*

Age
54
53
52
51
50
49
48
47
46
45
44
43
42

Year	1945	1946	1947	1948	1949	1950	1951	1952	1953	1954	1955	1956	1957	1958	1959	1960	1961	1963	1965
No. of members*	25	19	21	31	28	28	28	28	28	23	25	36	36	36	40	38	40	33	33
Average age	43.7	42.1	42.8	42.6	44.8	46	47	49	49.6	50	51	50.4	49.3	50.6	51	52.6	52.7	51.8	53.9

Source: Who's Who in France and data obtained from SFIO library.

* The number of members is frequently less than total executive committee membership because of lack of information for all members.

5. World War II experience of executive committee members

Deported, condemned to death, imprisoned, or arrested by Gestapo	1
External Resistance (London, Algiers), charged with mission by de Gaulle	4
Founder or chief of Resistance network, commander of Free French Forces, or chief of clandestine organization	10
Cadre or active member of Resistance network or other political or union organization	12
Holds a Resistance medal	22
Holds Croix de Guerre, 1939–45	10
Prisoner of war	2
Total members for whom information was available	61
No information	61

Source: Who's Who in France and data obtained from SFIO library.

6. Tenure rate of executive committee members, 1945–1966

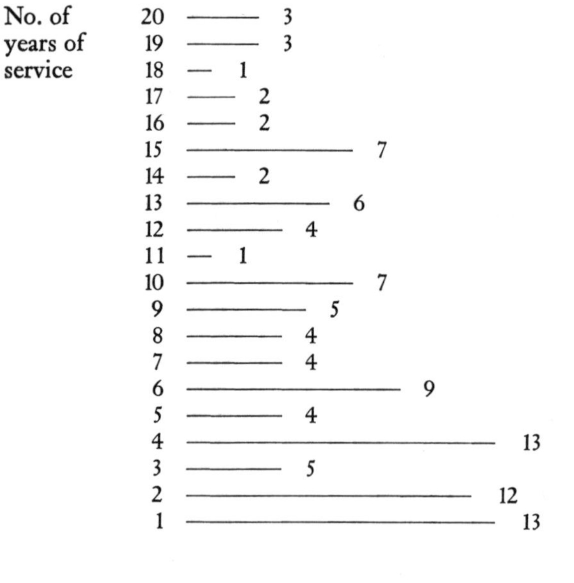

Source: Reports of SFIO congresses published by SFIO in various issues of the *Bulletin Intérieur*.

7. *Re-election rate of executive committee members*

Year	% re-elected	Year	% re-elected
1946	41	1956*	66
1947	77	1957	91
1948	80	1958	82
1949	90	1959	93
1950	90	1960	95
1951	90	1961	86
1952	90	1963	80
1953	90	1965	91
1954	80	1967	85
1955	84		

Source: Reports of SFIO congresses published by SFIO in various issues of the *Bulletin Intérieur*.

* Executive committee was enlarged from 31 to 45 members in 1956.

Chronology of the Principal Events in the Internal Politics of the SFIO from 1956 to 1966

1956

January 14–15	Extraordinary National Congress votes unanimously that Republican Front seek to constitute a government.
February 8	Pierre Commin assumes post of interim secretary-general of SFIO as Guy Mollet becomes Prime Minister.
May	Report of commission assigned to study question of reinstituting proportional representation on CD published in interior bulletin of SFIO.
June 28–July 1	Forty-eighth National Congress held in Lille. Modification in composition of CD voted. Party discipline is tightened. Criticism of government's Algerian policy is voiced by André Philip, Daniel Mayer and Pierre Rimbert. Vote on motion asking approval of government policy receives 3,308 votes, minority motion receives 363 votes.
September 20	André Philip warns government against using force during Suez crisis.
October 27	Benbhamed resigns from SFIO and joins FLN in Cairo.
November 10	Mme. Andrée Vienot resigns from SFIO in protest over Algerian policy.
December 6	Twenty-five Socialist notables, including seventeen deputies, sign letter protesting pacification methods in Algeria and Suez invasion.

1957

January	André Philip bitterly attacks party organization action and Algerian policy in CD meeting.
January 29	Socialist minority forms Socialist Study and Action Group for Peace in Algeria.
April 10	Bureau of SFIO calls for dissolution of Socialist Study and Action Group for Peace in Algeria.
May 12	National Council debates government policy. Majority motion approves government policy and receives 2,997 votes. Minority motion condemns government Algerian policy and asks for opening of a free tribune in party press and receives 401 votes. There are 425 abstentions. The federation of Bouches-du-Rhône abstains.
May 21	Mollet government falls.
June 3	National Council debates question of participation. Majority motion sets forth SFIO conditions for participation in Pflimlin government and receives 2,464 votes. Minority motion rejects participation and asks for moderation in Algerian policy and receives 1,071 votes; 398 abstain. The federation of Bouches-du-Rhône splits, two-thirds voting with majority and one-third with minority.
June 6	CD and Socialist parliamentary group reject participation in Pflimlin government.
June 8	CD and Socialist parliamentary group vote for participation in Bourgès-Maunoury government by 51 to 33.
June 27–30	Forty-ninth National Congress held in Toulouse. Debate on Algerian policy. Pineau, Defferre, and Verdier present separate motions. Pineau supports Mollet leadership;

Defferre asks for free elections in Algeria and for granting Algeria a large degree of autonomy and criticizes the record of the Mollet government. Verdier motion calls for recognition of "national vocation" of Algeria. Vote: 2,547 for Pineau motion, 779 for Defferre motion, 498 for Verdier motion.

July 19	Nineteen Socialist deputies express disapproval of government bill extending special powers legislation to metropole by not taking part in the vote.
September 10	National Council debates Algerian policy and deputies who broke discipline.
September 30	Bourgès-Maunoury government falls.
October 28	Mollet fails to obtain investiture from National Assembly.
November 3	National Council debates participation in Gaillard government. Majority asks for participation and receives 2,087 votes; minority opposes participation and receives 1,732 votes. Bouches-du-Rhône votes with minority.
November 6	Félix Gaillard invested as Prime Minister.
December 14–15	National Council debates questions of free tribune in party press and continued participation in Gaillard government. Majority motion opposed to free tribune receives 2,539 votes; minority motion receives 1,196; there are 119 abstentions. Bouches-du-Rhône votes with minority. Majority motion advocating continued participation receives 2,650 votes; minority motion opposing participation receives 1,121 votes; there are 83 abstentions. Bouches-du-Rhône votes with minority.

1958

January	*Tribune du Socialisme*, monthly newspaper of Socialist minority, begins publication.
March 15–16	National Council debates continued participation in Gaillard government. Majority motion advocating continued participation receives 2,754 votes; minority motion opposing continued participation receives 1,157 votes. Bouches-du-Rhône votes two-thirds for minority, one-third for majority.
April 15	Gaillard government falls.
April 29	Mollet accepts resolution of Socialist International in London calling for negotiations on Algeria without any preconditions.
May 2	National Council unanimously opposed to participation in Pleven government.
May 5	Pflimlin government investiture voted by National Assembly with SFIO voting with majority. Mollet and Jules Moch participate in government.
May 16	Mollet poses three questions to de Gaulle.
May 25	Mollet sends letter to de Gaulle saying that de Gaulle's investiture would serve the interests of the Bolsheviks.
May 26	De Gaulle replies to Mollet. Vincent Auriol writes to de Gaulle asking him to disavow the seditious elements in Algeria.
May 28	Socialist parliamentary group states support of PCF–CGT demonstration against rebels.
May 28	CD votes 17–9 against common SFIO–PCF demonstration. Demonstration held, Communists join with other marchers.
May 31	Socialist parliamentary group votes 62–29 to approve Auriol letter to de Gaulle. Indicative vote of CD and parliamentary group shows 77 for and 74 against de Gaulle investiture.

June 1	Socialist group in National Assembly votes 42 for and 49 against de Gaulle's investiture. Mollet, Lejeune, and A. Thomas participate in de Gaulle government.
July 6	National Information Conference.
July 27	Representatives from 41 Socialist federations meet to voice opposition to proposed Constitution.
August 7	Socialist group votes that Constitution harbors serious dangers for the Republic.
August 20	Socialists voice misgivings on Constitution to de Gaulle.
September 6–7	Gaston Defferre and Frances Leenhardt state support for proposed Constitution.
September 11–14	Fiftieth National Congress debates question of supporting Constitution. Majority motion asks for "yes" vote and receives 2,786 votes; minority motion asks for "no" vote and receives 1,176 votes. Bouches-du-Rhône supports Constitution.
September 14	Edouard Depreux announces formation of Autonomous Socialist party (*Parti Socialiste Autonome*).
September 28	SFIO appeals for "yes" vote on Constitutional referendum.
November 23–30	Elections for first legislature of Fifth Republic. SFIO sends 40 deputies to National Assembly.
1959	
January 8	Socialist Ministers resign from de Gaulle government in protest over budget.
January 30	Jean Le Bail, Socialist Senator, resigns from party, criticizing its "opportunism."
March 8–15	Municipal elections. In some areas the SFIO and PCF run joint lists.
July 9–11	Fifty-first National Congress is held in Pu-

teaux. Jules Moch and Albert Gazier criticize the distinction drawn by SFIO between Debré government, which the party opposes, and de Gaulle, whom it supports.

1960

January 25 — SFIO creates Committee for Liaison and Understanding for the Support of General de Gaulle's Action to support de Gaulle against generals' rebellion that occurred on January 24.

April 28 — SFIO group in National Assembly deposes a motion of censure against the government.

May 5 — Guy Mollet attacks Debré over the refusal to convoke the National Assembly.

June 21–23 — Elections on Paris Municipal Council illustrate growing friction between SFIO and UNR.

June 30–July 2 — Fifty-second National Congress held in Issy-les-Moulineaux. SFIO still refuses to enter into systematic opposition.

1961

March 4–5 — Guy Mollet begins to emphasize "revolutionary" strain in Socialist doctrine.

September 27–28 — Extraordinary National Council condemns continued fighting in Algeria and government's attitude on *force de frappe*, Europe, and the UN.

1962

January 30 — SFIO decides to join a National Action Committee against the OAS along with Radicals, Independent-Center, Jacobin Club, and antifascist and antiracist organizations.

May 20	Party condemns de Gaulle for his "anti-European and anti-Atlantic" positions at National Council meeting held in Puteaux.
October 7	At National Council meeting held in Puteaux, SFIO condemns de Gaulle for violating Constitution.
October 28	Referendum changing Constitution to allow direct election of President is approved.
November 7, 9	Guy Mollet suggests that under no circumstances should one vote for a Gaullist candidate on either the first or second ballot of the legislative election.
November 18, 25	Legislative election gives Socialists an increase in National Assembly, but many Socialists elected only because of Communist support.
December 16	Mollet defends himself against accusations of having contravened decision of National Congress on election strategy.

1963

March 14	Guy Mollet, speaking before a conference of Socialist mayors, asks Communists how they stand on the "twenty-one conditions."
March 20	François Billoux replies for Communists, saying that situation in 1963 profoundly different from that in 1920.
May 30–June 2	Fifty-fourth National Congress approves Fundamental Program. Question of supporting the presidential system is raised but not settled. Party also decides to delay making decision on presidential election. Debate on question of regrouping parties is intense and divides party deeply.
July 1	Guy Mollet in an interview emphasizes

	points of agreement between PCF and SFIO.
September 12	Rumors begin to circulate that de Gaulle might resign from the Presidency and call a new election before the opposition has a chance to nominate candidates.
September 17	Socialist delegation travels to Moscow to meet with Soviet officials.
September 19	"X" campaign begins.
December 11	Maurice Duverger, writing in *Le Monde*, calls on "X" to unmask himself.
December 13	CD agrees to allow Defferre to solicit SFIO presidential nomination.

1964

February 1, 2	Extraordinary National Congress nominates Gaston Defferre as Socialist presidential candidate.
June 22	Defferre agrees to clear up confusion created by his distinction between a program and a policy, and makes specific policy statements.

1965

June 3–6	Fifty-fifth National Congress. Bitter debate on question of federation proposed by Defferre and especially on question of soliciting MRP adherence. Final resolution mentions reintegration of PCF and *laïcité*, but does not mention socialism or revolutionary mission of SFIO.
June 17, 18	Negotiations between SFIO leaders, the MRP, and assorted political personalities lead to failure of proposed federation agreement.
June 25	Defferre resigns from presidential race.

September 11	Agreement reached on the composition of the Federation of the Socialist and Democratic Left.
December 5, 19	Presidential election. De Gaulle defeats Mitterand on second ballot.

1966

January 21	Gaston Defferre, Georges Brutelle, Francis Leenhardt, Gérard Jaquet, Christian Pineau, and Albert Gazier resign from Bureau of SFIO. Pierre Mauroy becomes assistant secretary-general, replacing Brutelle.
March 13	Mitterand proposes the formation of a "countergovernment."
April 18	National Council of SFIO sees Guy Mollet and Gaston Defferre differ on how quickly SFIO should agree to fuse itself into the FGDS.
May 5	Members of the "countergovernment" include Guy Mollet, Pierre Mauroy, Gaston Defferre, and Georges Guille.
October 20	FGDS elaborates an election strategy that includes mutual support for Communist deputies on second ballot.
October 29–30	Extraordinary Congress of SFIO supports idea of an electoral agreement with Communists for legislative elections scheduled in March, 1967.
December 20	The FGDS and the PCF reach agreement on a common election strategy for the scheduled March, 1967 legislative elections.

1967

January 20	The FGDS and the PSU reach an agreement on election strategy.
March 12	Second turn of the legislative elections. The

FGDS wins 121 seats, of which the SFIO holds 76, the Radicals 25, and members of the Convention (*Convention des Institutions Republicaines*) 15. Four members of the PSU and one other deputy ask to join the FGDS group in the National Assembly. The Communist group holds 73 seats.

May–June — The SFIO and the PCF differ in their views on the Arab-Israeli conflict. The Socialists support the Israelis, while the PCF condemns Israel and echoes Soviet support for Nasser.

June 29–July 2 — SFIO holds its fifty-sixth National Congress. There is little conflict as the party votes motions on international politics attacking the American position in Vietnam and supporting the "security of Israel's frontiers." The party also unanimously endorses a motion calling on the FGDS to continue work toward fusion of the constituent organizations, as well as a motion endorsing further discussions with the PCF.

July 5 — Guy Mollet is chosen secretary-general of the SFIO.

October 1 — In the cantonal elections, the PCF increase their representation, but the FGDS loses some seats despite the election agreement followed by the two parties.

November 15 — The leaders of the FGDS reach agreement on a doctrine and the organization for the Federation as it moves toward fusion.

Selected Bibliography

Andrews, William G. *French Politics and Algeria.* New York: Meredith Publishing Company, 1962.

Arné, Serge. *Le Président du Conseil des Ministres sous la IVe République.* Paris: Librairie Générale de Droit et de Jurisprudence, 1962.

Aron, Raymond. *L'Algérie et la République.* Paris: Plon, 1958.

——. *Immuable at Changeante: De la IV e à la Ve République.* Paris: Calmann-Lévy, 1959.

Association Française de Science Politique. *La Dépolitisation: Mythe ou Réalité.* Paris: A. Colin, 1962.

——. *Les Elections du 2 Janvier 1956.* Paris: A. Colin, 1957.

——. *L'Etablissement de la Cinquième République: Le Référendum de Septembre et les Elections de Novembre, 1958.* Paris: A. Colin, 1958.

——. *Le Référendum D'Octobre et Les Elections de Novembre, 1962.* Paris: A. Colin, 1965.

Barale, Jean. *La IVe République et la Guerre.* Aix-en-Provence: La Pensée Universitaire, 1961.

Barsalou, Joseph. *La Mal-Aimée.* Paris: Plon, 1964.

Behr, Edward. *The Algerian Problem.* New York: W. W. Norton and Company, 1961.

Bilger, Pierre. *Les Nouvelles Gauches de Janvier 1956 à Mai 1958: Etude de Stratégie Politique.* Mémoire, Fondation Nationale des Sciences Politiques. Paris: 1960.

Blum, Léon. *For All Mankind.* Translated from the French by William Pickles. New York: Viking Press, 1946.

——. *L'Oeuvre de Léon Blum, 1945–47.* Paris: Albin Michel, 1958.

Bromberger, Merry and Serge. *Les 13 Complots du 13 Mai.* Paris: Librairie Arthème Fayard, 1959.

Chalmers, Douglas A. *The Social Democratic Party of Germany.* New Haven: Yale University Press, 1964.

Chapsal, Jacques. *La Vie Politique et les Partis en France depuis 1940.* 3 vols. Paris: Fondation Nationale des Sciences Politiques, 1962.

Chevallier, Jacques. *Nous, Algériens . . .* Paris: Calmann-Lévy, 1958.

Club Jean Moulin. *L'Etat et le Citoyen.* Paris: Editions du Seuil, 1961.

——. *Un Parti pour la Gauche.* Paris: Editions du Seuil, 1965.

Combes, Annie. *Monographie de la Fédération Socialiste de la Sarthe.* Paris: Institut d'Etudes Politiques, 1962.

Coston, Henri. *Partis, Journaux et Hommes Politiques d'Hier et d'Aujourd'hui.* Paris: La Librairie Française, 1960.

Defferre, Gaston. *Un Nouvel Horizon.* Paris: Gallimard, 1965.

Depreux, Edouard. *Le Renouvellement du Socialisme.* Paris: Calmann-Lévy, 1960.

Duquesne, Jacques. *L'Algérie ou la Guerre des Mythes.* Paris: Editions de Brouwer, 1958.

Duverger, Maurice. *Partis Politiques et Classes Sociales en France.* Paris: A. Colin, 1955.

——. *Political Parties.* New York: J. Wiley and Sons, 1962.

Elgey, Georgette. *La République des Illusions,* 1945–51. Paris: Librairie Arthème Fayard, 1965.

Faucher, Jean-André. *Les Clubs Politiques en France.* Paris: Editions John Didier, 1966.

Fauvet, Jacques. *The Cockpit of France.* London: Harvill Press, 1960.

——. *Les Forces Politiques en France.* Paris: Editions "Le Monde," 1951.

——. *La IVe République.* Paris: Librairie Arthème Fayard, 1959.

——. *Histoire du Parti Communiste Français.* 2 vols. Paris: Librairie Arthème Fayard, 1964–66.

Favrod, Charles-Henri. *Le FLN et l'Algérie.* Paris: Plon, 1962.

——. *La Révolution Algérienne.* Paris: Plon, 1959.

Godfrey, E. Drexel, Jr. *The Fate of the French Non-Communist Left.* New York: Random House. 1955.

Goguel, François. *Géographie des Elections Françaises de 1870 à 1951*. Paris: A. Colin, 1951.
——. *La Politique des Partis sous la IIIe République*. Paris: Editions du Seuil, 1946.
——, and Alfred Grosser. *La Politique en France*. Paris: A. Colin, 1964.
Graham, B. D. *The French Socialists and Tripartisme, 1944–47*, Toronto: University of Toronto Press, 1965.
Grosser, Alfred. *La IVe République et sa Politique Extérieure*. Paris: A. Colin, 1961.
Hernu, Charles. *La Colère Usurpée*. Paris: Editions C. H., no date.
Lavau, Georges. *Partis Politiques et Réalités Sociales*. Paris: A. Colin, 1953.
Lefranc, Georges. *Le Mouvement Socialiste sous la Troisième République, 1875–1940*. Paris: Payot, 1963.
Leites, Nathan. *Du Malaise Politique en France*. Paris: Plon, 1958.
——. *French Politics*. New York: Rand Corporation, 1962.
Levine, Eric. "The French Intellectuals and the Algerian War," M.A. thesis. New York: Columbia College, 1962.
Ligou, Daniel. *Histoire du Socialisme en France, 1871–1961*. Paris: Presses Universitaires de France, 1962.
Louis, Paul. *Histoire du Socialisme en France*. Paris: Librairie Marcel Rivière, 1950.
Luethy, Herbert and David Rodnick. *French Motivations in the Suez Crisis*. Princeton: Princeton University Press, 1956.
MacRae, Duncan, Jr. *Parliament, Parties and Society in France, 1946–1958*. New York: St. Martin's Press, 1967.
Marabuto, P. *Les Partis Politiques et les Mouvements Sociaux sous la IVe République*. Paris: Sirey, 1948.
Melnik, Constantin and Nathan Leites. *The House without Windows*. Evanston, Ill.: Row, Peterson and Company, 1958.
Micaud, Charles. *Communism and the French Left*. New York: Praeger, 1963.
Moch, Jules. *Confrontations*. Paris: Gallimard, 1952.
Mollet, Guy. *Bilan et Perspectives Socialistes*. Paris: Plon, 1958.

Mollet, Guy. *13 Mai 1958—13 Mai 1962*. Paris: Plon, 1962.
Morazé, Charles. *The French and the Republic*. Ithaca, N.Y.: Cornell University Press, 1958.
Oppermann, Thomas. *La Question Algérienne: Données Historiques, Politiques, Juridiques*. Paris: F. Maspero, 1961.
Philip, André. *Henri de Man et la Crise Doctrinale du Socialisme*. Paris: Librairie Universitaire J. Gamber, 1928.
——. *Pour un Socialisme Humaniste*. Paris: Plon, 1960.
——. *Le Socialisme Trahi*. Paris: Plon, 1957.
Planchais, Jean. *Le Malaise de l'Armée*. Paris: Plon, 1958.
Priouret, Roger. *La République des Partis*. Paris: Les Editions de l'Elan, 1947.
Savary, Alain. *Nationalisme Algérien et Grandeur Française*. Paris: Plon, 1960.
Servan-Schreiber, Jean-Jacques. *Lieutenant in Algeria*. New York: A. Knopf, 1957.
Siegfried, André. *De la IIIe à la IVe République*. Paris: B. Grasset, 1956.
——. *De la IVe à la Ve République*. Paris: B. Grasset, 1958.
——. *France, a Study in Nationality*. London: Oxford University Press, 1930.
Suffert, Georges. *De Defferre à Mitterand*. Paris: Editions du Seuil, 1966.
Tillion, Germaine. *L'Afrique Bascule vers l'Avenir*. Paris: Editions de Minuit, 1961.
——. *Algeria*. New York: A. Knopf, 1958.
——. *Les Ennemis Complémentaires*. Paris: Editions de Minuit, 1960.
Tournoux, Jean-Raymond. *Carnets Secrets de la Politique*. Paris: Plon, 1958.
——. *Secrets d'Etat*. Paris: Plon, 1960.
Werth, Alexander. *France, 1940–1955*. New York: Henry Holt and Company, 1956.
Williams, Philip. *Crisis and Compromise*. Hamden, Conn.: Archon Books, 1964.
——. *Politics in Postwar France*. London: Longmans, 1958.

Index